Craft of the Wise

A Practical Guide to Paganism
and Witchcraft

First published by O Books, 2009
O Books is an imprint of John Hunt Publishing Ltd., The Bothy, Deershot Lodge, Park Lane, Ropley,
Hants, SO24 0BE, UK
office1@o-books.net
www.o-books.net

Distribution in:

UK and Europe
Orca Book Services
orders@orcabookservices.co.uk
Tel: 01202 665432 Fax: 01202 666219
Int. code (44)

USA and Canada
NBN
custserv@nbnbooks.com
Tel: 1 800 462 6420 Fax: 1 800 338 4550

Australia and New Zealand
Brumby Books
sales@brumbybooks.com.au
Tel: 61 3 9761 5535 Fax: 61 3 9761 7095

Far East (offices in Singapore, Thailand,
Hong Kong, Taiwan)
Pansing Distribution Pte Ltd
kemal@pansing.com
Tel: 65 6319 9939 Fax: 65 6462 5761

South Africa
Alternative Books
altbook@peterhyde.co.za
Tel: 021 555 4027 Fax: 021 447 1430

Text copyright Vikki Bramshaw 2008

Design: Stuart Davies

ISBN: 978 1 84694 232 7

Printed by Digital Book Print

O Books operates a distinctive and ethical publishing philosophy in
all areas of its business, from its global network of authors to
production and worldwide distribution.

Craft of the Wise

A Practical Guide to Paganism
and Witchcraft

Vikki Bramshaw

BOOKS

Winchester, UK
Washington, USA

Links

www.craftofthewise.co.uk
Official website of Craft of the Wise with links to the Yahoo!
Group
www.earthspiritstore.co.uk
Providing quality wares for pagan and occult traditions.
http://annikagarratt.moonfruit.com
Cover image by Annika Garratt

BOOKS

MySpiritRadio

CONTENTS

Acknowledgments

With Special Thanks to:

Pete Lugh Lámhfhada, High Priest and friend who has accompanied me on this journey, so much of this material was built from our work together; Nat and Tony, who introduced me to the Craft and taught me the ways of the forest; Maureen Wheeler, who taught me the meaning of true dedication to the old religion; Morgaine, gifted High Priestess and Traditional witch who guided me on the path of the Gods; Somerset Oak, High Priest and friend from the west country who taught me the power of nature and of the self; Ron SilverEagleSpirit, Holly King and friend, entertaining us all with your wit and enthusiasm; and Janet Farrar & Gavin Bone, who read through my work in the early days and helped me immensely as this book came together.

Introduction

The Crooked Path

I took my Second Degree initiation on a cold winters' evening in the late 1990's. Shivering uncontrollably and up to my knees in mud, I stood in West Kennet Long Barrow and declared my commitment to the Gods, the ancestors and the Elders of the coven. It was about then that I realised what a breeze my last few years as a First Degree initiate had been!

I started my training some ten years ago, with a coven called Ytene based in the New Forest. We always worked outdoors; we would bundle into the High Priests' 4 x 4 and be taken into the forest to perform the esbat, come rain, hail or snow. My training with this first coven was both intense and exciting; we were set challenges, taught how to listen to the forest and overcome our fears.

A year or so later that particular coven dissolved, and soon after I was invited to join a new coven. My new teacher and initiator, Maureen Wheeler, was one of the most respected women of the Craft and an initiate of Gavin Bone. A Priestess of Isis, she demanded high standards from all her students. Her beautiful grove near the village of Bishops Waltham in Hampshire almost shone with energy, and we spent many an evening huddled around the fire pit after rituals, reading the tarot and fire scrying.

The years which followed my Second Degree were some of the hardest of my life. The Second Degree marks the start of The Test, a period which tries your commitment to the Craft. It is also the period of the Dark Moons, the point during your training when you learn to overcome your inner demons and go through the process of rebirth. For me, it was the time when I rediscovered myself and my passion for the Craft, and I began to write.

Two years later, I found myself beneath the boughs of ancient trees in the New Forest. I was back in the place I had begun my journey, and today was my Third Degree initiation. By this time I had taken my Second Degree again and had spent two years working with a coven in the west country. The two and a half hour journey which it took to get to the covenstead certainly took it out of me, and sometimes myself and my working partner Lugh were there for days at a time, training day and night. The period with the coven in the west country was possibly one of the most challenging of my life, yet it was also one of the most rewarding. We invariably worked inside in a dedicated temple, and although I craved the outdoor grove of my previous coven the temple was beautiful; to step inside was to immediately be in the presence of the Gods.

After my Third Degree, myself and Lugh hived off and formed our own coven in Hampshire. I managed to get back in touch with all the wonderful Craft teachers from my past who reminded me how much I still had to learn; and I continue to learn, both from teachers old and new. This book in part is dedicated to them; the wonderful people who have given their time and energy in order to teach me the true ways of the Craft.

The Offering

I started this project when I decided to bring my personal studies together with my coven training. My own notes, nine years of coven records held together in battered old files and scrawled on the back of shopping receipts, were hardly good enough to use as reference material within the coven! As the work continued to grow, people began positively commenting on my writing and eventually I turned what began as coven reference material into a successful correspondence course. As the course came to the end of its first year, I felt that I would like to bring more of my personal studies and experiences into the work and explore the idea of developing it into something else. The result was this book, which I hope will encourage you to begin your own journey of transformation; for witchcraft is not only a religion of the earth but also a journey of the self. It allows us to reclaim the spiritual connection to life that we may have lost, reuniting us with our primal instincts, our psychic wisdom and our sense of being.

The purpose of this book is to give the reader an insight into the true Craft. There are many books available nowadays which portray Wicca as something that it is not. Be under no illusion; this book will not tell you how innocent or harmless witchcraft is; this is not 'Pop Wicca'. The Craft, and magic, is wholly in the hands of the witch, and I have presented the Craft in all its forms and I leave it to you as a responsible person to make your own choices and decisions.

Whilst I honour my Alexandrian and Gardnerian roots, my practices are wholly eclectic and not limited to any tradition. Some people dislike the term eclectic, preferring to remain within one tradition and one way of doing things. This may work for them, but in my opinion it is limiting. Only now are we beginning to re-explore our ancient roots, the practices of our ancestors and the worship of the old Gods and Goddesses. Like the waves of the Wyrd, the Craft is forever moving and changing; we must move with it before we get left behind.

Ultimately, this book is my offering to the Gods. As they have guided me on this path and taught me the ways of the Craft, so I have written this book in testimony to my journey.

In European Craft, witches were known as 'hedge riders' or 'they who straddle the hedge' – the hedge representing the boundary between this world and the other. I hope that there will be something in this book to inspire you, and allow you to jump the hedge into a fulfilling and diverse tradition – the Craft of the Wise.

A note on the texts

Due to the nature of the standard texts used in modern witchcraft, many of the quoted passages repeated in this book (such as the chants, spells and extracts of rituals) can be considered as 'orphaned' material, which I have endeavoured to source from the most reliable texts and publications. Since the original material was first released to the public many of them have also undergone changes, omissions and additions by various other authors.

I have also included spells, charms, chants and rituals from my own coven's *Book of Ways*. Any excerpts, chants, folk songs or other material whose authors could not be identified at the time of writing are respectfully quoted as 'author unknown'.

Chapter One

The Craft of the Wise

What is Paganism? This is not such an easy question to answer. The practice of Paganism as we know it today is relatively new; however, it is based on some very old beliefs and principles which were set in motion by primitive man. And that could mean almost 100,000 years of Pagan history.

The Pagan ways have shaped our language, our myths and our society; an ancient past that has influenced our modern lives to the core. Many towns and cities all around the world are named after Pagan Gods and Goddesses and numerous national holidays also find their roots in the ancient festivals of our forefathers. A myriad of folktales and superstitions echo the Pagan beliefs of antiquity which have been integrated into modern life, with skills such as mathematics, literature and science also finding their origins in the Pagan civilisations of the past. Indeed, these same civilisations boasted the architecture of the pyramids in Egypt, the breathtaking temples in Greece and the awesome structures of Avebury and Stonehenge in Britain.

The term 'Pagan' is a broad one and many meanings have been given to it, including 'one who worships false Gods; an idolater' and 'a person who has no religious beliefs'. The Middle English translation for the word Pagan comes from the Latin 'paganus', meaning 'country dweller' or, 'one who lives off the land'. Looking at these definitions you can see that there is no reference to any religion, or even a belief system. Then again, when that belief system is so ancient that it precedes language, reasoning and the written word, it comes as no surprise that for every era in history people have viewed Paganism in different ways. The result is that many meanings are based on misconception and are in no way true reflections of the practice today.

Due to the practice of Paganism becoming more accepted by society in the last one hundred years, many dictionaries are starting to change their definitions and it is now in the 21st century that the forgotten ways of Paganism are beginning to be followed once again. Today, the word Paganism describes an umbrella of eclectic belief systems which are based upon the practices of our ancestors, but for a modern world. It embraces a wide variety of traditions, and as individuals we may each choose our preferred path to follow.

Paganism and Witchcraft

Fire flame and fire burn, Make the Mill of magic turn
Work the will for which we pray, io! Evo-he
Air breathe and Air blow, Make the Mill of magic go
Work the will for which we pray, io! Evo-he
Water heat and water boil, Make the Mill of magic boil
Work the will for which we pray, io! Evo-he
Earth without and Earth within, Make the Mill of magic spin
Work the will for which we pray, io! Evo-he!
'The Mill Chant', author unknown

The art of witchcraft has captured the imagination of the human race for thousands of years, and it is just as difficult to place one certain definition on the word 'witch' as it is to define the word Pagan. As with many words, the meaning of the word 'witch' has changed with time and cultural differences and has been at the mercy of religious trend. The witch has been the wise-woman and the shaman; the soothsayer and the Priestess; the Maiden and the Hag. In Egypt she was a healer and midwife, whilst the Anglo-Saxons called the witch 'a conjurer of evil spirits'.

The word 'witch' is not confined to any specific religion or country; neither does it point to any particular form of magic, gender, or ethics. It incorporates the shamanic practitioners of the Maya, the Strega witches of Italy, the ceremonial witches of western Europe, and the Cunning Craft of Britain. So where does the word come from, and what is the meaning behind it?

Although opinions are mixed, the most popular theory for the origin of the word 'witch' is that it traces back to the Proto-Indo word 'weik', meaning 'to consecrate', and 'to practice religion and magic'. This word was also associated with seasons and cycles of the earth. The related Germanic words, 'wikken' or 'wikker', meant 'to use magic, divination and sorcery' and the Old English 'wit' or 'witan', meant 'to know'. It is believed that a combination of these words later developed into the Old-English 'wicce' (feminine) and 'wicca' (masculine). From these came the Middle-English 'wicche,' and of course with time the modern day word 'witch'.

Another theory is that the word originates from the Old-English 'wican', meaning 'to bend'. The old name for witch hazel, 'wice' also comes from this word. Although this particular theory is generally disproved by modern etymologists, it was probably the theory that Gerald Gardner, the 'father of modern witchcraft' favoured, due to his spelling of Wica with one 'c' rather than two.

We will probably never know which theory is correct, however one thing is certain; no matter which theory we favour, or where we look in the world, the witch has always been a symbol of power, transformation and magic.

So why are modern witchcraft and Paganism such good partners? If we consider that the modern word 'Paganism' describes an umbrella of religions whom all revere the earth as sacred, then, although it is not necessary for a witch to be Pagan, the tradition of the Craft is by nature an earth orientated practice and wholly conducive with Paganism. And most importantly, modern Initiatory Craft pays reverence to the old Gods.

The Craft is often described as a reconstructionalist religion, built upon what little we know about the practices of our ancestors. Its interesting; 'Old Religion', 'Old Craft', 'Old Ones', 'Traditional Ways'. We find ourselves drawn to the ways of our ancestors, those people who were in tune with the earth and lived in touch with the seasons. Perhaps we crave their simple lives, their connection to nature and their understanding of the cycle. We should not forget, however, that their lives were extremely difficult. Food was scarce, times were hard, laws were few and violence was frequent. Our ancestors were people just like us, and religion allowed them to comprehend life and death, and ponder on meaning and consequence. Their rites were based upon the necessities of life; the need to hunt, the need to mate, and the need to bury their dead.

My own coven practices eclectic Initiatory Witchcraft, a tradition in which we embrace old Pagan rites, develop our occult understanding and progress with our own personal development through the mysteries. It blends the early religions of Britain, Egypt, Mesopotamia and Greece; the mysteries of Freemasonry, Qabalah and Hermeticism; and the ways of European Cunning Craft, whilst absorbing various different magical systems from around the world. In my opinion, our modern Craft borrows all the 'best bits' of ancient and modern mysticism and combines them all in one honey pot, altering the way we see the world on both a conscious and subconscious level. In the following chapters, we will be looking at some of the origins of the Craft, and how we can blend these different mystery traditions and Crafts into one practice.

Chapter Two

The Ritual and Magic of our Ancestors

Ritual and Magic in Britain and Northern Europe

At the start of the Palaeolithic age, Europe was almost exclusively home to a species of pre-human named Homo neanderthalensis – the Neanderthals. Early Neanderthals were the first creatures to recognise life and death, and ponder on meaning, consequence and life itself. They were also the first of the pre-humans to practice burial and display sentimental culture, such as laying flowers within the graves of their dead. Although Homo neanderthalensis looked similar to humans, it is argued that they are in fact not related to us at all. Approximately 30,000 years ago, after dominating Europe for over 150,000 years, they simply disappeared. It is thought that this could have been due to some sort of conflict between the Neanderthals and Homo sapiens (modern humans) who had migrated from Africa, Southern Europe and Asia. So, although the Neanderthals probably never added to our modern gene pool, it is possible that their understanding of life and death became integrated into that of the Homo sapiens during their time of coexistence.

The people of the Mesolithic Age (approximately 13,000 years ago) were largely nomadic, yet managed to thrive despite the harsh living conditions. They used tools made from flint, bone and antler to hunt; they domesticated dogs from wild wolves; and their lives revolved around the hunter–gatherer lifestyle. The best hunting was carried out at night under the cover of darkness, with only the light of the moon to help the hunters stalk their prey; in time, the moon began to be worshiped as provider and giver of sustenance and abundance. As time progressed, the people began to recognise another effect of the moon; the mysterious power of the female menstrual cycle, a pattern which followed the cycles of the moon. The female and the moon, counterpart symbols of abundance, became synonymous with one another and the moon became regarded as feminine; the Goddess.

In hand with the worship of the Goddess as provider, the male God came to be worshiped as his role of hunter and gatherer, and Animism began to be practiced within society. From the earliest beginnings, it was believed that a soul or spirit existed in every object, and in a future state that soul or spirit would exist as part of an immaterial soul. Our ancestors believed that drawing the spirits of the animals which they were hunting would assure a successful hunt and countless cave art images, particularly in France and Italy, preserve such paintings within their cavernous depths. This type of practice we now call 'sympathetic magic'. Hunting deities were often depicted as half animal half man, (called a *theriantrope* – from the Greek *therion* 'wild beast' and *anthropos* – 'man'). Sometimes, women also featured as hunting deities, such as the 'Bison Women' in the caves of Pech Merle in France.

Along with the illustration of their prey, our ancestors also depicted other animals in their cave art, such as bears and horses. Did ancient people imagine themselves as taking on the power of the bear, or the swiftness of the horse, when they illustrated them so vividly in their caves? We will probably never know the true meaning behind ancient cave art, but we can focus on its meaning to us today.

Images in the caves also depicted forms of shape shifting; that is, the animal or man in the process of changing from one form to another. This may also have aided the hunter to connect with the beasts and blend in with their prey, approaching their quarry unnoticed. Our ancestors would dress up as the animal that was being hunted to take on the power of the animal spirits; the costume would usually consist of the fur hide of the animal together with a headdress made from its skull. An example can be seen in the British Museum in London: an antlered red deer skull which has been modified in order that it could be worn as a headdress.

Early Neolithic groups, approximately 9,000 years ago, shared the same basic characteristics to those of the Mesolithic. Communities were small, between 50 and 100 people, and in the early years were extremely nomadic. There were still no real hierarchies within communities, and the group worked together as one to hunt and to gather. However, the Neolithic Age was also to be the dawn of more successful farming techniques such as the cultivation of land and an increased interest in the domestication of animals. The nomadic hunter-gather ways were beginning to be abandoned for a more sedentary lifestyle, in which the people began to settle and claim boundaries of land for farming. The more settled lifestyle in turn lead to population increases, and changes in environment to a scale that had not been seen before, as people began to clear the land to make way for farming and grazing for domestic animals. With the arrival of people from Southern Europe came even more advanced methods of farming in Britain, together with heavily fortified settlements like Windmill Hill in Wiltshire and Maiden Castle in Dorset.

The landscape of Britain is abundant with the sacred monuments of our ancestors: long barrows, round barrows, standing stones and henges which echo the forgotten heritage of ancient Europe. And these sites are not positioned at random; many are connected by ceremonial pathways, named 'ley lines' or 'serpent lines' and almost all correspond to the turn of the seasons. In Wiltshire, the Marlborough Downs was the epicentre of ancient monuments which were built by hand using rudimentary tools such as antler pick-axes and flint chisels; yet they aligned perfectly with the movement of the planets and the stars in the sky.

However, it is the way that our ancestors dealt with death that gives us even more insight into their beliefs; the long barrows and round barrows - their monuments to the dead.

Long barrows were constructed with chalk, earth and stone and built to serve as mortuary houses for the dead where loved ones could be laid to rest and offerings made. Often, just a skull would be offered to the barrow which had been cleaned of its flesh beforehand; it could be that the ancestors believed that just a token part of the body was necessary to ensure reincarnation. Long barrows were also sometimes reopened at particular times of the year, and skulls taken out to be used in ceremony.

There is evidence to suggest that the use of the long barrow was just as ceremonial as it was practical. Our ancestors believed in reincarnation; to place their dead into the mound was synonymous with the foetus in the womb, and giving the body back to the Mother Goddess where it could be reborn. Burial places would often be painted with red ochre to symbolise the blood of rebirth and the power of the Mother Goddess.

So who was this originator Goddess? Julian Cope, author of 'The Modern Antiquarian' offers a theory using 'root words' or 'root sounds' of our native language. He speculates that many of the Goddess names we know today, and indeed many common words and place names, come from these ancient root sounds. He identifies the Goddess Ur as the first of the named deities, a root name which would later lead to such Goddesses as the Scandinavian Urd or Urtha, which means earth. He also identifies Koer the Goddess of Agriculture, Ma the Goddess of Motherhood and Bree the Goddess of Fertility, who would lead to such modern Goddess names as Kore, Madron and Brigid respectively.

Round Barrows were constructed as round hillocks of earth and stone. Many barrows were built in close proximity to others and near other sacred monuments, suggesting a cemetery-type arrangement. Whereas the long barrow could hold ten or more individuals, the round barrow was usually dedicated to just one person, and once closed the round barrow was rarely reopened. Round barrows are also the most common of ancient monuments; there are almost 40,000 round barrows in Britain alone.

Stone circles and henges are by far the grandest of Britain's ancient monuments: enormous agricultural calendars which tracked the seasons and allowed astronomical observations. As well as mapping the seasons of the earth and the movements of the stars, the stone circles were used for seasonal rites and offerings, but over all they were solar temples, dedicated to the worship of the sun as agriculture became more important in the lives of the people of Britain.

Although the Moon Goddess was still worshiped for her mysterious qualities, as time progressed her importance in relation to the supply of food was more or less abandoned as people stopped hunting by night and began to farm. Our ancestors watched the sun warm the land and the grain swell as if made fertile by the heat, and began to attribute the sun as the masculine force and fertility giver – the God.

Ritual and Magic in Mesopotamia

Mesopotamia was the ancient land of modern day Iraq and western Iran, and lays claim to some of the world's first complex societies including Sumeria, Babylonia and Assyria.

The city of Sumer was one of the first advanced civilisations of the world and known as the 'Land of the Lords of Brightness'. True civilisation began in Sumer around 6,000 years BC, when it became a centre of thriving trade and economy, a place of settled city life and large religious centres. Sumer was divided up into city states, each with impressive temples dedicated to particular deities. The first Sumerian religious centre was Erudu, which mythology says was founded by the Sumerian creation God Enki. As Sumerian agricultural centres began to grow, dedicated temples to Gods and Goddesses called 'Ziggurats' were built, which were run by Priests. Ziggurats were humble wood shrines to begin with, but as society developed these old structures were reinforced and made more aesthetic by applying mud cement and brickwork.

Arts and crafts were also an important part of culture, and aided the development of the creative mind. Most temples housed a library, and both men and women learnt to read and write. Sumer was one of the first places where writing was used, along with Egypt, India and China and was also the first religion to be properly recorded. The Sumerian language was later replaced by the Akkadian, but continued to be used in ritual as a magical text by the Babylonians until the arrival of Christianity.

The Sumerians were a Polytheistic society; that is, they believed in many separate Gods. They had a complex and interesting belief system which surrounded the sea, sky and earth and were one of the many cultures who embraced the notion of the Primordial Waters, and the marriage of the sky (the Sumerian God 'Enki') and the earth (the Sumerian Goddess 'Namma'). Like other religions to come, they believed in deities for all things; they also erected statues to their ancestors, and mounted skulls for the ancestral spirit to inhabit.

The Akkadian Empire came to height of power around 4,000 years BC. The Akkadians were people from northern Mesopotamia who invaded the Southern Somerian city states no less than thirty times before incorporating the cities as their own. After this conquest, Akkad became the capital of Mesopotamia. However, their period of rule only lasted about 100 years before they were invaded by Gutian barbarians from the mountain ranges of Mesopotamia, and eventually became absorbed into the unified state of Babylonia.

The state of Babylonia, 'Gateway of the Gods,' unified the cities of Mesopotamia. Much of the Babylonian culture and religion continued on from that of the Sumerian, just as the

Babylonian religion and philosophy would in turn influence the Greek culture of the future. Babylonia was a spectacular epicentre of trade, architecture, crafts and religion. They were one of the first civilizations to incorporate a monarchy into their culture, but unlike their neighbours the Egyptians they did not deify their Kings and Queens as Gods. The Babylonians were also the first culture to conceptualise the zodiac, and use it together with astronomy.

In 539BC (approximately 3000 years ago) Babylonia was invaded by the Persians, and although Babylon continued to act as an administrative city for Persia for many years the city lost its independence, and gradually its culture, in the mists of time.

Ritual and Magic in Egypt

The unified Kingdom of Egypt was established around 3,000 BCE when individual settlements of Egypt, which had already been living and working along the Nile for thousands of years, came together to create one Empire. It is from this era that we find evidence of the earliest known hieroglyphic writing and advanced language. By this time, the inhabitants of most of the rest of the world had only just begun to start building rudimentary earth passage graves, and certainly had no written language. In addition to a head start in organised agriculture and literature, the Egyptians already had a strong concept of life, death and spiritual purpose, and worshiped local animal and vegetation deities to ensure prosperous harvests and successful hunts. Later, they even expanded their belief system to include the Gods of the elements.

The Egyptians called Egypt 'na neteru', which means 'Land of the Gods'. Religion was intrinsic to everything that the Egyptians did and was woven into the very fabric of their lives. Indeed, the Egyptians had no word for 'religion' because to give it a name was to separate it from everything else, and that in their ideology was impossible. They believed in 'Heka,' the magical and spiritual force within the universe, but also believed in the Gods in their own right who manifested as personified deities. The outer appearance of the Gods was not limited either, as one God or Goddess could be depicted in multiple guises, which often occurred between administrative districts in Egypt. Each district or 'nome' had a cult centre that usually followed a particular divine family or myth, i.e. the divine family of Isis, Osiris and Horus. Many Gods would not have been recognised in one district as they would have been recognised in the next, and this often lead to the syncretism of two Gods into one when those districts became closer through trade, marriage or politics. For instance, worship of the God 'Amun-Re' came about when Thebes (whose patron deity was Amun) and Heliopolis (whose patron deity was Re) made a political alliance. Re also took on another new form, 'Re-Horakhty', who was a combination of the falcon God Horus and Re. Gods could also appear as separate deities, to display the contrasts and polar opposites in their personalities. For instance Hathor, Goddess of Love who was illustrated as part-cow, could transform into Sekhmet, the malevolent side of her personality who was depicted as a lion. However, even the more severe Egyptian deities such as Sekhmet were not seen as negative, as they played just as an important part in the processes of life as their benevolent counterparts.

Egyptian religion revolved around the Nile, which was the source of all life in Egypt. Their calendar followed the Egyptian's own unique agricultural cycle composing of three seasons: the Season of Flood, the Season of Planting and the Season of Harvest. The flooding of the Nile brought fertility to the hot, lifeless desert soil and the Egyptians interpreted this in their myths and festivals; they referred to the Nile Valley as the 'black land' in reference to the black fertile soil deposited by the Nile, and the dry outer desert as the 'red land' the place of death. Later, these two parts of Egypt were personified in the tales of the God Osiris (the fertility God of the black land), and Set, Osiris' twin brother (who ruled the red land). Ironically, Set also appears in the Bible, as the little known third brother of Cain and Abel.

The myths of Set and Osiris tell how Set is constantly battling with Osiris over the reign of Egypt. The battle rages on even after Osiris' death, between Set and Osiris' son, Horus. Osiris is described as a 'dying and rising God' a God who is sacrificed, yet who will rise to make the soil fertile once again. This belief revolved around the agricultural cycle of the Nile, but also reflected the Egyptian's interest in life after death.

The Egyptians called the afterlife the 'shining realm of heaven' and they had many strict beliefs about what must be done to ensure passage to this place after death. They also believed that the body had many separate layers of consciousness after death. The 'Khat' described the physical body of the corpse. The 'Khaibit' described the 'shadow' of the person (a negative aspect that could be left lingering once the person had died) and the 'Ka' described the higher self, or soul. It was believed that the Ka was created at the time of the person's birth, and therefore it was also the Ka that was released from the body after death. It would then journey to be judged by Osiris before moving on to the afterlife. Food was left in the tomb to nourish the Ka, and false doors were constructed in the walls so that the Ka might move though from room to room whilst awaiting judgement. The 'Akh' described the spirit body 'shining form' or ghost, and the 'Sah' described the body once it had been transformed into a mummy and imbued with magic. The Egyptians mummified their dead because they believed that the body must be intact for the spirit of the person to reach the afterlife, and so that the Ka could identify it and the Ba could perch upon it. It was also believed that the main organs of the body would be required in the afterlife, so organs such as the heart were buried along with the body in Canopic jars.

The Egyptians saw their journey through the afterlife in a similar sense to that of the journey of the sun through the sky. It was said that during the day the sun God Re travelled in his 'golden sun boat' east to west across the skies, inspecting Egypt. But then at dusk Re disappeared beneath the horizon and the land was cast into darkness. They believed that during the hours of night Re made his journey through the Netherworld in his boat, a perilous twelve-hour journey with many challenges, after which he emerges victorious at dawn together with the appearance of the sun. This story is just one of the ancient myths which led to the popular 'Ferryman' tale.

An alternative Egyptian myth which which also explains the origins of day and night says that the sun is swallowed by the Goddess Nut (daughter of Shu, element of air and Tefnut, element of water) and travels through her body during the night, being born again the next morning.

Although the movements of the planets were often interpreted as symbolic elements within Egyptian mythology, the Egyptians were also highly developed in astronomy and understood the cycles of the planets. They observed and recorded the movements of the planets as we do today, and illustrations of the lunar months and the constellations decorated the ceilings of tombs and temples, enlightening the viewer with the powers of the universe. Rituals were held to mark the new and full moons, the position of the sun and other auspicious astronomical occasions.

The Egyptians provided us with a wealth of magical and occult knowledge, some of which we can still read today in the Pyramid Texts, Coffin Texts, Book of the Dead and the texts of Coming Forth by Day, to name just a few; we can also study the archaeological evidence of amulets, statues and depictions on the walls of temples and tombs. Talismans were commonly worn upon the person to protect the wearer from evil and were also placed upon the body of the dead for the same purpose, often inscribed with a magical formulae or words of power.

The 'Tyet Knot' or 'Girdle of Isis' was a popular amulet which was incorporated into the funerary wear of the dead. It was usually made of Red Jasper and Carnelian and worn about the neck, to ensure the protection of Isis. It was known as the 'Blood of Isis' associating it with the magical properties of menstrual blood, and also as the 'Knot of Isis' which can be recreated with a tied robe cord today. The 'Tet Tree' amulet was also associated with Isis and represented the tree truck where the slain Osiris, husband of Isis, lay. The Tet symbolised the resurrection of Osiris, and so was an important magical symbol of rebirth, new life and hope.

> *Rise up thou, Osiris! Thou hast thy backbone, O Still Heart! Thou hast the fastenings of thy neck and back, O Still Heart! Place thou thyself upon thy base, I put water beneath thee, and I bring unto thee a Tet of gold that thou mayest rejoice therein.*
> 'The Egyptian Book of the Dead'

The Ankh is possibly one of the most recognisable amulets of Egypt and another symbol of rebirth. It was often referred to as the 'Key of Life' and was said to have risen from the Tet. Not only did it have the powers of regeneration and rebirth, but it was also the key to the mysteries and the unknown; it was said that to have the Ankh upon you ensured your access to ancient occult records, called the Akasha. The term 'Akasha Records' is also sometimes used to describe the collective unconscious.

Sometimes parts of the body acted as amulets themselves, such as the Amulet of the Heart. The person's real heart was mummified separately to the rest of the body and placed within a Canopic jar. The body was then given a heart double, the Heart Amulet, which was made of Lapis Lazuli, Green Basalt or Quartz and carved into the shape of a scarab. It was believed that the 'Ka' of the deceased person would, by possession of the Amulet of the Heart, gain power to go where it pleased and journey to the Judgement Hall of Osiris. There, the heart of the deceased would be weighed against a feather to consider whether they would be allowed permission to enter into the afterlife.

The Utchat, or Eye of Horus, was another important symbol and talisman of ancient Egypt. The eye was usually made of Gold, Silver and Lapis Lazuli. There were two forms of the eye: one facing to the left and one facing to the right, representing the two eyes of Horus and the sun and the moon. The Eye was worn as an amulet of protection and also to represent the balance between light and dark and summer and winter. Offerings were made to the Eye at times of particular solar significance, such as the Summer Solstice and other astronomical events.

There were several full time positions to be held as an Egyptian Priest, and jobs were open to all sorts of people from the highly educated to the illiterate. Scribes and scholars worked in the sacred libraries and study halls, where subjects such as astronomy, history, herbs, medicine and the occult were studied. One chief Scribe, Kenkirkhephshef, was famed for his historical and occult writings. He also wrote the *Book of Dreams and Interpretations*, and spells for dispelling negative dreams and evil demons. Kenkirkhephshef was a follower of Set, the mysterious God of the desert.

'Lector' Priests trained as physicians, and 'Sem' Priests oversaw funerary rites and the preservation of bodies prior to burial. 'Ka' Priests were in charge of the upkeep of the offering tables and replenishing the food for the dead, and other Priests oversaw the daily rituals and the use of the temples. 'Phyle' Priests and 'Wab' Priests (or 'Wbt' Priestesses) were lower ranking employees, often working part time and carrying out supportive roles such as cleaning and assisting the other Priests. Other temple roles included the role of 'Mrt' Priestess, who organised and took part in the daily running of the temples as well as the administrative side, and lesser Priestesses, who were often part time and who had been called upon from the local community for 'temple duty'. They would perform such tasks as the washing and feeding of the statues in the temple and sharing out food between the Priests once the offerings had been made.

The Pharaoh represented both God and High Priest within society. Often the Kings were deified, many before their death, and proclaimed as sons of Gods. The Heb-Sed ritual, a festival held when a Pharaoh reached thirty years on the throne and then held every three years after, was a celebration to mark both the strength of the King upon the throne and the power of the God he personified.

But it was not just Kings who were deified. Queens took the title of 'God's Wife', and were deified in their own way. Queen Hatshepsut, who took the position of Pharaoh by default as there was no suitable male heir to take the throne, was also deified and proclaimed the 'Son and daughter of Amun, and incarnation of Horus on Earth'. Imhotep, a Priest originally of no royal relation who served under King Djoser in the 3rd Dynasty, was also deified after his death. He was announced the 'Great Son of Ptah, the Great God', and known for his skills of architecture and medicine.

Egyptian religion was largely polytheistic, worshiping multiple Gods side by side. However, during the short reign of the Pharaoh Akhenaten, 1352-1335 BCE, the idea of worshiping just one sole God was introduced, and Egypt was declared a Monotheistic society. This new God was 'Aten', a male God who was a composite deity of Ra-Amun-Horus. Solar deity cults had become increasingly popular in Egypt prior to Akhenaten's reign, with cities such as Memphis leading the way in the adoration of such solar Gods as Atum and Re. Even local deities were being solarised by adding Re or Ra to the end of their name. The name 'Aten' had been introduced as a reference to the sun disc that was now being placed upon the heads of deities such as Horus and creating new names, in this instance proclaiming him Re-Horakhty. When Akhenaten came to power he responded to this rise in solarism and began commissioning architecture depicting God just as the sun disc, proclaiming Aten as the supreme God of Egypt. The worship of other Gods and Goddesses was still permitted, however, until Akhenaten's ninth year in reign when a new law was passed announcing that Aten was the only God. It was at this time that the worship of other Gods was banned, old temples destroyed and the names of Gods other than Aten scratched out from temples, walls and tombs. There was also a ban on idolatry, with the only image allowed being the sun disc with its rays shining down on Akhenaten, who had now pronounced himself mediator between God and the people. Akhenaten even had a city built for himself called Akhetaten, in which everything was orientated towards the east, the place of the rising sun. However, the change was not taken well by the people of Egypt who felt that abandoning their ancient Gods could only lead to chaos. There were rumours of curses from the old Gods as death struck Akhenaten's family and plague, polio and influenza swept the land during the time of his reign. Political relations were also affected, as alliances made through marriage and the synchronism of Gods no longer seemed valid.

Akhenaten had ruled Egypt for 17 years before he died in 1335 BCE. The cult of Aten died along with him and the land was quickly re-established to a Polytheistic religion by his successor, Tutankhamen. The city of Akhenaten was abandoned and the ruins used to rebuild temples to the old Gods and Goddesses. Egypt continued to be a polytheistic empire until circa 33AD, when the Romans invaded and it became part of the Roman Empire.

Although it may not be immediately obvious, many Egyptian ways were brought to Britain by the Romans, especially the worship of Isis, the 'Goddess of a thousand names', who we know was worshiped at Isis Temples in London, York, and Silchester.

Ritual and Magic in Greece

The extent of the Greek Empire spanned from the tail end of the Minoan and Mycenaean periods of the Bronze Age right though to the conquest of Greece by the Roman Empire in the year 146 BCE.

The Minoan Empire established itself on the Greek Island of Crete between the years 2700 and 1600 BCE, and is believed to have been the most ancient civilisation of Europe. The Minoan religion was almost entirely matriarchal; that is, only female deities were worshiped. Although symbols within nature (such as animals and the sun) were sometimes seen as symbolically 'masculine' they were not worshiped as deities in the same way as their female counterparts. Despite Minoan religion being essentially matriarchal, their attitude was not in any way disagreeable towards the male and on the whole their culture was largely based on equality. Rather than being seen as inferior to women, men were seen as equals (in contrast to patriarchal attitudes during the later periods of Mycenaean and Ancient/Classical Greece). Women carried out the same positions within society as men, performing the same job roles, took part in the same sports and joined the same priesthoods. They also held a similar social standing to men, and both women and men played an important part in the politics and the decisions made in the empire.

The Minoans were keen merchants and traded in saffron, ceramics, gold, silver and other precious wares, as well as being known for their beautiful and well-tailored clothing. They were on the whole a peace-loving society; they avoided war when they could, and developed alliances rather than hostility with their neighbours. It is believed that their religious practices were highly influenced by that of the Egyptians who the Minoans traded with on a regular basis, and many aspects of the Goddesses from Egypt were absorbed into Minoan culture.

There is very little written evidence to provide us with the names of the Goddesses who were worshiped by the Minoans at Crete. Sculpture and artwork that remains tells us that Goddesses of Harvest, Goddesses of the Seasons and Goddesses of Hearth and Home were worshiped, as well as the serpent who was called the 'Minister of the Goddess'. Although the archetypes of these Goddesses can be identified in Mycenaean and Classical Greek mythology, there is very little evidence to show that their names were absorbed into the Goddesses of these later cultures.

The Mycenaean civilisation extended their control to Crete and defeated the Minoans in 1600 BCE. The Mycenaean's incorporated much of the Minoan art and refined culture into their own, particularly their skills of fashion and trade. Unlike the Minoans, however, the Mycenaean's were raiders as well as traders and accumulated much wealth through their conquest of other societies.

With the Mycenaean culture came the worship of Gods as well as Goddesses, and it is this range of Gods and Goddesses that made the transition into later Classical Greek worship with familiar names such as Zeus, Athena, Hera and Ares. Mycenaean writing is recognisable as Classical Greek and the structure of their society certainly leaned toward the coming era of Ancient/Classical Greece. Mycenaean culture was also highly influenced by Egyptian practices. The practice of mummification was popular, as was burying the dead within burial chambers and stone tombs with a golden mask upon the face.

The Mycenaean Empire came to an end in 1150 BCE, when Greece and the surrounding area suffered from famine and poverty. The period that followed was described as the 'Greek Dark Ages'.

The Archaic/Classical Greek era began around the year 1000 BCE. Greek society was divided by the legal status of those who were free and those who were enslaved, and slaves were legally bought and sold. However, people could change classes depending on their education and wealth. Slaves could also be freed, although they would not become citizens but instead join a class called the Metics, who although free had no citizen rights.

Although Priestesses were still important within the structure of worship, the society as a whole was much more patriarchal than it had been in the times of the Minoans and the Mycenaeans. Women were in general seen as inferior to men and were often obliged to cover the head and neck; they were also subject to arranged marriages. However, many powerful Goddesses still held positions of high importance in Greek belief, and tales of mighty Goddesses with formidable power over their men folk was very common.

In general, the Greeks worshiped twelve major deities: Aphrodite, Apollo, Ares, Artemis, Demeter, Dionysus, Hephaestus, Hera, Hermes, Hestia, Poseidon and Zeus. As with many other cultures, Greek deities often displayed a local nature, such as 'Artemis the Fertile One' in Ephesus, who was also known as 'Artemis the Huntress' in Sparta. Just like the Egyptians, the Greeks had no specific word for 'religion' as their beliefs were part of their everyday life and they saw no separation. The Priests and Priestesses of the Temples were considered as representing the Gods and Goddesses, and conse-crated food offerings were often eaten by the brethren on behalf of the deities, a practice which continues in some modern Craft covens today. Political relationships were also built between leaders and deities, with public rituals, holidays and festivals held to appease the Gods.

The Greeks are well known for their Lesser and Greater Initiatory Mysteries, systems which trained participants in occult knowledge, mythology and the secrets of living and dying. One of the most famous of these secret systems is the Eleusinian Mysteries, which studied and celebrated the legend of the Goddesses Demeter and Kore. Another was the Dionysian Mysteries, which taught the secrets of fertility, prosperity, and wine. Although the true Mysteries were practiced in secret with wisdom only shared with the initiated, there were also street festivals in honour of the mysteries, which were held for the common people.

Ritual and Magic in Rome

The rise and fall of the Roman Empire lasted almost 2000 years. Although the Romans were a highly successful society who introduced new technological advances to both civilian and military life, they owed a high proportion of their language, architecture, philosophy and religious beliefs to the Greeks. Much of the Greek culture had been absorbed into Roman society when Greece became part of the Empire.

Early Romans were keen practitioners of Animism; that is, they saw the Divinity in all things and the early deities of Rome were known as the 'Numina', meaning 'divine spirit'. On the whole, Romans paid homage to these spirits rather than specific deities. The Numina spirits included 'Lates', the spirits of the ancestors whom inhabited small statues, the 'Penates', who were larder spirits and the 'Genius' the serpent spirit. However, the Romans were also firm believers in syncretism; that is, they believed that the same Gods existed everywhere, just by different names. As contact with Greece increased, Roman spirits became associated with the more humanised Greek Gods and the people of Rome began to absorb the Greek mythos and God names into their own. The Romans also began to embrace the Grecian esoteric mystery traditions which surrounded Greek mythology.

As the Romans spread to Egypt and Asia, the worship of new deities such as the Egyptian Isis and the Persian Mithras also became popular. Pagan worship in Rome had become almost multi-cultural, with various deities becoming popular depending on who was Emperor at the time. Emperors often pronounced themselves as Gods, and after they died were deified and worshiped, in a similar way to the Pharaohs of Egypt.

Although the popularity of individual Gods in the Empire as

a whole often varied depending on who was Emperor, two particular deities were important to the Romans more or less throughout the entire period of the Roman Empire. These were Vesta, the Goddess of the Hearth, and Janus, the God of Doorways. Vesta and Janus were deities of the people; not limited to any particular class and worshiped by many. The Roman Empire was rigidly class orientated, with slavery common and individual laws and rights depending on birthright; Vesta however was a Goddess who was very much a part of everyone's lives. She was worshiped in great temples which were built for the imperialist upper class, but also worshiped by poorer people in their homes.

The Temples of Vesta housed a sacred fire that was kept burning at all times by the Vestal Virgins: women who were ordained as Priestesses of Vesta from an early age. The Vestal Virgins performed rituals of worship to Vesta and held much prestige in society. However, there was a considerable price to pay if a Vestal Virgin broke her vows and lost her virginity – usually the sentence of death, or even worse, being bricked up into the walls of the city alive.

Other deities were popular within Roman culture including Diana, Jupiter, Mars, Mercury, Minerva, Neptune, Pluto, Saturn, Uranus, Venus and Vulcan.

The Romans were, on a whole, a rather ruthless society and under a firm rule of imperialism. In a similar way to Classical Greek society, the state was divided by the legal status of the free and of the enslaved, and although human sacrifices for religious causes were rare they were not entirely unknown. The person to be sacrificed was called the 'sacer' meaning 'given to the Gods'. Criminals were usually the victims of the sacrifice, killed in order to restore divine order. However, the majority of sacrifices were those of animals, with as many as 100 white oxen being sacrificed at one time for particular rites. The use of animal by-products for divination was also common, such as studying the entrails of the sacrificed animals in order to foresee the future. Other forms of offerings included incenses and statues, wine, milk and honey and even gold. Elaborate feasts were held in the name of the Gods, in conjunction with holiday festivals and the Amphitheatre games.

When Christianity eventually reached Rome it was met by much persecution by the Pagan leaders of the Empire. Some of the worst persecution of the Christians is said to have occurred during the reign of Diocletion: a devout Pagan Emperor. However, the following Emperor, Constantine, was a keen Christian, and so Christianity became very popular during the height of his reign.

Christianity continued to be popular even many years after Constantine's death. Emperor Julian the Apostate briefly tried to bring Paganism back during his reign, but by then the popular faith of the masses was Christianity, and he failed to convert the Empire back to Paganism.

Emperor Theodosius was a committed Christian and sought to convert the whole of the Roman Empire to his religion. He was fairly tolerant of Pagan beliefs to begin with, only banning some of the more unethical practices such as blood sacrifice, but soon into his reign he had sent troops to Egypt, Asia and Syria to destroy Pagan temples. Any Pagan festival that had not been absorbed by Christian holy days were changed back into working days, and the games which accompanied many of the Pagan festivals were cancelled. Temples which still existed (such as temples to Vesta) and libraries that had been held by Pagan scholars and Priests were either closed or destroyed, and to follow the Pagan religion became heresy. The De Obitu Theodosii, a document written after the death of Theodosius, contains a detailed account of the suppression of the Pagan faith by the Emperor, which led to Christianity becoming the official state religion of Rome.

TASK: Tapping the Bone - A Journey to meet the Ancestors

Meditation is an important skill for any witch or practicing Pagan, as it allows you to relax and to focus your mind. When practiced effectively, meditation lets you enter 'the alpha state': an altered state of consciousness similar to the experience of dreaming, or trance. Through meditation we can access the otherworlds, receive advice from spirits, manipulate energy and even contact the Gods. Don't worry if it doesn't happen straight away; meditation, visualisation and how to improve your technique will be discussed in more detail later. If you are artistic, a keen reader or someone with an active imagination you may find meditation easier to achieve, as the skill of meditation is in the first instance the ability to allow your mind to visualise and imagine. However, with practice anyone can meditate.

This meditation will take you to meet with one of your ancestors. The ancestor may be from your bloodline, from a past incarnation, or even a spiritual ancestor. He or she will be someone who has influenced your spiritual life or shaped you in a positive way. Working with the ancestors is called 'tapping the bone', a term first published by Traditional witches Robin Artisson and Peter Paddon which describes the art of tapping into the knowledge and wisdom of our forefathers.

For this mediation you need to find somewhere that you will not be disturbed. This could be a bedroom, a locked study, or even outdoors. Turn off the phone, and tell anyone who may interrupt you that you wish to be left alone for a while. For beginners, it is best to meditate at the end of the day when there are no pressures to rush off anywhere, and you feel relaxed and calm.Most people find it helpful to light a candle or some incense to help them relax and to focus their mind. If you are the sort of person who tends to drop off to sleep easily it is best to sit up for the meditation, but if you can trust yourself to stay awake then you can lie down if it is more comfortable for you.

Read the text below several times so that you have a good idea of what will happen in the meditation. If possible, have someone read the meditation to you, or record it onto a tape and play it back to yourself; listening to a meditation being read is by far the easiest way of following a guided meditation. When you have an image in your mind of the journey, you can begin. Don't worry if the meditation deviates from the original story; go with whatever happens in your mind, even if it is different to what you had expected.

Close your eyes and take a few deep breaths. Focus on your breathing – in, and out, in an out. With every breath in, feel yourself calm and at peace. With every breath out, feel the tension of the day drain away. Your heartbeat becomes slower, your body becomes heavier. Breathe in peace, breathe out tension. All thoughts of the day and other distractions leave your mind as you become completely relaxed and focused. There is no rush. When you feel completely calm and relaxed, you can begin.

See yourself stood upon the crest of a hill, breathing in the cool, refreshing air. You feel revitalized by the breeze and admire the beauty of the rolling fields beneath you. Above you soar birds of prey, calling to one another across the valley.

To the right of you lies a path through the long grass, meandering gently down to a cluster of inviting trees at the base of the hill. You follow the path down the slope, towards an ancient yew grove. As you approach, you marvel at the yew trees, whose low, damp branches have entwined into one another over the ages. The canopy of branches seem to be arching now, and invite you to enter the forest.

You step into the forest of yews, safe in the knowledge that you are protected, and nothing can harm you here. You follow the path which continues beneath the shady boughs above; you touch the gnarled bark of the yews as you start to walk deeper into the forest, feeling the wisdom within this place resonate through your soul.

Soon you see that the forest is beginning to thin out to a clearing, revealing a mighty yew in its centre. This yew is the oldest in the woods, and is home to the ancient spirits. You marvel at the size of the tree, which dwarfs the others around it. Its roots are strong, and reach deep into the earth.

But now you sense someone else is present in this quiet forest glade, and watch as a figure begins to step out from behind the mighty yew. This is your ancestor – he or she has been waiting for you.

You approach the tree and greet the person. You sit with your ancestor, as they recall tales of the past and reveal wisdom to you that will aid you on your spiritual path. Listen carefully while your ancestor speaks.

Now he or she offers you a gift, a small round stone with a hole running through its centre. It is a Hag Stone, a tool of otherworldly wisdom, which your ancestor places into your palm. Thank them for this gift, and if you have any questions, ask them now.

After a time, your ancestor gestures that it is time for you to leave. He or she walks back behind the ancient yew tree, and becomes part of the forest once again.

Now, when you are ready, the image of the trees begins to fade away and you start to feel yourself returning to this world. When you are ready, open your eyes.

'Ancestral Meditation', from the Coven Book of Ways

Paganism vs. a New Religion

It is difficult to say when Christianity began to spread to Europe as it was not the immediate mass conversion that is often suggested. Countries began to be classed as Christian when in reality it was often only the rulers who had adopted the religion, and superficially at that. Paganism in its many different forms continued to be openly practiced for at least the first 1,000 years of Christianity.

The first real attempt of mass conversion was made by Pope

Gregory (ca 540-604 AD). He commissioned churches to be built over the sites of Pagan temples and holy ground. In an attempt to convert the local populace, many sacred sites were adopted as well as the local customs and festivals; this conversion was widespread in the British Isles from the time the earliest missionaries arrived. One example of this is Knowlton Church, which lies about six miles north of Wimborne, in Dorset. It is the ruin of a fourteenth century church which sits in the centre of a Bronze Age Pagan earth circle, and it is widely believed that the standing stones, which were a feature of the surrounding henge, were broken up and used within the construction of the church. If this is the case, then the location of the church within the central henge at Knowlton is clear evidence of the christianisation of older Pagan sites. However, the common people employed to build the new churches had a few tricks up their sleeves themselves. In many instances they actually incorporated their own deities, particularly the foliate-faced Green Man, into the woodwork and masonry of the very churches and cathedrals they were building.

TASK: The Green Man

Parallels are often drawn between the Green Man and the Pagan Vegetation Gods, such as Tammuz, Woden and Cernunnos. He is also closely associated with the Vegetation Spirits of folklore, such as John Barleycorn and Jack in the Green. In some ways, it can be said that the Green Man personifies the unified spirit of all of these vegetation characters.

Research the history of the traditional foliate-faced Green Man, and the use of his image in churches and cathedrals. Look at his mythology throughout the ages, and discover his different guises.

Then make your own Green Man out of clay, leaves and whatever other materials you feel you can express yourself with. If you can, visit a woodland and collect fallen vegetation, berries and acorns to create a totally organic piece of art. If the materials you use are *completely* natural, you could take it back to the woodland and leave it there as an offering to the spirit of the Green Man.

The Old Myths Reinvented

In addition to the Christianisation of older Pagan sites, Pagan mythology also became incorporated into early Christian belief. Some of the earliest gospels suggest that Jesus was inspired by ancient Pagan mystery traditions and many tales from the Old Testament in particular also run parallel with ancient Pagan myths, containing characters who can be identified as ancient Gods and Goddesses.

One story evident of this is that of Adam and Eve. The story actually finds its roots in an earlier Middle eastern creation myth which has an additional character, named Lilith. In Pagan tales, the ancient Lilith was portrayed both as Mother and Crone – the Dark Goddess – who represented the primordial Mother who gave birth to the first man, named Adam. Lilith then became her son's lover, a notion which was unacceptable to the beliefs of the emerging patriarchal systems, although a concept that was common in Pagan mythos as a symbolic way of demonstrating the cycle of life within nature. Like many Pagan deities, Lilith also had an opposite polarity: her lighter side, named Eve. Eve was accepted into the new faith of Christianity as she fitted into their belief system: virginal, innocent and subordinate to man. Eve was placed at Adam's side and quoted in the bible as his 'helper' and it was written in the bible that Eve was formed from his spare rib – 'the part least needed by man'.

In the Christian story, Eve takes an apple - the forbidden fruit - from an evil snake on the 'Tree of Good and Evil' which eventually leads to her demise and their rejection from the Garden of Eden. However, in ancient times, both the snake and the tree were seen as symbols of enlightenment, rebirth, strength and knowledge, and the apple was seen as a symbol of initiation and learning. The Garden of Eden, therefore, can be seen as representing the unconscious and 'blissfully unaware' state of mind and on taking the apple from the tree of knowledge, Eve takes the gift of conscious awareness and initiation (see more about the apple in Chapter Ten). It is also interesting that Lilith is sometimes depicted in Christian art as the snake itself. In this way, Lilith is offering enlightenment, rite of passage and the gift of choice to Adam and Eve. The snake or serpent spirit was an important symbol in many ancient cultures, symbolising the energy of the earth, the powers of fertility and the philosophy of cycles. As modern Pagans, part of our challenge is to overcome the centuries of cultural oppression which has instilled a fear of the snake in our subconscious. When Christianity rose to power, the snake was demonised as a symbol of Satan, probably because of its importance in Pagan beliefs. This fear of snakes has been passed down from generation to generation, and if we are to pay due respect to the Ancient Ones then we must face this fear and overcome it.

Lilith was later demonized and the story was changed, and today it is very difficult to find any biblical literature that does not mention Lilith as a demon or evil spirit. However, this demonization of the ancient Gods and Goddesses spread much further than just the obscure Lilith. The ancient God Cernunnos, horned with stag antlers to represent strength, wisdom, fertility and protection, was also reinvented by Christian converters into their Devil: the anti-God. In fact before this reinvention,the original Christian 'devil' did not have horns at all, and was usually pictured with bat-like ears and bullish features - far from the stag-like horned God or goatish Pan of the Pagan Craft. It was only later in history that goat-like 'devils' began to be illustrated, which was most likely a Christian reaction to the Pan's growing popularity in poetry and literature at the time.

However some deities, such as the Celtic Brigid, were too

important to the local people and were absorbed into Christianity as Saints, to ease the transition from Paganism to Christianity. And so, the Goddess Brigid became St Brigit.

The temple of the Great Goddess should be despised, and Her magnificence should be destroyed, whom all Asia and the world worship.
New Testament 19:27

The story of Mary, the woman who gave birth to Jesus with her virginity intact, could also be a variation of an older myth recalling the Primordial Mother Goddess giving birth to the God. In Paganism, the Mother Goddess is highly revered; however, in the Christian myth Mary plays a subordinate role and there is very little mention of her after her son's birth. Nevertheless, Mary fits many of the roles of the Pagan Mother Goddess, in particular the Egyptian Goddess Isis and her lover/son Osiris. The birth of Jesus was prophesised by a star, as was the birth of the God Osiris, whose name is connected with the word Sirius; the star which the three wise men followed to Bethlehem. Osiris was worshiped in a grove of trees which shaded a small village in Israel; a village that was later named Bethlehem. Osiris even had twelve disciples, he turned water into wine and one of his symbols was the fish: the symbol of death, rebirth and the underworld, the domain of Osiris. Osiris died and was reborn as was Jesus: reminiscent of the Pagan 'dying and rising' Gods.

In the early fourteenth century in Europe and beyond, the church was becoming a powerful force and behind this power were some equally powerful and wealthy people. There was a lot of money in the church; it was big business. Wars, taxes and laws were all created in its name, and mainly for the profit of the people behind it. A few of the common people in Britain still followed the native ways and even those who did not often consulted the local cunning woman for cures, midwifery and advice. It was these women who the church saw as standing in their way. Why? For one; Christianity, the church and the Christian way was, essentially, patriarchal. That is, women were not seen as being as equal to men.

It is not unreasonable that this scum of humanity should be drawn chiefly from the feminine sex.
Judge N Remy, c. 1595, on witches

It was also against Christian belief for any person to have healing or magical abilities, as this was seen as a gift from the Devil and not from God. Therefore the wise women, who were seen by their village as the heart of the community stood for everything that the church detested. The rise of Christianity brought an end to the divine partnership between the Goddess and God that had lasted thousands of years, and left the God without his lover.

The Witch Hunts

Thou shalt not suffer a witch to live.
'The Bible', Exodus 22:18

The Witch Hunts, or 'The Burning Times' describes an infamous period of almost four centuries of witch hysteria and persecution which began in the fourteenth century with the publication of document called the Malleus Maleficarum – 'The Witch Hammer'. The Witch Hammer was written by two Dominicans named Jakob Sprenger and Heinrich Kramer, Inquisitors of the Catholic Church under the 'Holy Office of the Inquisition' in Rome. The Holy Office of the Inquisition was an institution set up to *'defend the* (catholic) *faith and trial heresy or false doctrines* (other religions)' and was one of the most feared offices in Europe. It approved in the use of torture and execution as forms of punishment, and many of its other victims included Cathars,

Hindus, Jews, homosexuals and even other types of Christianity. The Witch Hammer clearly outlined the prosecution of witches. It was divided into three parts, the first detailed that witchcraft was indeed real, and declared that to not believe in the Craft was, in itself, heresy. The second detailed the 'pacts with the devil, evil misdoings and other horrid crimes' that witches were alleged to be committing. The third detailed how to trial and prosecute a witch. The book was based on the biblical pronouncement, 'thou shalt not suffer a witch to live' together with the superstitions and folktales of members of the church. In fact, this phrase of the bible originally read 'thou shalt not suffer a poisoner to live' but was changed by Pope Gregory in the sixth century to suit his personal agenda.

There is very little original content in the Malleus Maleficarum. Most of it is based on earlier publications regarding occultism written by monks and other members of the church, who in truth would not have had any experience of true witchcraft or Paganism to base their writing on in the first place. Even the church itself eventually condemned the book as being 'illegal and unethical' and placed it in the 'index of banned books'. However, before the ban it managed to be published sixteen times and was generally *believed* to be accepted by the church. Shortly after the book became widespread, mass hysteria began in the villages and towns and people began blaming witchcraft for the failing of crops, sickness, ill health and even for the milk turning sour. This began almost 400 years of horrific persecution against women and men alike.

Cunning people withdrew from the public eye and refrained from performing the healing arts, midwifery and from making cures, except in secret. More than often the men and women arrested on the charge of witchcraft were just middle aged, middle class people who had bickered with their neighbours or fallen out of favour with the community. Others were just poor and uneducated, with no influential friends or social standing who were suspected of witchcraft just because they owned a cat, grew herbs or had some sort of body blemish. A large percentage of convicted 'witches' were in fact practicing Christians, taken to the gallows by people of their own religion for something as simple as having a crooked nose or being the local busybody. Witch hunters made a small fortune by charging local magistrates for each and every person they executed and some of the infamous and cruel practices that the witch hunters employed on the continent included torture by hot pincers, thumbscrews, mutilation, limb dislocation, disembowelment, gouging out of the eyes, cutting off parts of the body and sexual humiliation. In Britain, the inquisitors employed less violent but equally effective methods, such as sleep deprivation and indefinite imprisonment.

But witch hunters did not just rely on forced confessions. There were also a number of tests which were used to identify witches. These included the water test (if you sunk and drowned you were innocent, if you floated you were guilty, and hung!) the scales test (when the suspect was weighed against the bible) and the identification of 'witchmarks' (such as unusual moles, birthmarks and other blemishes upon the person). Before the witch hunts, wise women sometimes marked themselves with sigils such as the 'Witches Foot', the six pointed star, or 'Crows Foot', a triple-pronged pitchfork pattern and the rune of 'Algiz', which was a sign of their Art. Although this tradition probably stopped during the Burning Times, it was still a good enough reason for the witch hunters to condemn anyone with any sort of unusual mark to the body. Other bizarre tests were also carried out to 'identify' witches, such as 'witchpricking'. The method of witchpricking used a sharp needle-like instrument called the 'Bodkin' to pierce the skin of the suspect. If they did not show any signs of pain, or lost no blood, then the victim was declared a witch. The sad matter was that many of the witch hunters used phony bodkins with retractable blades, so that when they were pushed into the skin the blade appeared to penetrate the body, when in fact it did not. This way, the witch hunters could prosecute yet another 'witch'. The magistrates paid the witch hunters per head, and it is estimated by Professor Ronald Hutton in his article, 'Counting the Witch Hunt', that approximately 40,000 individuals were burnt, hung or tortured to death on the charge of witchcraft in Europe alone; it is highly unlikely that even a small percentage of the accused were even witches.

The Witchcraft Act was changed in 1736. The new document stated that witchcraft did not actually exist, and if you said that you had occult powers you would be charged with fraud. This law meant that the hysteria which had led to almost four centuries of torture and slaughter ended, however to practice witchcraft was still taboo under this law and so the Craft continued to be practiced in secret. And that is how things stayed until the 20th century, when the Witchcraft Act was finally repealed in 1951.

The repeal was a milestone for modern Craft, and lead to a boom of modern Wicca in Britain and America. Finally free to admit their beliefs, many witches began to appear on television and some even wrote books under their real names. For all the safety that the repeal gave modern witches, it is still unsettling to know that whilst its methods of torture and execution have since been made illegal, 'The Holy Office of the Inquisition' is still very much in operation. It underwent a name change in the 1960's and is now called the 'Congregation for the Doctrine of the Faith' - its most prominent 'work' in recent years being the persecution of homosexuality and abortion. At the time of research it was difficult to ascertain whether the 'Congregation for the Doctrine of the Faith' still kept any of the old tools of torture at their offices in Vatican City, nor what their attitude to modern witchcraft was.

Chapter Three

Revival of Witchcraft - 1951 to Today

Within the following pages I have covered some of the personalities of the modern witchcraft movement in the 20th century. There have been many other individuals who have also left their mark on modern witchcraft but I cannot possibly cover them all here, so here are a few of the better-known characters to get you started.

Gerald Gardner 1884 – 1964

Gerald Gardner was born near Liverpool to a well to do family. Early in his childhood he developed asthma and his family was advised to move to Asia, where he lived much of his young life. It was in Asia that he first became interested in the occult, influenced by the native belief and ritual practices.

Gardner claimed that he was initiated into one of the New Forest covens (which some say was one of the nine covens that were allegedly founded by 'Old George' Pickingill, the famous witch of Essex) by High Priestess Dorothy Clutterbuck who lived in Christchurch near the New Forest. Although there was originally much controversy over whether Dorothy Clutterbuck was in fact real, her existence can no longer be disputed since research by Doreen Valiente has proved Dorothy's date of birth and place of residence, which was not far from where Gardner himself lived. However, further research by Professor Ron Hutton has shown that it was very unlikely that Dorothy was involved in the Craft, and it is more probable that Gardner used her name to cover the identity of his real High Priestess who we now know as Edith Woodford-Grimes, or 'Dafo'.

Gardner   was   heavily   influenced   by   the   works   of

Anthropologist and Egyptologist Dr Margaret Alice Murray, who had written several controversial papers on ancient religion and witchcraft. Gardner based much of his work on her thesis, and Murray and Gardner would continue to be acquainted throughout their lives. Murray even wrote a foreword for one of Gardner's books, *Witchcraft Today*, in 1954. It was in this book that Gardner admitted to his beliefs, making reference to Margaret Murray's work. 'What Margaret Murray has theorised is quite true,' Gardner wrote, 'I know, because I am a witch myself.' The release of the book soon encouraged other covens to emerge out of the woodwork and admit their beliefs.

Another influence to Gardner's work was Reverend John Ward, the leader of the 'Confraternity of Christ the King' who ran a social history museum at Abbey Folk Park in New Barnet, London. Ward was also a Freemason, and had published several books about Masonry. When the Abbey Folk Park was forced to close due to the war, Ward sold Gardner a small brick and timber building from the Park which Gardner rebuilt on a few acres of land that he owned at Bricket Wood in Hertfordshire. The little cottage would go on to be the meeting place of Gardner's Bricket Wood Coven. Gardner also wanted to buy out the Fiveacres Country Club, which was in close proximity to the cottage, probably to form a folk museum but he and Dafo could only manage to buy part of the Club. They approached Gardner's friend, Cecil Williamson, to buy the other part; however, Williamson ended up buying an old windmill on the Isle of Man in 1948 instead, which he turned into his own 'Folklore and Witchcraft Centre'. Cecil eventually sold the windmill to Gardner in 1954 and moved his own collection to Boscastle, Cornwall. The Museum of Witchcraft still exists in Boscastle today, under new ownership.

One of Gardner's published works includes the famous novel *High Magic's Aid* in 1949. At the time, it was still against the law to say that you were a witch or to practice witchcraft, but

Gardner was able to get information out to the public by weaving the truth of Paganism and witchcraft into fiction.

The eventual publication of his training notes *Ye Bok Ye Art Magical,* and subsequent release of the *Gardnerian Book of Shadows* as complied by Aidan A Kelley in his book, *Crafting the Art of Magic,* lead to the standard structure of many modern rites in Wicca today.

Doreen Valiente 1922 – 1999

Doreen Valiente was born in London to devout Christian parents, but from an early age she felt a calling to witchcraft and magic - a curiosity which would grow later in life.

It was in 1952 that Doreen was initiated into the Craft by Gerald Gardner and became his High Priestess under her Craft name, 'Ameth'. She helped Gardner to re-write his fragmented rituals and also wrote many beautiful poems together with Gardner, such as *The Charge of the Goddess* (adapted from a version written by occultist Aleister Crowley) which are still used by many initiates of the western mystery tradition.

However, Gardner's preoccupation with publicity began to cause conflict with Valiente, and finally in 1957 when Gardner wrote a new list of rules that Doreen simply could not agree with, she parted company. After working with Robert Cochrane for a short period of time, Doreen decided to created her own working group.

In the 70s Doreen wrote a number of books, including *An ABC of Witchcraft, Witchcraft for Tomorrow* and *The Rebirth of Witchcraft,* and thereafter Valiente became one of the most influential leaders of the modern witchcraft movement. One of her most commendable achievements was lobbying parliament in 1972 to prevent the return of the Witchcraft Act. She was also one of the co-founders of the Pagan Federation, a government recognised organisation which stands for Pagan rights and develops the Pagan community.

Robert Cochrane (1931 – 1966)

The inherent philosophy of the craft was always fluid, and fluid it must become again before it gasps its last breath under a heap of musty nonsense, half-baked theology and philosophy. Witches cannot retreat from the world any longer, there is no room for us in this society unless we have something valid to offer it, and participate in its social evolution.

Robert Cochrane, 'The Craft Today' printed in Pentagram magazine 1964

Robert Cochrane was born Roy Bowers in 1931 in London. Despite his family having converted to Methodism, Cochrane claimed that he was a hereditary witch who was taught by older members of his family such as his grandfather and his aunt.

Cochrane founded the 'Clan of Tubal Cain' in his mid 20s, a group who followed 'The 1734 Tradition', which he himself had founded. In one letter to a friend, Cochrane explained the meaning behind the numbers within the name of the tradition: a combination of magical numbers which related to the 7 states of wisdom, the 3 elements (the 4th, fire, allegedly being 'owned by man') and the 4 winds.

Cochrane was a contemporary of Gardner; however, Cochrane did not hold Gardner in high regard, and described him as an 'out and out fake'. His contempt for Gardner, together with his increasingly unpredictable behaviour, would lead to one of his most influential High Priestesses Doreen Valiente resigning from the group only a few years after being initiated.

As well as being an avid poet and philosopher, Cochrane published many articles throughout the 60's outlining the tradition's practice, such as 'The 1734 Tradition', 'The Craft Today', 'The Faith of the Wise', 'On Cords' and 'Witches Esbat'. However, Cochrane is best known for his letters to fellow Craft members, from which the basis of much of his tradition was gathered after his death.

Cochrane wrote that the 'real mysteries' and the 'peasant ways' are separate. In a direct contrast to modern Pagan views Cochrane wrote, *'the natural forces are means to us, not an ends, and all that sort of stuff died out with the primitives'* and *'Nature worship is a thing that belongs to genuine peasants or to twee old ladies at borderline medicine associations'*.

However, it becomes apparent as we read more of Cochrane that although his comments are indeed based on his true beliefs, they are also a meant to be read with 'tongue firmly in cheek'. Cochrane certainly has a sense of humour, and we cannot criticise him for expressing his views in his own comedic and contemptuous way. For Cochrane then goes on to say, *'Pantheism still exists, but it is the lesser force for a witch of my tradition, not the greater.'* In later writings, he also states that *'the real witch instinct seems to have gone...been trained out by too much deodorant, and not enough nature'* ... and then continuously presses the importance of working outdoors.

There is much contest throughout the Pagan community as to how genuine Cochrane was. Having read much of his correspondence to his friends and colleagues, and having followed some of his subsequent ideas and traditions I believe that Cochrane made a very different, but wholly valid, contribution to the Craft today.

Robert died at Litha (the Summer Solstice) in 1966 after ingesting a lethal dose of Deadly Nightshade. It is not known if his death was an accident or a ritual suicide.

Alex Sanders (1926 – 1988) and Maxine Sanders (1947 -)

Alex Sanders was born in Manchester in 1926. Possibly one of the most influential characters in the modern history of the Craft, Alex first became involved in the Craft in 1962 when he joined a Gardnerian coven run by Patricia Crowther. After leaving Patricia's coven Alex joined a group run by Medea, another initiate of Gerald Gardner. When Medea resigned, she left Alex to run the coven together with Sylvia Tatham, who was part of

Medea's coven but was initiated by Scotty and Monique Wilson whilst visiting Gerald on the Isle of Man. When Sylvia moved away, Alex went on to start his own circle and formed a tradition called 'Alexandrian' Witchcraft, a term coined by Stewart Farrar who was one of Sander's initiates. It was during the mid 60's that Alex met his wife to be Maxine Morris, who he initiated into the Craft.

Maxine was born in Cheshire in 1947. Her mother had a fascination with the occult, and Maxine was still a teenager when her mother made contact with a group practicing the Egyptian Mysteries. Whilst apprehensive about joining the group herself, her mother wholeheartedly encouraged Maxine to train, and it was with the Egyptian Mysteries group that she had her first experiences of ritual and initiation which would be so much a part of the rest of her life.

Maxine began training with Alex Sanders in the mid 1960's and soon started to show her abilities as a teacher as well as a witch; when Alex told her that the coven needed someone to represent the Goddess, Maxine took the title of Witch Queen within the circle. Maxine became Alex's wife in 1968 and although they separated a few years later, the pair had two children and continued to work together to form new covens under the Alexandrian tradition.

In 1969 Alex released his autobiography, *King of the Witches* and shortly after the pair appeared in the film *Legend of the Witches*. Alex soon found himself being asked to appear on television and radio more and more. Although many others in the Craft disliked Sanders' relationship with the media, Alex and Maxine believed that people should be educated about witchcraft. Regardless of the bad press that Alex is often accused of creating, he did a lot for the modern Craft movement and in particular his Alexandrian Craft, which continues to be one of the most practiced forms of modern witchcraft today.

Maxine released her first book in 1976, titled *Maxine: The*

Witch Queen. This was followed by a further book, *The Ecstatic Mother* which was a biography written by Richard Deutch in 1977. Most recently, she published *Fire Child: The Life and Magic of Maxine Sanders* which was released in 2007; a wealth of information about her life with Alex and a testimony to how far modern Craft has come from its beginnings in the 1950's.

Alex died in 1988, and Maxine continued the Alexandrian tradition thereafter. She has now retired from Craft training, but continues to give talks and offers counseling around the country.

Stewart Farrar 1916 – 2000

Stewart Farrar was born in Essex in 1916, and brought up in a middle-class family as a Christian Scientist. Even before his involvement in witchcraft, Farrar was a prolific journalist and author and wrote many articles during his time at University. He met Alex and Maxine Sanders in 1969 when he was sent to conduct an interview with them following their involvement with a short film called *Legend of the Witches*. Stewart found himself warm to the philosophy of witchcraft and shortly after in 1970 was invited by Alex to begin training with the coven. It was in Alex Sanders' coven that he met his wife and co-writer to be, Janet Owen.

Farrar later collaborated with Alex Sanders to write a book called *What Witches Do*, which was published in 1971. The book was a milestone for the witchcraft movement, written in a straightforward manner with intelligent, inside knowledge of the Craft. Along with his wife, Stewart aided the revival of Britain's culture, mythos and ancient lore and help re-establish the Witches Wheel of the Year, making witchcraft accessible to all.

Janet Farrar (1950 -) and Gavin Bone (1964 -)

Janet Owen was born in London in 1950 and was brought up as a member of the Church of England. By the age of 20, Janet Owen had met Alex and Maxine Sanders and in October 1970 Janet was initiated into their coven. It was also here that she met her magical partner and husband to be, Stewart Farrar. Stewart and Janet worked together towards their Second Degrees in Alex's coven, but later that year decided to leave the group to start their own coven. They were married in 1975, and soon after moved to Ireland.

Janet and Stewart co-authored many influential books on witchcraft and Paganism, all of which have become well known and respected reference books on the subject.

Working alongside Stewart, Janet helped revive the mysteries of the Wheel of the Year and the forgotten folklore of the British Isles, as well as many other magical traditions from all around the world. Their book, *A Witches Bible*, contains, in one volume, two of their earlier books *Eight Sabbats for Witches* and *The Witches' Way*, and has become a must-have handbook both for beginners and experienced witches alike.

Gavin Bone was born in Portsmouth in 1964. He trained as a registered nurse, and practiced many different holistic therapies such as reflexology and spiritual healing. Gavin was introduced into the Craft in 1986, and initiated Maureen Wheeler in the 1990's. Maureen went on to become a respected occult teacher and Elder of the Wicca, and is commended in particular for her commitment to developing the Craft community in the south of England.

Shortly after meeting Janet and Stewart Farrar at a Pagan Federation Conference, Gavin began to collaborate with the Farrars and accompany them on tours, eventually co-authoring with the couple. When Stewart passed away in February 2000, Janet and Gavin continued to carry on with the work together and have released several new books and DVDs. Their latest book, *Progressive Witchcraft*, has been very influential in changes to coven structure and procedures in covens in both Britain and America.

Sybil Leek 1923 – 1983

Sybil Leek was born in Staffordshire to a well to do family. Her immediate family all played a part in encouraging her to follow the Craft and she learnt much from her father about nature, animals and the power of herbs. Her grandmother taught her astrology by decorating biscuits and cakes with astrological symbols, asking Sybil to put them in order and describe what each symbol meant.

Sybil claimed she only had three years of orthodox schooling; her family continued to school her at home but her grandmother focused on her esoteric training, such as the knowledge of herbs, astrology, the psychic arts and divination. However, despite the lack of schooling that Sybil had, she was in no way uneducated and Sybil's family played host to some very scholarly characters including HG Wells and poet and occultist, Alistair Crowley. Alistair was a regular visitor to the family home and used to read his poetry to Sybil, who soon became a keen poet herself and published her first volume of poetry when she was just a teenager.

When she was 18 Sybil became friends with the Romany Gypsies in the New Forest, learning much from them about local folklore, natural remedies and even more about the practical use of herbs than she had learnt from her grandmother. She lived with the gypsies for a year and also attended rituals with the Horsa coven in the New Forest.

When she was 20, Sybil moved to Burley, also in the New Forest, and opened an antique shop there. She refused to sell anything to do with witchcraft in the antique shops, much to the disappointment of visitors; however, Sybil became well known for her psychic healing abilities and people would travel from far and wide to ask for healing.

Sybil's open attitude about being a witch caused problems too. As media interest grew, Sybil found herself constantly being pestered by news reporters and tourists, who travelled to Burley and would turn up on her doorstep day and night. Sybil even had to create decoys in order to be able to escape out of the village to go to the secret coven meeting places, for fear of being pursued by cameramen. Although the village itself thrived on the extra tourism and visitors, some people were not so happy about the extra traffic and noise, and her landlord eventually asked her to move out.

At the same time, an American publishing house had approached Sybil to speak about her new antique book, *A Shop in the High Street*, on a TV programme in the States. She took the opportunity to go and flew to New York. While in New York, she was contacted by a parapsychologist named Hans Holzer, who invited her to join him in investigating psychic phenomena; they went on to do numerous TV and radio programs on the subject together. Sybil then moved to Los Angeles where she met Dr Israel Regardi, an authority on Qabalah and ritual magic, and they spent much of their time together discussing and practicing the Golden Dawn rituals.

Strong in the defence of her beliefs, Sybil sometimes differed and even quarrelled with other witches. She disapproved of nudity in rituals (a requirement in some traditions) and was strongly against the use of drugs. She was also at odds with most other modern witches in that she did agree with cursing; however, she was also one of the first of the modern day witches to take up environmental causes.

Sybil died at her Melbourne home on the 26th October 1982. She will be remembered as a remarkable woman of many accomplishments: a gifted psychic, astrologer and writer who did much to influence the revival of the modern day movement.

Chapter Four

The Elements and tools of the Craft

The Divine Without: An Introduction to the Elements

To the Elements it came from, everything will return;
Our bodies to earth, our blood to water, heat to fire, breath to air.
'Empedocles on Etna'

The elements are a core principle in European Pagan culture and ritual, and in fact European Pagans are not alone in this belief, as many ancient traditions from all around the world hold the concept of the elements close to their heart. The elements of air, fire, water and earth are the building blocks of life, both physically and spiritually; take one of these elements away and life as we know it ceases to exist. The air that we breathe, the heat that warms us, the water that hydrates us and the food which nourishes us are all in a fragile balance, which keeps us and the world we live in alive.

Mankind has grown further and further away from the elements of nature: the rain, the sun, the wind and the soil. We are able to block out the elements that we dislike and enhance the ones we favour, but without these four key elements – earth, air, fire and water – it would be impossible for life to survive on this planet. After all, the elements are equal parts in a cosmic equation, in perfect harmony with one another. It is important to appreciate each of these elemental energies in order to embrace the natural balance of life.

It doesn't take much to see the misuse of the natural elements due to the ignorance and disregard by mankind: the pollution of the air, the exploitation of the land, the destruction of the forests, and the contamination of the seas. Mankind has wildly underestimated the power of the natural elements and has created an imbalance in the natural way of things, the consequences of which governments and authorities are only just beginning to acknowledge as a global issue.

In the Craft, we learn to embrace each element and acknowledge its nature in our lives. The elements rule our emotions, our skills, our thoughts and our actions, and therefore an understanding of the elements allows us a greater understanding of ourselves and the world that we live in. We begin to appreciate things which seemed insignificant before, and understand their important roles in the cycle of life. We begin to not only embrace the sunny days, but the 'rainy ones' too, so to speak, and to see every part of our world as sacred.

The elements are also closely linked with the seasons, the festivals, the moon phases and even the time of day. They are of special significance in the tarot deck, and also play a part in a magic circle. In our coven, we take each potential trainee through four months of elemental training before they are officially dedicated into the circle. Within these training sessions, we run through the outer qualities of the element followed by its inner psychological and magical qualities, and in that period of time the trainee learns the basic correspondences of each element.

In ritual itself, the elements play a key role in the stages of magic and their symbology is often used within talismans and other magical praxis. The elemental symbols of the elements are as follows:

EARTH	AIR	FIRE	WATER	SPIRIT
North	East	South	West	Centre

Using the Tattvas

Some other elemental symbols, which are often ignored in modern practice, are the tattvas. Each tattvic symbol represents the basic elemental forces of that particular element and can help you to understand the inner and outer qualities of each one. The tattvic symbols are as follows, in the colours of yellow, blue, red, silver and black from left to right:

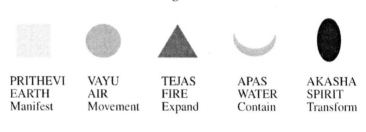

PRITHEVI	VAYU	TEJAS	APAS	AKASHA
EARTH	AIR	FIRE	WATER	SPIRIT
Manifest	Movement	Expand	Contain	Transform

In addition to the five main tattvic symbols, it is also possible to combine the shapes to create up to 25 other symbols, or sub-elements. Using a sub-element allows us to be more specific about the intended outcome of the ritual or spell that we are doing.

To learn more about each element through tattvic vision, you should cut out the shape of your chosen tattva from paper or card of an appropriate colour. Then gaze at the tattvic symbol for at least 60 seconds before transfering your focus to a plain white surface (i.e. a white wall) and observing the shape in its complimentary 'spirit' colour. After practising this several times, you can then work on imagining the symbol in your mind's eye only. With practice, you will be able to enlarge the symbol in your mind and 'step through' the tattva, in order to explore the world of that specific element on the other side of the door.

The Elementals

The elementals are the spirits, or outward expressions, of the qualities of each classical element and reside within their respective compass directions.

The elementals were first mentioned in the 14th century occult writings of Paracelsus, who gave them their names and assigned them to each element: the Sylph of air, the Salamander of fire, the Undine of water and the Pygmy, or Gnome, of earth. Although the elementals are often romanticised by some as appearing 'fairy like' the elementals are not fairies – they are archetypal energies of their particular element, and can take on a form if they wish - or if a magician asks them to do so. As they are the personification of an element, their primal and instinctual energy makes these creatures extremely creative and powerful.

Magical Tools of the Elements

Cords and censer, scourge and knife, powers of the witches' blade
Waken all ye into life, Come ye as the charm is made!
'The Witch's Rune' written by Gerald Gardner and Doreen Valiente, and sourced from 'Eight Sabbats for Witches', by J&S Farrar

Many witches assign a magical tool to each element which is regularly used within ceremony, either actually or symbolically. These four main altar tools are usually the wand of the east, the athame or sword of the south, the chalice or cauldron of the west and the pentacle disc or pentagram of the north. The fifth element, spirit, is usually symbolised by the altar itself, or the centre of the circle.

Very often, the use of a tool in a magical or spiritual manner is derived from its mundane application in day-to-day life. This is because the people who first used the tools within their ritual did not choose them for theatre or appearance; they chose them for practicality and direct symbolism. These were items that were used every day which people could relate to, such as the cup (the chalice of west) and the knife (the athame of south). This down-to-earth and practical approach to the tools works on a psychological level too, because it allows our minds to understand the type of energy that we are working with by relating it to the mundane use of the item in the material world.

The wand of east and pentacle disc of north are more recent additions to the set; however, their origins and meanings are just as ancient. The wand, representing the male, originates from the staff – a phallic representation of the God, a tool used prolifically in shamanic cultures. The staff was also associated with the guardian spirit of the magic circle of Art and the doorway to the otherworld, and is reflected in the Cunning Craft 'Niding Pole' and pitchfork or 'Tine'. The pentacle disc originates largely from ceremonial magick, but it may have been used previously in other cultures as a designated sacred area in which to work magic or used to grind herbs and incense upon.

Due to the wide use of these four key tools in different cultures and magical traditions, the quarter designation for tools can vary. Designation also varies in the tarot deck, which can be confusing when you first start out. The best way is to use your intuition, and go with whatever feels right to you.

Other basic tools which are used in the Craft, but which are not necessarily attributed to an element, include the Besom (or broom), the Boline (or white handled knife), the bell, and the Book of Ways or Grimoire (more commonly known as the Book of Shadows).

The Element of Earth

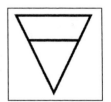

Colours: Green, Black, Brown
Time of Day: Midnight
Season: Winter (Yule, Winter Solstice)
Zodiac Sign: Taurus, Virgo, Capricorn
Magical Tool: Pentacle
Name of Wind: Boreus
Rules: The Body

Earth is the foundation of all elements. Its symbol is the inverted and crossed green triangle, and its function, or state of being, is 'to do'. Its talismanic tattvic symbol is Prithivi, the yellow or green square, and its magical use is 'to manifest'.

Whilst it is the element we are most familiar with it is also the one we most take for granted, since we live upon the earth and interact with it in our daily lives. Therefore, earth can be seen to rule the more ordinary aspects of our lives such as working, playing, sleeping, and eating. However, to be without the element of earth would be to be without form or structure; without this binding element we would fall apart and be no more.

As well as its ability to hold form, earth is also vital in the form of the food that we eat, as we take in the earth's nutrients which give us energy and sustenance. Although it is water that makes up most of our body it is earth that gives us form, which in turn allows us to process other elements such as air into our lungs, and warmth through our skin.

Earth is the element upon which all others rest. It is foundation, balance, perseverance, and focus. It is the manifestation of an idea in the material world. Without the element of earth all ideas, hopes, wishes, dreams and spells would amount to nothing, for earth is the element of manifestation. Earth is also the most stable of all the elements, a symbol of successful completion and a foundation on which the future is created. It is grounding and comforting whilst bringing realism, ideas and concepts into the real world, although it can cause stubbornness and resistance to change.

The elementals of earth are the Pygmies, or the Gnomes. Due to the popular picture book Gnomes with pointy red hats, people can be rather apprehensive about using Gnomes within their spellwork and ritual, and quite understandably; however, the original Gnome was nothing like this at all. Paracelsus gave the name of Gnome to these creatures after the Greek word

'Genomos' meaning 'earth dweller'. He recorded that these creatures looked rather goblin-like, and they lived under the earth and guarded treasures. According to Paracelsus, they cannot stand the light of the sun for even one ray would turn them to stone; his story may have lead to the inception of the humble garden gnome.

Other spirits associated with the element of earth are the Dryads (spirits of the trees) and the Woodwives, Woodwose or Wild Damsels, who appear as beautiful women from the front but hollow trees from the back.

The Pentacle: The Magical Tool of Earth

Thou shalt perfume the pentacle with sweet scents and perfumes, and afterwards having wrapped it in a piece of prepared silk cloth, thou shalt put it in a place fit and clean, which thou mayest open whenever it shall please thee.

'Key of Solomon' Book Two, original author unknown

The word 'pentagram' comes from the Greek word 'Pent', meaning 'five', and 'Graphen' meaning 'to write'. Although the name is of Greek origin, the symbol of the five-pointed star is much more ancient, and is believed to be more than 8,000 years old.

The pentagram is one of the very few symbols which are made up of one, single unbroken line, and has been used by many religions and magical traditions to mark magical enclosures and define sacred space.

The pentacle (a pentagram within a circle) resides in the north, the earth element, and symbolises divine equilibrium being perfectly round in shape and displaying all five points of the circle equally and in perfect balance. In short, both the pentacle and the pentagram represent the natural balance of things, and the divine perfection of the universe.

The pentacle and pentagram have both been subjected to an unfortunate reputation. Just the thought of this five-pointed symbol is enough to send shivers down the spines of most people, who consider it a sign of darkness and evil. Satanism later adopted the inverted (upside-down) pentagram as its own symbol, which did no favours for the already misunderstood five-pointed star. However the question remains, *why* has this symbol been tarred with this ill-fated reputation? To answer this question, we have to look at the real meanings behind the pentagram, and its inner mysteries.

The first mystery is the mathematical properties of the pentagram. The shape of the five-pointed star conforms to the 'Golden Ratio', the mathematical proportion known as 'Phi', which can be found everywhere, from the curl of a ram's horns to spiral of a snail shell.

Secondly, the shape of the pentagram is connected to the 'Holy Grail' – the word Grail itself derived from the Mesopotamian word, *Graal*, the term for the five sided pentagon shape in the centre of the pentagram made up by the lines of the star itself. The Holy Grail was originally a symbol of the Goddess (see 'The Chalice').

Finally, and the piers de resistance of the story of the pentagram; during an eight-year period, the planet Venus creates the five-pointed shape of the pentagram around our planet earth.

The pentagram is a symbol of both divine and mathematical significance. Before the inquisition, there were absolutely no negative associations to the pentagram, but a medieval fear of mathematics, science and the 'supernatural' powers of nature condemned all of these things and caused people to regard the pentacle as a symbol of evil. Unfortunately, this uneducated view has been inherited from generation to generation since. It is said that during the persecution, witches would make pentacles out of clay, dough or wax so that they could be quickly destroyed if danger approached; since we no longer need to fear such persecution, pentacle discs are now made from wood or metal, materials which channel earth energy much more effectively than other materials. I favour the wooden pentacle disc, which epitomises the steady and yet powerful character of the earth – just like the tree it was cut from.

Earth Magic and the Witch Ways

Earth rules the north, the place of darkness and winter. It is a feminine element; nurturing, comforting, moist and fruitful. Its colour is green, and it governs knot and stone magic among others, as well as divination such as the Ogham and the Runes. Earth can also be associated with Totem animals and nature spirits.

Despite many of us striving to rise above the mundane world to become more spiritual, we must not forget that earth is an integral part of spirituality itself and cannot be overcome. We are incarnated into this life as physical beings, for the reason of experiencing the highs and lows of an earthly life; to block this out will cause an unbalance in our lives, both physical and spiritual. All things that the earth rules – food, shelter, death and rebirth – are necessary for life here on our planet; a sacred cycle of life which would not be possible without the earth.

Earth quite literally radiates power, which can be used in healing, spell work and ritual. Ley lines, paths of energy known in the Craft as 'Witch Ways' or 'Serpent Lines', connect sacred sites and places of power all over the earth. Where two Ley lines cross a particularly powerful place will be found, and these crossroads are thought to be entrances to the otherworld. Physical crossroads can also signify a place of power, where either two roads cross or one road forks into two, and a 'watch fire' can be lit at the crossroads to release the energy from the point of power.

Earth power is a potent and direct form of natural energy, and can be used for material benefits such as prosperity, stability and harmony in the home. It is also a form of progressive magic;

bringing things into manifestation. In ritual, the invocation of deities associated with earth are performed - such as Gaia the Earth Goddess and Dagda the God of Plenty. Deities of sacrifice and harvest are also invoked, such as Ker the Harvest Mother and Lugh the Sacrificial God.

In a witches circle, earth is used to both consecrate the space and ground the energy after the rite has ended. Salt, a natural mineral, is often used to represent earth within the circle, and is mixed with water to evoke its purifying qualities.

Humans have used the earth and its materials to create stone circles, pyramids, temples, statues and all sorts of religious art. Patterns have been carved out of the land and rock to sanctify a special place and devote it to the Gods or to the Ancient Ones, and carved mazes, labyrinths and mandalas are symbols which relate to the Underworld and earth wisdom. They are also closely related to the psychology of the mind, which brings a different attribute to the element of earth that is not often appreciated: the qualities of thought, decision and the subconscious.

TASK: Getting in touch with the Element of Earth

To become connected with the element of earth, go out to a natural place such as a forest or a meadow. Sit against a tree or lie out on the grass and begin to breathe slowly and deeply, so that your body starts to run the same steady rate as the energy of the earth.

Take off your shoes and socks and feel the grass or the leaf litter beneath you; visualise tree roots growing from your feet and reaching deep into the ground. Feel the power of the earth all around you, and the rising earth energy beneath you.

If you are lucky enough to live near one, visit a sacred site such as a stone circle, a long barrow or a tumuli. If you can get hold of pair of dowsing rods, walk in straight lines across the site and see where your rods cross; this is a sign of Witch Ways (points of earth power) and underground streams.

TASK: A Magical Working of Earth: The Magical Maze

From the Nazca lines in Peru to the Cretan Labyrinths of ancient Greece, the maze has been used throughout history to access the magical power of the creative and subconscious mind. Try the exercise below for some simple yet powerful earth magic. You should prepare for this ritual by placing candles in each quarter of your working space, and switching off any electric lights.

Choose one thing in your life that you would like to achieve, but with which you have encountered obstacles that have stopped you from reaching your goal. For instance, you may want to find a new job, but you don't know where to start looking. Or you might want to find a new place to live, but you don't have the funds.

Now design a maze. It can be as simple or as elaborate as you wish, but it must reflect how you feel about your journey towards this goal. Is it full of dead ends, twists, turns, backtracking? Focus on the goal, and your journey towards it, as you design the maze. Make sure you have a beginning (the entrance to the maze) and an end (the centre of the maze). And make sure there is at least one pathway that leads to the centre. If you wish, you can draw images at the dead ends, twists and turns, which symbolise the problems that you have encountered on your way to achieving your goal. Don't worry if you can't draw well – it only matters that the images mean something to you.

Once you are happy with the maze, write your goal in the centre. The centre of the maze symbolises what you would like to achieve, and the pathways of twists, turns and dead ends symbolise the obstructions that you may encounter on the way to achieving our goal.

Now light a candle and focus on the flame. Feel yourself become calm, your breathing and heartbeat begins to slow, and feel yourself enter a meditative state.

Now turn your focus to the maze, and begin to trace your way to the centre. Stay calm and centre your attention on nothing but the maze and your goal, at the centre. Try not to anticipate your next move; just allow your intuition to guide you through the maze and when you encounter dead ends, accept the mistake and backtrack. When you eventually reach the centre of the maze, say:

> *The centre of this maze is the thing I desire*
> *As I trace this path, so I manifest my goal*
> *As above, So Below. As Without, So Within*
> *As my mind wills; So mote it be!* *
> 'The Spell of the Maze', from the Coven Book of Ways

* I was taught this affirmation *'as above so below, as without so within, as my mind wills, so mote it be'* by my teacher and Craft Elder, Maureen Wheeler, who used this rhyme to affirm the connection between the microcosm and the macrocosm when working with spellwork and ritual.

Keep the maze to symbolise your power to achieve the goal of your desire.

The Element of Air

Colours: Yellow, Light blue
Time of Day: Dawn
Season: Spring (Eostara, Spring Equinox)
Zodiac Sign: Gemini, Libra, Aquarius
Magical Tool: Wand
Name of Wind: Euros
Rules: The Mind

Air is the conception of a new idea; the seed of knowledge from which all ideas, plans and projects grow. It is the element of intellect, the first step in any cycle of creation, and the inspiration to dream up ideas, plans and goals. It is also associated with knowledge and all matters relating to knowledge and learning, such as perception, analytical thought, communication and memory. Its symbol is the yellow crossed triangle and its function, or state of being, is 'to think'. Its talismanic tattvic symbol is Vayu, the blue circle or swirl, and its magical use is 'movement'.

Air provides us with the intense concentration required when we are working on a difficult problem, and is present in any superior craftsmanship or artistic skill. It can inspire us to create great masterpieces and fantastic works of beauty; although on a more negative note it can cause a sense of detachment and a distance between us and others, as we can become consumed by our thoughts and ideas.

Air is an essential ingredient to all life on this planet. Everything that lives breathes, from the trees and plants that take in carbon dioxide and produce oxygen to the animals and people which breathe in oxygen and produce carbon dioxide. This cycle is in perfect balance and it is of the utmost importance that it remains this way, which is why keeping the air clean and the forests healthy are both so very important to all life.

The air within ourselves is the oxygen we breathe into our bodies in order to live. It is the substance that fuels our blood, keeping our bodies running, and without the initial breath of life we would have never been born. The lungs are the part of the body which connects us with the element of air, allowing us to breathe in and out; we can survive a matter of months without food, a few days without water but only a matter of minutes without oxygen.

The elementals of air are the Sylphs. They are a part of the creative force of air, and it is their work that results in the tiniest of breezes to the mightiest of tornadoes. Sylphs are said to be elusive creatures, and it is necessary for you to know your own mind and your true will for them to show themselves to you.

Sylphs also function as muse-like beings, inspiring humans with great ideas, writing, music and poetry, as well as astral projection and spiritual progress, providing us with great epiphanies and realisations. However, if someone becomes too influenced by the energy of the Sylphs it can be all too easy for them to become addicted to this captivating inspiration.

The Wand: The Magical Tool of Air

There are differences between Craft traditions regarding whether the wand belongs in the east (the air element), which is common in modern Craft, or the south (the fire element) which is used in ceremonial magic and the tarot deck. However this is a personal decision, and only you can decide which you prefer. In our coven, the wand resides in the east: the place of new beginnings, thoughts and invention. This tool is used for creative and mindful magic, directing the thoughts and the will of the practitioner. It is gentle and persuasive, and has the power to direct and command in a just and fair manner.

The wand is essentially a branch or twig that has the power to root itself and grow new life – power rising from within. In the same way, the wand is often partnered with the cup or chalice (symbol of water) to create the 'divine marriage': the joining of male and female. The wand usually has one pointed end, representing the male and one rounded end, representing the female. These two different points are also related to the inner potential of the wand: the power of both containment and release.

Another magical tool associated with the modern wand is the European Craft 'stang' a 'Y' shaped ashwood staff whose forked tip represents the horns of the God. Its associations with the God and the rites of fertility are particularly poignant. I have given some instruction on how to use the stang later in the book.

The wand also symbolises the metaphysical principle of 'As

Above, So Below', a motto that is used in the Craft to epitomise the universe and our relation to it. This iconography can be seen in the tarot card 'The Magician' in which the archetype holds his wand high up towards the sky channeling the heavens above, whilst the other hand points down, channeling the energy of the earth beneath him. In this posture he epitomises perfect balance and harmony, and this stance is often used in ritual to symbolise equilibrium of the universe, the magic circle and the practitioner themselves. This position can also be used in ritual at the sabbats of Yule and Midsummer to represent the exact balance between day, night, summer and winter, before the season changes.

The modern wand is often inscribed with the planetary symbols, in order to evoke the powers of the planets as well as the power of 'As Above, So Below.' In northern European traditions, the wand also represents the World Tree, with its branches reaching up to the sky and its roots reaching down through the earth.

Witches cut their wands from a variety of trees, but the most common is hazel, a wood which is associated with inspiration and wisdom. The length of a wand is traditionally taken from the fingertip to the elbow, although nowadays many people find shorter wands more practical. *The Key of Solomon* Grimoire states that the wand should be cut in a single stroke, on the day of mercury, at sunrise.

The wand that we use today is a fairly modern design; originally a staff was used for the activities we use the wand for today. The staff has always been a symbol of fertility and sexuality due to its phallic appearance and the power to spring forth new life and therefore, both the staff and the wand are used to represent the male in ritual and magic. The snake, a symbol of regeneration and sexuality, is often depicted interweaving around the staff as a symbol of virility and abundance. Two the famous staffs are the Hermes Caduceus Power Wand – which is two snakes entwined around a rod – and the Staff of Asclepius – which is one snake wrapped around a knotty, branch like rod. In Egypt, the 'Serpent Wand' was a symbol of authority whilst in Greek and Roman times, people used to keep Aesculapian Adders as pets in their homes for luck and prosperity. This tradition also reached some parts of Britain, and was followed by many of the European Craft.

Another origin of the modern wand is that of the Egyptian 'Wand of Horus', a hollow and cylindrical magical tool that was filled with precious stones and used for healing rituals. These wands could transverse the worlds of the living and of the dead, and Pharaohs were often depicted holding these wands to assure guidance in the afterlife. An Egyptian tool that preceded the modern wand was the 'Throwing Stick' or 'Apotropaic Wand': a flat, semi-circular disc not dissimilar to a boomerang which was carved with symbols, animals and creatures. It was said that when the wand was thrown it could turn evil back onto its source, and soon became a symbol of 'Maat' - order over chaos. The Apotropaic Wand was also used to draw circles of protection in the sand.

The ancient Greeks used the 'Thyrsus', a hollow rod with a pine cone at its tip, which represented the delicate balance of both the tame and the wild sides of human nature. The Thyrsus also acted as a tool to promote fertility, and was often depicted in paintings and sculptures along with the chalice for this purpose.

In European Cunning Craft, a crook was sometimes used in a similar way as the modern wand. Originally called the Crommenstick, it resembled a shepherd's crook or irregularly shaped walking stick and was used for both healing and cursing; it was made in a variety of woods depending on its purpose. The crook also appeared with the Gods of death and resurrection in Egypt, and was also used in imagery as a symbol of the Pharaohs' power. In the 'Horseman's Word', a British secret society, the 'Gad' was used in a similar way as the wand, and was associated with mastering horses.

Air Magic and the Wists

Air is a masculine element; dry, expansive and active. It rules magic and ritual which involves travel, instruction, freedom, learning, change and visualisation. It rules the east, the direction of the sunrise and the birth of each day, reflecting its qualities of newness and birth. Its colour is yellow of the radiant sun and its season is spring, the time of new buds and shoots and the start of the cycle of growth for the year. The negative aspects of air, however, can quickly reveal themselves in hurricanes, cyclones and monsoons, blizzards and storms, strongly reflecting air's dual nature as both a gentle and destructive force.

Air is the pure, clear and uncluttered frame of mind that is so important in affecting change in magic. It is movement, the catalyst that sends this visualisation out towards its first steps into eventual manifestation, and the element of truth and justice.

The element of air has long been associated with the quality of purification. The power of the air to clear the mind is practiced in many cultures, and even in a non-religious context air is often described as 'blowing the cobwebs away' to clear the head and freshen the spirit. Being the place of beginnings, air also corresponds to the season of spring, the time of new growth and the start of the year, bringing new ideas and opportunities into the fore. Unlike the emotional fluctuations of water, the constant change in the element of air is decisive and purposeful - transformation with intention. Therefore, the air of the east can also be linked to the intellectual, scientific and inquisitive mind. It also rules over consciousness as a whole, and can provide the qualities of forethought and foresight, the 'upper hand'.

In a witches circle we use the purifying qualities of air to cleanse the sacred space, which is usually symbolised by incense. Native American practice also uses this technique, 'smudging' the circle and its occupants to banish negative spirits and purify the sacred site. Catholicism also recognises the cleansing powers of air, using incense within ceremony.

Incense itself has long been associated with religion, ritual and offering. The ancient Egyptians used incense on a regular basis as a gift to the Gods; this was echoed later in the myths of Christianity, when gifts of Frankincense and Myrrh, two expensive and prized ingredients of incense used by the Egyptian Priests, was said to have been offered to Jesus.

As well as its purifying abilities, air is also involved in travel and navigation and weather vanes which are used to predict the movement of the sea. The power of the wind can also be harnessed to carry us to our destinations and can even provide us with electricity. This connection to power and travel also links air with our own personal journeys and new experiences within our lives. It denotes a strong relationship with freedom and escapism, both physical (i.e. travelling, moving jobs or starting new relationships) and spiritual (i.e. through meditation and astral journeys).

The totem animals of air sum up the attributes of this element wonderfully: the birds, insects and other winged creatures are animals which live by constant flux and change. Some of them, like the swift, live in the skies all their life. Birds are also the world's most experienced travellers, covering thousands of miles on the wing to voyage to more pleasing climates every year; for air is also an element of independence, and the creatures of air which live independently to man demonstrate this most clearly. They are some of the very few creatures that still remain truly free. With the help of birds and insects, air begins to represent another quality – fertility. In fact, winged creatures play a huge part in fertility as a whole, pollinating plants and carrying seeds to new places.

Spiritually, air can develop your mind like no other element. It will help you to concentrate on your studies, encourage you to read and grow in wisdom. However, one must be careful as the element of air can also breed procrastination, such as that brilliant invention that will never be built, or the intellectual

Magus who has read many books on his field of study but has never practiced his subject. If someone is too influenced by air, they may spend their whole lifetime planning for something that they will never actually get round to doing. In order to achieve the goal, you need not only good planning, but also drive, which of course is a quality of fire. The east is the place of beginnings, but once we have formulated our plans and imagined our goals we must then move to the south, the element of fire, to put our ideas to form.

Witches are practical people; philosophy to them is not just an intellectual exercise, they have to put it into practice in their everyday lives and in their working, if philosophy is to have any meaning.
Janet and Stewart Farrar, 'A Witches Bible' part 2

TASK: Getting in touch with the Element of Air

To connect with the element of air you need do nothing more but delve into your imagination and the mental realms within yourself. Write a poem, a story, or maybe start to record your dreams. Go outside and feel the wind through your hair and the breeze touching your face. Lie down and gaze up into the clouds, watch them as they change and transform.

Now focus your attention to the top of your head; the place of ideas, epiphanies and imagination and allow voices of the Sylphs become present in the sound of the wind around you. Listen to what they have to say.

TASK: A Magical Working of Air: Whistling up the Winds

If crows fly low, the wind will blow
If crows fly high, the wind will die.
Author unknown

Whistling up the Winds is a Craft method of raising the wind and using its power. The word 'whistle' comes from the Old English 'hwistle', 'whist' or 'wist' meaning 'to wish'. The sound of whistling is believed to evoke the magical forces of the element around you, and is based on an old belief that whistling at sea will cause a storm to rise.

You can tailor your work to the nature of the wind on that particular day. First, ascertain which direction the wind is blowing, in order to use that knowledge to your advantage. Although whistling up the winds can be used to raise wind on a still day, for this particular working the technique should be carried out somewhere high up where wind is already present, in order to take advantage of the wind that is already there.

Use your knowledge of the area or the position of the sun to determine which way the wind is blowing. Making a rough assessment of the direction of the wind by the position of the sun is not too difficult – the sun rises in the east and sets in the west, so depending on the time of day you can judge the cardinal directions by the point of the sun. If all else fails, acquire a compass.

Each wind is associated with a particular element and season, and is also named after one of the four Greek Gods of the wind.

Euros – The Eastern Wind:

The Wind of Euros is fresh, revitalizing and pure, and associated with the seasonal properties of spring. It corresponds to the compass direction of east and the colours yellow or white. Work magic in an eastern wind to bring insight, inspiration, new beginnings and purification.

Notos – The Southern Wind:

The Wind of Notos is passionate, powerful and intense, and associated with the seasonal properties of summer. It corresponds to the compass direction of south and the colour red. Work magic in a southern wind to bring passion, fertility and strength.

Zephyros – The Western Wind:

The Wind of Zephyros is cleansing and compassionate, and associated with the seasonal properties of autumn. It corresponds to the compass direction of the west and the colours blue or turquoise green. Work magic in a western wind to bring emotion, creativity and cleansing.

Boreus – The Northern Wind:

The Wind of Boreus is strong and wise, and associated with the seasonal properties of winter. It corresponds to the compass direction of north and the colours brown, dark green or black. Work magic in a northern wind to bring an end to bad habits, destroy negative thinking and work towards prosperity.

Consider your intention and how the present wind could aid you. Maybe you are looking for a new job. If it is an eastern wind, you might ask for new beginnings. If it is a southern wind, you might ask for strength and courage at the interview. If it is a western wind, you might focus on the happiness that the new job will give you, and if it is a northern wind you might focus on how the job would bring you stability and financial security.

The power of the wind is raised by sounding a constant, extended whistle whilst lifting the arms up and toward the direction of the wind you are calling, facing into the breeze. Focus on the power of that particular wind as it rushes about you, breathe in its power and feel it rising within. Feel the fresh oxygen purify and strengthen you. Even if the wind is inter-mittent, feel its presence and know that its energy is listening to you. When you feel the power at its greatest (normally indicated by a sudden strong blow around you) declare your intention to the wind. Listen for guidance as the wind rushes past your ears. Tune in to the language of the wind; it is a language you will never forget. When you are finished, thank the air for its aid and bring your arms back down to settle the wind if necessary.

The Element of Fire

Colours: Red, Gold, White
Time of Day: Midday
Season: Summer (Solstice, Litha)
Zodiac Sign: Aries, Leo, Sagittarius
Magical Tool: Athame/sword
Name of Wind: Noteos
Rules: The energy of the body

Fire is the most primal of the four elements. It is the element of will, passion, change and intensity, inner desire, life force, and fundamental transformation. It is the essence of sex and passion, yet it is also the spark of divinity that burns within us. Its symbol is the red triangle, and its function, or state, is 'being'. Its talismanic tattvic symbol is Telian, symbolised by a red triangle, and its magical use is 'to expand'.

Fire is the most active of the four elements, representing motivation and determination. It symbolises the will to create or destroy, to move towards something, or simply to move 'for the sake of moving'. Fire emotions are those which are intense and urgent although they pass quickly, such as lust, anger, joy and panic. Fire is the element that pushes the other elements along and keeps the world from settling into an uninteresting and fixed state.

Fire also rules the creative spark within us all. It is the beautiful poem or captivating painting; it is the great novel or enchanting piece of music. Air is what inspires us to act in the first place, but fire is the skill needed to transform that inspired thought into form. Take some time to name the activities in your life that fire you up, that make you feel vital, and that make you feel truly alive. What are the flames that light up your life? When we engage in the things filled with passion and meaning for us, we feed our life force which keeps ourselves vital and energised.

Fire in nature can be seen in various forms, but most obviously in the sun that provides us with the heat and light that is essential for our survival. Without the sphere of burning gases that is the sun we would not survive, and its powerful effect on mankind has remained constant throughout the ages. The sun also contributes to our sustenance; plants convert its light via photosynthesis, and when we eat those plants we take the sunlight (fire) into our bodies. Without the sun's energy we would have no growth, and consequently there would be no life. In our modern world we use fire to warm the food we eat, and to heat the water we bathe in. We use it to power the cars we drive, and to forge tools out of metal.

The elementals of fire are the Salamanders. Salamanders are the embodiment of every open fire, every bolt of lightning and every charge of electricity. Salamanders make up fire's qualities of heat and light, and are ever present, in the tiniest spark to the raging power of the forest fire. You can observe the Salamanders in the flicker of the candle flame, and the shapes created as the flames curl and lick in the hearth. They are wild, passionate and untamed, and therefore can be difficult to work with due to their uncompromising nature. It takes a skilled witch to be able to truly control or contain them and if allowed, Salamanders can be incredibly destructive.

However, Salamanders can also help you achieve the drive to succeed, the passion for life and the warmth of love. With time and practice, you can learn to work with these elementals and make use of their benevolent aspect without allowing your own nature to become too impulsive, aggressive or destructive.

The Athame: The Magical Tool of Fire
There are three types of magical blade commonly used in modern

witchcraft – the white handled knife or 'Boline' the Sword, and the black handled knife or 'Athame'. In our tradition, the athame resides in the south – the element of fire, the force that forged the blade. Fire is the element of transmutation, and through the destruction of the old it has the power to create the new. Therefore, the athame evokes the masterful force of destruction and creation, storing, focusing, transmitting, transforming and amplifying life force energy.

The blade is a primitive but effective tool. It commands authority; it is severe, aggressive and distinctive, and the double-edged nature of the athame blade is synonymous with its power to both wound and defend. A situation with two possible outcomes is often referred to as a 'double edged blade' and the knife can also be associated with the two polarities of life and death - being the first tool in contact with a newborn as the umbilical cord is cut, whilst at the same time being capable of bringing that life to an end.

It is a tool which relies upon the owner's intent and carries it out effectively, and without exception. Both physically and symbolically, the blade is an extension of one's will projected through the blade; whether that is a deadly thrust into an enemy's side or the action of cutting fruit from a tree to feed your family.

Man has used the blade in one form or another since he first learnt how to use tools to hunt. Hunting was not only a way of providing food for the tribe, but also a symbolic, sacred act: a form of magic which represented future hunting success and even gave the power of the animal spirit to the hunter. The blade was also linked to lifeblood, and blood sacrifice. Although modern Paganism does not indulge in these practices, it is beneficial to have an understanding of the blade's use in early belief systems so that we can apply these beliefs symbolically in our own way. In early belief systems (and this continues in some voodoo practices today) sacrifices would be performed with

69

sacred blades to ensure good hunting and prosperity for the tribe involved. As with sacred hunting, it was also believed that the powers of the animal were released by the sacrifice, and transferred to the attending priest. The chosen animal would first be decorated, fed well, and revered as a laudable spirit before its sacrifice. The cut itself was ritualised: the priest tracing the blade across the animal three times to suggest the cut and show their intent to the spirit of the animal before any cut was made. Nowadays in Pagan ritual, physical cutting is usually limited to the carving of candles, sharing of bread and other harmless activities and the white handled knife the 'boline', is used for these purposes – the sword and athame being employed for magical use only and not for any physical cutting. Incidentally, it is traditional when cutting wood for magical purposes (i.e. for wands, stangs and staffs) to offer a little of your own blood to the wound of the tree as an offering of thanks. Many choose to use their spittle for the same purpose today.

The larger relative of the athame is the sword, an archetypal representation of righteousness, truth, equality and fairness. The sword is often featured in the Justice Tarot card as a symbol of balance and universal law, and continues to be used in such a way in Initiatory Craft. A prominent sword of British mythology is Excalibur: King Arthur's sword that was said to have healing properties and shone with the light of 30 torches and dazzled Arthur's enemies. The pre-Christian version of the story, however, calls this sword Caledfwlch and says that it was forged in Avalon (old Glastonbury). It was decorated with two serpents which writhed about the golden hilt, and roared flames of fire at Arthur's opponents. The Caledfwlch was used by one of Arthur's warriors to kill the Irish King Dilwrnach in order to steal his magic cauldron, and the link between the blade and chalice (divine marriage) is evident in this myth, which resonates in the later Arthurian legends of Excalibur and the quest for the Holy Grail.

The athame is traditionally a black handled knife with an iron blade which is used for casting the circle, calling the quarters of the compass, cleansing and blessing the elements and other magical operations. The word 'athame' is believed to have originated from the manuscripts of the Key of Solomon, where it is named 'Artave', 'Arthana' or 'Arthame' although another origin of the magical knife may have been the Arrow; writer Robert Graves suggests an Arabic etymology, from the word 'Al Thame', which literally meant 'the Arrow'. Although at first the Arrow appears to belong in the eastern quarter of air, it would have been used in early hunting and this links the blade with the qualities of keen observation, deadly accuracy and, of course, blood.

The use of the athame in modern witchcraft is directly attributed to Freemasonry and later the Golden Dawn in the arts of High Magic, in which the athame is used to direct and command spirits.

The Runes of the Athame

These witches runes can either be carved or painted onto the hilt of the athame, and serve to empower the tool as follows, left to right: The initials of the Goddess, the waxing and waning moon, the scourge, the initials of the God, the sign of the Horned God, the Eightfold Path, the inherent power of the athame and the symbols of male and female.

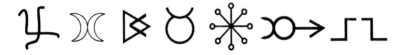

Fire Magic and the Cunning Serpent

Fire is masculine and rules the south, the place of greatest heat. Its colour is red and its season is summer. Fire rituals involve energy, sex, healing, destruction and purification, and fire rites can include candle magic and spells of transformation – that is, using fire to burn something and transform it into smoke to send it from the earthly plane to the astral plane.

Fire magic rules the creative force of the universe. Due to its intense character, it rules the drive behind ecstasy, life force, progression, inspiration, creativity and action. Fire emotions are those that are intense and urgent, yet usually 'burn out' and pass quickly. The effects of the element of fire in nature can be devastating, manifesting in the form of powerful lightning storms, volcanic eruptions and forest fires which can cause the loss of large areas of woodland. The destructive power of fire is tremendous, and it is important to remember the dual nature of this element when working with it magically.

Fire also denotes the spark of divinity and magic within all of us, and using the power of fire we can awaken this Divine and Magical Self and become more sacred within ourselves. There is a line of Craft power which is passed down through generations; this is sometimes called the Distaff line. Although all people have the potential to work magic and recognize the divine self, most will ignore it for many lifetimes. Working with fire allows us to awaken the 'witch within' and start to recognise true consciousness.

Fire is also the power behind sexuality, passion and fertility, providing the drive to procreate and multiply. The fire force behind these drives is called the Kundalini, which is usually depicted as a coiled serpent lying at the Base Chakra in the body. This fiery energy plays a key part in the practices of Tantric and Taoist lovemaking, and also in the Voodoo customs of spirit possession and ecstatic dance of Africa. However, serpent stories can be found all over the world with connections to the fire element, including Europe. Carvings of serpents and statues of snake goddesses have been discovered which were used in fertility ritual and magic, and symbols of the serpent, such as the Ouroboros which swallows its own tail to form a never ending circle, represented creation and eternity. Serpentine patterns can also be seen depicted in the land itself, such as the Great Serpent Mound in Ohio and the Nazca Snake in Peru, and even in the stars – such as the great 'Draco the Serpent' constellation in the sky.

Fire magic is often used in protection rites, purification and healing. It is also related to the hearth and home and the Mother aspect, because of its nurturing qualities. In fire rituals, invocations of deities associated with fire are performed such as Brigit the Fire Goddess, and Bel the Fertility God, and because of fire's destructive tendencies, deities such as the powerful Sekhmet or Bastet and the cunning Set or Bes may also be invoked.

Fire can be great gift, but it can also be a terrible burden. However, when used sensibly and in balance with the other elements, there is no reason why fire cannot be beneficial to your rites and magic.

TASK: Getting in touch with the Element of Fire

To connect with the element of fire, gaze into a candle flame or into the flames of a roaring hearth; feel yourself empowered by the elementals of fire, and feel their energy blaze over you and purify your spirit. If you have access to an open hearth, a log burner or a bonfire, try scrying into the simmering ashes after the flames have died down to see what shapes you can see. Feel the power of fire awaken your inner primal senses and forgotten memories.

TASK: A Magical Working of Fire: Candle Magic

Using a candle in magic allows the witch to focus their intention in order to manifest a particular outcome. A certain colour may be chosen which relates to your goal (i.e. green for prosperity or maybe red for love) and oils can be used to anoint the candle which also correspond to the aim. You should be aware that there is no power in the colour of the candle; it is simply an association or 'trigger' which helps your subconscious make a connection between the candle, the action and your goal; a plain candle can be just as effective for an experienced witch (although, colours do share 'vibrations' with other things in the universe, and so using colour in this way could indeed be beneficial)..

The candle is used within ritual to represent the means of achieving the goal, as well as representing the goal itself. Other forms of fire magic include scrying into a flame, which can reveal prophecies, or burning a piece of paper with your wish written on it, which allows you to transform your wish into form. Try the exercise below to manifest a goal in your own life.

Colour Correspondences

BLACK   Divination, Protection, Darkness, Restriction, Binding, the Underworld

BLUE   Protection, Healing, Emotion, Divine Power, the compass direction of west

GOLD   Colour of the Gods, Attraction, Prosperity, Sun Magic, the God

GREEN   Healing, Nature magic, Financial Gain, the compass direction of north

PURPLE   Magic, Powers of the Ancients, Wisdom, Mysticism

RED   Love, Passion, Energy, Heat, the compass direction of south

SILVER   The Goddess, Moon Magic, Night Magic, Divinity

WHITE   Righteousness, Purity. Can be used to substitute any colour if need be

YELLOW   Intellect, Healing, Change, the compass direction of east

Choose a goal which you would like to see manifest through this spellwork. What would you like to bring about in your life? We will be covering 'Ethics in Magic' in more detail later in the book (Chapter 16), but for now look at this quick check-list to see that you are not breaking any ethical rules:

Never work to influence any other person's will or freedom of
   choice
Never work to cause harm to others
Never work for ego or unreasonable financial gain

If possible, make the effort to achieve the goal on the physical
plane (in everyday life) as well as the astral plane. For instance,
if you wish to get a new job, you need to apply for the position
and write a good CV as well as doing the spellwork. Magic does
not mean you can be lazy!

If you are working for another person, always consult the
person and tell them that you are planning to do a spell for them.
To not consult them is breaking rule no.1 of the ethical rules in
spellwork, no matter how well-meaning you are. You should also
finish the spell with an affirmation such as 'for the good of all, so
be it done'. This is a fail-safe action which means that if the spell
would have inadvertently caused harm to someone then that
energy would immediately be dissolved by the words of your
own spell.

Once you have chosen a goal and matched a colour to our
specific goal, it is time to prepare the chosen candle. You may
decide to anoint the candle with an essential oil that you feel is
appropriate, or carve a symbol on the candle which you feel will
encourage the success of the spell.

Carving the Candle
It is best to do this before anointing the candle otherwise it can
be a bit messy. Carving should be done with the white handled
knife, the boline, and not the athame.

You can carve symbols, names and pictures into your candle
to empower it further. You don't need any special knowledge of
magical symbols for this method – any symbol that represents
the goal to you is sufficient. For instance, if you were working to
bring love into your life, you might choose to carve a heart.

However if you do want to research a little more, you could carve a particular Ogham or Rune glyph into the candle.

Anointing Candles

Different oils correspond to different goals, such as orange oil for prosperity and lemongrass for purification. A good reference book for oil and herbal correspondences is *The Complete Book of Incense, Oils and Brews*, by Scott Cunningham. This book also teaches you how to blend your own oils.

Anointing a candle works in two ways; the first is that it releases the powers of the oil that you have chosen as it burns; the second is that it works on a psychological level, as you inhale the scent. Dress the candle from the base toward the wick with your chosen oil, focusing on your goal as you do so. You should anoint your candle as follows:

> *To bring something into your life, smooth the oil towards you (wick facing your body)*
> *To banish something from your life, smooth it away (wick away from your body).*

Visualising the goal

Once the candle is prepared, place it into the middle of your working space or table. Light it, and look deep into the flame. Visualise yourself achieving your goal. See yourself experiencing the outcome of the spell – perhaps you are at work enjoying your new job, or spending quality time with the person who has been very ill and is now well again. The candle acts as a focus for your mind, and uses the creative force of fire to enhance your desire and transform it from the astral plane into the physical.

At this point you can push a needlework pin through the softening candle about 5-10mm down from the wick; as the candle burns down, the pin will drop, signifying the release of the magic and the success of the spell.

As this candle burns, so my wish turns to form
As this pin has fallen, so my magic is done;
As above, So Below, As Without, So Within
As my mind wills; So mote it be!
'Candle and Pin Spell', from the Coven Book of Ways

Extinguish any other candles and then ground yourself by placing your palms upon the ground or stamping your feet.

Allow the spell candle to burn right down – place it in a dish of sand or in the sink with a little water to keep the flames contained. Sometimes however, if we need to go out of the house after casting a spell and we cannot leave the candle burning for safety reasons the candle *can* be extinguished so long as it is then re-lit again at the stroke of midnight, and allowed to burn down completely.

The Element of Water

Colours: Blue, Grey, Indigo
Time of Day: Dusk
Season: Autumn (Autumn Equinox)
Zodiac Sign: Taurus, Virgo, Capricorn
Magical Tool: Cup/Cauldron
Name of Wind: Zephyros
Rules: The Emotions

The elemental symbol of water is the inverted blue triangle, and its function, or state of being, is 'feeling'. Its talismanic tattvic symbol is Apas, the pale blue or silver crescent moon, and its magical use is 'to contain'.

Although soft to the touch and mild in nature, water shapes our coastlines, lakes and riverbeds by the constant pull of its tides. Where ancient seas used to flow now stand awe-inspiring rock formations shaped by the seas, such as the 'Cheese Rings' in

Cornwall or the Jurassic coastlines of Lyme Regis.

In evolutionary terms water was the first element to spawn life, which led to the development of the rest of the flora and fauna on our planet. Water is the giver of life; it is also the primary transporter of nutrients through our body, just as the oceans, lakes and streams transport nutrients to the land. As a solitary element, water breeds life, and has very few negative attributes.

However, when another element is introduced to water it can quickly change character. For instance, if heat (the fire element) is introduced to water, the water evaporates. This process is vital in the water cycle, transporting water from one place to another and creating fresh water from salt water, but it can also cause drought in extreme cases. Adding wind (the air element) can cause flash floods and tidal waves, leading to disastrous consequences. However, some cultures actually rely on flooding for their livelihoods, and the ancient Egyptians who lived with no rainfall for the majority of the year depended on the floods to fertilise the land. They purposefully positioned their farming plots directly next to the river Nile, so that as the river burst its banks fertile soil flooded onto their farms. Their religion was largely based around the flooding, the Egyptian myths and deities interwoven with the ways of the Nile.

However, stories of much more devastating floods also run through the mythology of ancient cultures, reflecting the sheer force of water at its most destructive.

One such cataclysmic event, often termed the 'Great Flood' or the 'Deluge', is said to have occurred somewhere around 12,000 years ago. According to both folklore and factual evidence, the flood affected a vast number of people all over the Middle East and Europe. Although there have been many theories for the cause of the Great Flood, including a sudden glacial melts, storm floods, earthquakes, volcano eruptions and meteor impacts, the cause of the Deluge was most likely the result of a combination of these disasters, which are scientifically recorded to have all happened within the same period in history.

Many theories put the origin of the flood near or in the Tigris-Euphrates river valley in Mesopotamia, modern Iraq. In the myth Epic of Gilgamesh, the God Ea (or Sumerian Enki) tells a wise man named Utnapishtim that a Great Flood will come, so Utnapishtim builds a boat in readiness for his family and animals. Consequently, they survive the flood. This tale was probably brought to Canaan (where the Israelites settled) and reshaped into the Biblical version we know today. It is argued that the Biblical version was the true story of the two, due to certain parts of the story seeming more convincing than the   Utnapishtin story; in particular the seaworthy dimensions of Noah's boat against Utnapishtim's rather ill-designed cubic raft. However, expert studies show that the Babylonian texts significantly pre-date the Biblical version, by at least 1,500 years.

Indeed, water is the element of mysteries and mythology, of deep emotions, the subconscious mind and primal change. The change that water brings is slow but constant, like a trickling stream which erodes a cliff over thousands of years. It is the element of strong, enduring love, and yet also of the deepest sorrow.

Water emotions just as fluid and changeable. They are also reflective, like the surface of water, offering us a glimpse of ourselves and our emotions that we might not otherwise see.

Just as water holds the power to bring new life, it also brings death. In Greek lore two important bodies of water, the River Lethe and the River Styx, ran through the Underworld of Hades. The River Styx acted as a boundary between the world of the living and the world of the dead, and its companion, the River Lethe, was known as the 'river of forgetfulness'. On drinking from this river, the dead would forget the memories of their previous life. The Lethe was also said to run through the cave of

Hypnos, the Greek God of drowsiness and sleep and it is this mythology that reflects the hypnotic power of water and its connection to scrying and divination. The connection between water and the otherworlds is a common theme in Craft lore, and the crossing of the river is often seen as an initiation or rite of passage in itself. As well as symbolising the journey into the afterlife, it also represented a place between the worlds: a point of transition for the witch between the mundane world and the spirit world.

Casteth a flint stone over (the) left shoulder, towards the west, or hurleth a little sea sand up into the element, or wetteth a broome sprig in water and sprinkleth the same in the aire.
  'To Make Rain and Storms', from 'Discoverie of Witchcraft', Reginald Scot

The elemental spirits of water are the Undines, from the Greek 'Unda' meaning 'wave': insubstantial creatures made of water and foam. The Undine is a type of water spirit from the family of Greek 'Naiads', the water nymphs. In their natural form they can rarely be seen by the casual eye but they are detectable psychically or if caught unawares. They assist in psychic and emotional feelings and work with empathy, intuition and creativity.

Another form of water spirit is the Mermaid, usually depicted as a beautiful woman to the waist with a fish tail below the waist. Part human, part fish creatures are common in the mythology of the sea and generally they are benevolent souls, helping sailors who have lost their way and guiding ships from the rocks.

The Mesopotamian 'Oannes' were curious creatures who also had the body of a fish. Beneath the head of the fish was a man's head, and beneath the tail of the fish was a pair of human legs, and these water spirits were said to come on land to teach science, art and literature. However other water spirits, such as the 'Lorelei', are malevolent creatures who disguise themselves as beautiful women and lure sailors to a watery grave.

As the element of water is ever changing and transforming, shape shifting spirits are often found in this element. The most fabled of all shape shifting water spirits is the Selkie 'the seal woman' from Ireland and Scotland. Folklore says that many a sailor has tried to capture a Selkie and marry her, because in her human form she is very beautiful indeed. In order to capture a Selkie one must steal the sealskin that is shed when the Selkie takes on a human form; however, Selkies cannot be kept out of water for long as their skin soon becomes dry, and they become unwell. Only by returning the sealskin to the Selkie can she survive and then return to the sea.

The Chalice: The Magical Tool of Water

The chalice (cup, cauldron or holy well) represents the receptive feminine form and is the embodiment of the Goddess and the womb. Out of the chalice springs new life, a belief which is echoed time and time again in countless myths and legends from around the world.

As well as its association with physical conception, the chalice is also viewed as an important symbol of spiritual attainment and initiatory rebirth. The chalice resides in the west, the water element and its ability to contain liquid, the element of the mysteries, connects the chalice with the powers of water of wisdom, inspiration, enlightenment, intuition. A vessel of water is often used for scrying: a form of divination and this is depicted in the tarot card the Queen of Cups where the Queen, the keeper of the mysteries, gazes into the chalice using her psychic powers of foresight.

The chalice is a magical tool that has survived the test of time and in one form or another has been incorporated into almost every spiritual path. The church also permitted a Christianised version of the ancient mythos of the chalice to occupy a place in the imagination, the Grail. The Grail (or 'Sangreal') was a chalice that Joseph of Arimethea was said to have brought to Britain from the Last Supper, which had the power to lead a hero from death to immortality - although it would leave the hero speechless. However, before the Christian Grail story came from the East, the people of Britain already had their Grail of eternal life. An older Celtic story imparts a tale of 'Bran's Cauldron' in which Celtic warriors also emerged from the vessel alive but also unable to speak. The tale of Cerridwyn, the Welsh Goddess of the mysteries and rebirth, also echoes the powers of the magical vessel; in this myth her cauldron holds a broth that endows the boy Taliesin with all knowing insight. Dagda the 'Good God' had a cauldron of plenty which overflowed with abundance. It is said that his cauldron was so big it had to be taken about on the back of a giant.

It is possible that integrating a Grail into Christianity managed to keep the Goddess in the subconscious of the people who once worshiped her, and made the conversion to Christianity in Europe easier. And, just maybe in the iconic myth of searching for the Grail, we still search for the Goddess, and the eternal life she offers.

Water Magic and the Domnu

Water is ruled by the moon, which regulates the pull and ebb of the tides. In fact, the moon affects all water even on the planet and the fluid in our bodies. The moon's energy also causes what is commonly known as 'moon fever', which describes the unpredictable behaviour that people display on and around the Full Moon. This too is caused by the effect of the moon's energy upon water in the body, influencing men and women alike.

Water rules the depths of our emotions and our subconscious. It is related to all that is hidden and mysterious, and mankind has always had a strange relationship with water, the sea being the one place in the world that man has never been able conquer. There is so much of the sea that still remains undiscovered, and many creatures which live beneath its surface which no man has ever seen. Water has always been shrouded by mystery, a closed book which led to endless sailor's tales of what might lie beneath the waves.

When I was small I lived near Bournemouth, a seaside town in Dorset on the south coast. Whenever I visited the beach with my family, which was quite often during the summer, I used to spend hours by the edge of the water willing the waves to rise and fall in accordance to my will. I remember being able to see shapes in the waves, white horses and messages in the churn of the sea. It was around that time that I started to feel I could make a connection with nature; for water is the chief element that rules psychic ability and intuition, the perfect element to connect with if you wish to develop your psychic senses and magical abilities.

The purification and healing powers of water is also well known in many cultures, and countless rivers, lakes and streams all over the world are said to have healing or purifying properties. 'Chalice Well' in Glastonbury is well known for its curative properties, as is the 'Healing Well' at Elwell in Dorset. Many cultures entertained the custom of blessing by water such as the Ancient Greek 'Lustration Rite' which purified the mind, body and spirit before entering the holy temples. In Initiatory Craft, water is used to purify a person in a similar way before ritual and also used to purify the space in which the ritual is to be held.

Due to the bewitching and mysterious nature of water, many bodies of water are believed to be entrances to the otherworld such as Lake Llyn Dinas and Lake Tegid in Wales. Tegid also has connections with the myths of the Goddess Cerridwyn, and the lake itself is said to symbolise her Cauldron of Transformation and Rebirth.

From Cerridwyn's Cauldron in Wales to Demeter's Jug in Greece, and even the Holy Grail of Christian belief, vessels and containers have long been associated with mythology and religion, in particular their association with the womb, pregnancy and childbirth. The Holy Grail in Christian belief is said to hold the power to grace eternal life; in older myths such as Celtic, Greek and Egyptian the idea of 'eternal life' was understood as not played out in this physical lifetime but in the natural way of birth, death and rebirth.

Domnu, an important Fomoire Goddess whose name means Abyss or Deep Sea, was strongly associated with immortality. The old Pagan beliefs viewed death as returning to the womb of the Mother, the vessel of rebirth and this belief is reflected in many of the rites of Initiatory Craft today. Within Craft, the word Domnu is sometimes used to describe the western gateway to the Underworld.

Paradoxically, water is also associated with many creation myths, with life first springing from the primordial waters, or from the tears of the Gods. Water is a reflective and deep element which offers it the properties of foresight, as well as allowing us to explore our own inner depths. It embraces such methods as scrying, dowsing, healing, cleansing and purification. Deities associated with the element of water, such as Neptune, Poseidon, Aphrodite and Morgana may be invoked in water rituals.

TASK: Getting in touch with the Element of Water

To connect with the element of water take a trip to a lake, a stream or a beach. Sit and listen to the waves as they crash against the shore, watch the ripples on the surface of the water and make note of the creatures that live in and around the sea. If you can, visit an aquarium where you can observe the creatures of the sea close up and read about them. If you live near a beach, an ideal offering to the Undines is to clear up some rubbish from the shore; make sure you take a pair of gloves and a plastic bag with you.

The Hag Stone

I have found a holy stone upon the ground;
O fate! I thank thee for this happy find.
Translated by Charles Leyland in 'Aradia: Gospel of the Witches', original author unknown

The Hag Stone is a folk name for any stone or pebble which has a natural hole running all the way through it, which was created by hundreds, if not thousands, of years of water erosion caused by the ebb and flow of the sea. There are various meanings behind the Hag Stone, and finding such a stone is believed to be extremely fortuitous.

During the medieval period, the Hag Stone was considered by the superstitious as a talisman to actually ward off witches; but in fact, somewhat ironically, it was originally a witches' symbol of prosperity, luck and fertility. The holey or 'Holy' Hag stone represented the sacred circle, the wheel of life, and the Mother Goddess. It was also considered a spiritual gateway, and it was said that if you peered through the hole at dusk you would see the creatures of the otherworld. The Hag Stone was also sometimes called a Wishing Stone, and could be held in the left hand and rubbed to make wishes true.

In Cornwall, our ancestors imitated the qualities of the Hag Stone and created 'Men An Tol': a triple stone megalith formation with a large holed stone at its centre. Still to this day, people believe that passing through the holed stone of 'Men An Tol' brings healing and fertility.

It is quite rare to find a natural Hag Stone; they are more common on beaches, but can sometimes be found inland, in the earth over which ancient seas used to flow. The best Hag Stones, however, are the ones which come to you. You can look for hours at the beach to find a stone and return home empty handed, but another day step outside into your garden and come upon one right away. In fact, to find a Hag Stone is believed to be a gift from the Gods themselves, and a Hag Stone which is found by accident is thought to be much luckier than one actively sought out.

TASK: The Hag Stone Knot

If you are lucky enough to find more than one Hag Stone, you can make a Hag Stone Knot. Take several Hag Stones and pass a red cord through their centres. Tie each stone at regular intervals along the red cord, focusing on the purpose of the Hag Stone as you tie each knot. The ideal number of stones for this spell is nine, if you are lucky enough to find that many. If not, tie your one or two Hag Stones onto the cord and add to it when you find more. The Hag Stone Knot can then be hung on the bed post to bring passion and fertility, or taken outside and swung around the head to chase away storms. If you hold it in your palm whilst you sleep, it will help you reach the otherworlds in your dreams; and traditionally, witches would use this method to 'go to the Sabbats' via astral travel whilst they slept.

When you are not using the Knot, tie it in the window to evoke the powers of prosperity and protection, and the strength of the sea.

A Hag Stone knot can be seen in the Natural History Museum in London, dated 1801-1900.

TASK: A Magical Working of Water: Hydromancy

Water scrying, or 'hydromancy' is a form of divination that allows us to look deep into our sub-conscious and receive messages from water spirits and even the Gods themselves.

Water scrying can be performed either outdoors on a still pond or lake, or indoors with a black scrying bowl. If outdoors, scrying can be performed with the light of the Full Moon reflecting on the surface of the water, which is a favourite for some witches. However, it is in fact the New Moon which is best for divination, so this is when I would recommend performing your scrying, because although the Full Moon empowers water, it also has the potential to disrupt its energy. The ink blackness of the water at a New Moon also creates a more effective scrying palette than the reflecting water of the Full Moon; but again this is something that you need to practice with and decide what works best for you.

I would, however, recommend using a bowl for your first practice rather than an outdoor body of water, as there is less interference from other elements and you can take your time in the comfort of your own home. Ideally, the bowl you choose needs to be jet black.

The art of scrying lies in the ability to switch off your mind, allow the everyday clutter of your thoughts to disappear, and give your sub-conscious and your creative mind the ability to take over. Practice the water scrying below, to develop your psychic abilities and connect with the otherworlds.

Place the black bowl of water in the centre of your sacred space and dim all of the lights. I find it most effective to extinguish all of the candles except one, which should be placed behind you so that that its reflection does not interfere with your scrying.

Close your eyes and take a few deep breaths. Focus on your breathing, in and out, in and out. With every breath in, feel yourself calm, and at peace. With every breath out, you feel the tension of the day drain away. Your heartbeat becomes slower, your body becomes heavier. Breathe in peace; breathe out tension. All distractions leave your mind as you focus on this one task, breathing in ... and out, in ... and out. Give this process as much time as you need and allow yourself to become completely relaxed and focused. There is no rush. When you feel completely calm and relaxed, you can begin.

Holding your palms over the water, say:

Spirits of water show unto me, the mysteries which lie beneath thee
Allow me to see the inner depths, the mysteries and the unknown;
I call upon the spirits of water; lend me your gifts of insight and
wisdom. Spread apart the Veil of being, that I might look beyond.
'Hydromancy', from the Coven Book of Ways

If you have any questions that you want answered, or any particular insight you wish to look for, ask for it now. Look deep into the water. Allow your eyes to relax; do not strain to see anything. Look past the water if you can; allow shapes to form in their own time, and in their own way. If you feel your eyes go out of focus, that's okay too. You may find it takes a bit of practice to get images coming through; however, even in your first few attempts, you should see movement in the black of the water, and the sense that the water is changing in some way. Give this process time, I would recommend you remain scrying for approximately 5 or 10 minutes, having a break to rest your eyes, and then returning to scrying. It is important that you do not strain your eyes; things should come naturally in time. Do not dismiss any images you receive in your mind, either – the power of water also works through our intuition and imagination, so anything that you see in your mind is also valid.

When you have finished scrying, thank the water spirits for their help, extinguish the single candle and cast the water on the ground outside or into a running stream as an offering to the spirits.

The Element of Spirit

There is a fifth element that the Craft recognise: the element of spirit, or Aether, which flows through everything. This is the element that transcends, yet is part of, all the other elements and binds them together as one. It takes the name of Akasha, from the place on the astral plane where records are kept of all that has happened in the past and all that is to happen in the future.

Akasha is an eastern-Indian word which means 'inner space' reflecting the belief that the universe and the spirit is both within and without ourselves. Its talismanic tattvic symbol is also named Akasha, its shape a black oval and its magical use is 'to transform'.

The ethereal element of spirit has no direction, yet encompasses all directions. It is the centre, the circumference, the above and the below. It is a purely spiritual element – the realm of The All; it is protection and justice, movement and mastery, life, death and rebirth. It is often symbolised by the turning wheel, the Spinners distaff, or the sign of infinity.

The element of spirit in nature is present in every animal, plant and tree; every rock and stone in the fertile soil, and within the rushing streams. It is alive in mountains, volcanoes and raging fires. The element of spirit is present in absolutely everything that exists within our universe. It is The All, the collective consciousness, the web that connects all things together, the great primeval ocean from which we all came and to which we all return. It is the Chinese concept of Chi and the Japanese concept of Ki – the energy that flows through all things. In European lore, spirit is the key to 'Wyrd', 'Spirament' or Fate, the motion of cause and effect throughout the universe. Fate is the potential for all things, which lies dormant in the otherworld and waits to be woven into the fabric of life by the spinning Sisters: Urd, Verthandi and Skuld of Norse mythology or Klotho, Lachesis and Atropos of Greece. We human beings, and all living things, are expressions of the strands of Fate's thread, granted life by spirit. In sympathy with this belief, the coven copy of Liber Umbrarum states that the Cord is one of the magical tools for the element of Spirit.

Spirit is the element that allows us to use the other elements together in order to make magic, whilst also acting as the subtle connection we feel to one another and to the earth itself. When the element of spirit is lacking we may feel isolated, disconnected and alone. In our modern world it is all too easy to lose our connection to spirit, and so it is important to strengthen this bond through meditation and ritual so that we may feel a part of the all, breathe as one with the universe, and learn to flow with the Wyrd.

We are walkers in between worlds, we profess to work with the currents of the Wyrd and may, at times, influence their flow. This is our magic. The Goddess has put things in motion, we must learn to ride the surging waves of change. Be as a surfer, watch the waves, read them, be in the right place at the right time, chase the crest and rise the energy throwing caution to the wind and let Her take you where she will. Keep your balance, stay in control of yourself, while her energy controls our flight.

'Wyrd', written by Greenman Wildhunter

The Spirit Evocation

In our coven, we perform a spirit evocation after the other elements have been called. The spirit evocation differs slightly to the other elemental quarter calls, in that spirit is called at the centre of the circle (called 'the nowle') rather than the edge, and also is not banished at the end of the rite. This is because the element of spirit is within all things, and so stays with us always.

All should come into the centre of the circle directly after the other quarters have been called, and join hands whilst one appointed person recites the following:

Spirit, all encompassing element that binds the other elements into one, that connects us with the powers of unity, the God and Goddess and the web of Wyrd, join us this night and strengthen our bond. We bid you Hail, and Welcome!

'Spirit Evocation', from the Coven Book of Ways

The Altar: The Magical Tool of Spirit

*And he raised the holy altar as the ancient writs ordain
Decked and graced with scented garlands grateful unto gods and
men.*

Valmiki, 'Epic of Ramayana'

The word 'altar' is derived from the Latin meaning 'high place'.
Some of the first altars were built almost 75,000 years ago high
up in the French Alps, whilst in Britain oak groves were planted
on the top of hills so that people might worship closer to the
heavens. The ancient Nordic people, who named their altars the
'throne of the Gods' built their shrines out of conical piles of
stones the apex of which reached up to the skies, on which they
worshiped and placed offerings.

The altar acts as an offering in itself, as its creation demonstrates devotion to the deity or spirit to whom the altar is
dedicated. It acts as a gateway between this world and the realms
of the Gods, a place where we can communicate our magic, our
prayers and feel the powers of the universe. It is also the place
where we can perform our personal devotions, give offerings
and listen to our intuition. It is often at the altar where we can
most easily communicate with universal energy, the spirits and
the Gods. But how does it work?

An altar aids the human mind to perceive omnipotent forces,
by giving us something physical to direct our attention towards,
and with which to focus these energies. The same applies for
statues and images with which we decorate our altar; we are not
worshiping the statue or altar itself, but the divinity it represents.

The physical items that we place upon the altar and the way
we choose to compose them also represents our personal beliefs,
concepts and ideas. The subconscious mind adores imagery and
visual tools help the mind focus on the goal that we are working
towards. In the past altars were often used as canvasses for

religious imagery, with illustrations carved into them depicting ritual items and ceremonial tools. The cup or vessel was a common image that was used to decorate altars in this way, usually with Priests or Priestesses shown pouring offerings upon the earth. Particularly in Greece, Egypt and Rome, the Gods themselves were painted stood or sat on altars. This is reflected in modern Initiatory Craft today, in which the High Priestess will sit upon the altar to demonstrate her role as representing the Goddess.

Artwork carved into altars could also be used to depict the achievement of the rite which was to be performed upon the altar, as a form of sympathetic magic, illustrating the image of success before the event in order to help manifest the desired outcome. For instance, the Edo people of Nigeria live by the belief that personal action lies in the palm of the hand, and erect shrines in private chambers of their own homes which represent the achievement of their goals. Such shrines, called 'Ikegobo', are usually made of wood and brass and are decorated with scenes of sacrificial items and images of success. They often depict the owner of the shrine at the top of the altar, celebrating the success that they had achieved by their positive actions and magic. Another example is an altar to Neptune which was commissioned by Lucius Aufidus Pantera, a high ranking military officer, who offered it to Neptune to promote a fortuitous voyage and trade overseas. This engraved altar was exposed to the sea in as an offering and was left in the water for some time; probably until the fleet returned home safely.

Dressing the Altar

The altar represents the divine balance of the male and the female. Chinese sages described these two polarities as 'Yang' and 'Yin' two complementary forces locked together, one unable to exist without the other. To your right hand side, the altar represents the male and the sun, and therefore all of the masculine tools and correspondences should be placed on the right. These include images of the God, the wand, the athame, incense, the candle and other symbols of the masculine.

To your left hand side, the altar represents the female and the moon, and therefore all of the feminine tools, and correspondences should be placed on the left. These include images of the Goddess, the chalice, the salt and water, the scourge and other symbols of the feminine.

When working with a coven, the High Priest of the circle will always stand and work at the right of the altar whilst the High Priestess will always stand and work on the left. This is also the position of the Bride and Groom during a wedding ceremony today - a living memory of the ancient and sacred balance between man and woman.

The left can also be attributed to the feminine because it is the side where the heart sits in the body, the heart being the organ of blood and therefore linked to female menstruation and compassion. Evan John Jones writes in his book, *The Roebuck in the Thicket,*

> *By positioning the cup to the left* [and the blade to the right] *not only does this symbolise the feminine mysteries, it also refers to the protecting mother aspect of the Goddess who looks after her own. Just as the shield is held in the left hand while the sword is held in the right, so the Goddess shields us, for are we not her children from the moment we first step into the circle?*

Another magical path that places the female on the left and the male on the right is the Jewish mystic tradition of Qabalah: a belief system that employs the Pillars of Severity, Mildness and Mercy as three states of being which are part of the structure of the Qabalistic Tree of Life. The left hand of the pillar represents 'the constrictive and passive' – the feminine. Its key word is 'understanding' due to the psychic and intuitive nature of the female mind. The right hand pillar of the tree represents 'the expansive and active' – the masculine. Its key word is 'wisdom'. These polarities convey the extreme opposites of the masculine and the feminine, two halves of a whole. The central pillar represents this perfect harmony of divine balance, and is named the 'Pillar of Equilibrium'. Therefore, the centre of the altar also represents perfect balance and the centre of the universe, and makes it the ideal place to perform magic.

TASK: A Magical Working of Spirit: Creating the Altar

Your altar is a sacred space which is an expression of your own beliefs and spiritual consciousness, and therefore should be tailored to suit you. You should decorate it however you wish, and allow it to express your own personality and your relationship with the Divine. The altar is not only a magical tool and an offering to the Gods, but also an offering to yourself. It is a reflection of your personality, your goals and achievements, and should suit your own specific needs to aid the ritual or magic that you are performing. Try creating your own altar, using the guidelines below.

Any risen surface will suffice for your altar - from an ornate wooden chest of drawers to a small coffee table that can be tucked away when it is not being used. In our coven, we cover

our altar with a cloth before we place the tools upon it, and we often change the colour of the cloth depending on the ritual we are performing, or the time of year.

Once you have chosen a table to act as your altar, place it in the north within your sacred space, gather the required tools together and put them upon your altar. As discussed, the masculine tools are usually placed on the right of the altar, the feminine usually on the left, and the generic or central tools (i.e. the pentacle) are placed in the middle. Two altar candles, one for the male and one for the female, should be placed on either side of the altar as additional symbols of the God and the Goddess. Remember that the tools we use within the Craft are simply extensions of our own personal power; if you cannot afford, or cannot get hold of, any of the tools then a substitute will do. For instance, a simple cup can replace the chalice, and an everyday kitchen knife can replace the athame. The important thing is to use those tools for ritual and magic only. A great place to find tools is at boot sales; we often find some real gems at our local boot sale, especially chalices, censors, dishes, candlesticks and sometimes even God or Goddess statues, particularly from the Greek and Roman pantheon.

When you have gathered the tools together and dressed your altar, perform the ritual following this chapter to cleanse and consecrate both the altar and your tools in order to prepare them for magical use.

Bringing the Elements Together: The Magic Circle

The use of the magic circle is a powerful method of protection and empowerment, and through the ages variations of magical circles have been used by different cultures and religions from all around the world. Some are drawn on the floor and others simply visualised; some are conjured by a long and drawn out ceremony and others by a single thought or gesture. But all magical circles have the following common aims:

- To define and empower a sacred or magical space
- To create a mini-cosmos to symbolise and evoke the powers of the universe
- To open a portal 'a place between the worlds'
- To create a vessel in which we contain and transmit the energy we raise

- To protect those inside (and outside) the circle.

By casting the circle of art and calling in certain elements we are creating a focused portal of energy in which we can work magic and create change; a place of balance, equality and infinity and a place between the worlds. This is similar to the purpose of the pentacle disc which also symbolises the five elements together in balance within a circle – a continuous line with no end.

The symbol of the circle, both on the pentacle disc and the magical circle itself is synonymous with the never-ending expanse of the universe. When we create a magical circle we create a 'mini universe' with all the elements which make up that universe immediately present to empower our ritual, our workings and ourselves. The witches' circle is a microcosm, and what we do within the microcosm affects the macrocosm, or 'the bigger picture'.

It is also the process which allows us to make the transition from our own mortal world to the world of spirit. In European Cunning Craft, the process of casting a circle was called 'drawing the compass round' or 'Treading the Mill', which involved scribing the circle upon the floor with the stang or staff and entering a shamanic ritual consciousness.

In my coven, the circle is usually cast with the athame or the sword and a specific set of words. Although the casting is usually performed by the High Priestess in Wicca, this is largely due to the influence of Doreen Valiente on Gardner's later works; in Gardner's original *Ye Bok Ye Art Magical* the circle casting is a joint venture between the High Priest (or Magus) and the High Priestess. In our coven, the High Priestess performs the majority of circle castings, although it is not unusual for the High Priest to cast a circle for particular rituals, particularly if they focus on the male mysteries.

The High Priestess or High Priest creates a force of energy around the working space in a deosil (clockwise) motion starting at north, and seals the circle back at north. The circle can offer extra protection if also scribed once round with a piece of ash, or swept with an ash besom.

In our coven, the High Priestess then makes the 'Three Times Pass' in which she 'cleanses, consecrates and seals' the circle by encircling the space three times and intoning those respective words.

Each element corresponds to a compass direction, and we apply these to the magic circle. We call the quarters and their corresponding elements to attend our ritual and to guard and guide the rite, and the invoking pentagrams are used. The pentagrams given here are the individual elemental pentagrams for each quarter; some covens use just the earth pentagram for all of the quarters, but the ones illustrated here are the specific pentagrams given in the traditional *Book of Shadows*:

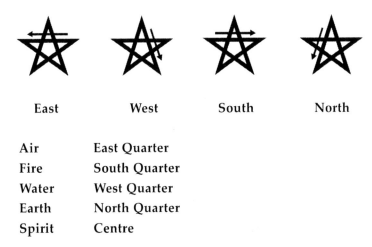

| East | West | South | North |

Air	East Quarter
Fire	South Quarter
Water	West Quarter
Earth	North Quarter
Spirit	Centre

Although these particular correspondences are generally accepted as standard in western occultism, it is appropriate to mention here that not all practitioners of the Craft use these particular associations. For instance, some European Cunning Craft ascribe the east to fire, the south to earth, the west to water and the north to air, and many shamanic cultures place air in the south, water in the west, earth in the north and fire in the east. Ultimately, this is a decision that only you can make. The elements also correspond to the Wheel of the Year and the witches sabbats; so then, by casting a magic circle we symbolise all of these correspondences, and we can then use them within the ritual.

Some people find it quite hard to remember how each elemental pentagram is drawn. It might be of help to remember that when calling the eastern and western quarters, the first horizontal line of the pentagram is always drawn *towards* the northern altar, from right to left for east and left to right for west. When banishing, the opposite is done and the first horizontal line is drawn *away* from the altar, left to right for east and right to left for west. The south is associated with fire, and is therefore drawn *sun-wise* (clockwise) from the top point to call and *anti-clockwise* from bottom right point to banish. The north is the opposite of the south so is drawn the opposite direction to the sun, *anti-clockwise* (widdershins) from the top point to call and *clockwise* from the bottom left to banish.

Once the circle is cast, no one should leave it. The boundary of the circle forms a barrier of energy, and someone passing though the circle can cause damage to the circle and the energy within it. I always tell my students to treat the edge of the circle as if they were surrounded by a brick wall; solid and impenetrable. Within reason, it is only safe to leave the circle when a door is cut, or the circle has been closed.

TASK: A Psychic Circle Casting Rite

A full magic circle should only be cast by someone who is fully prepared. In a coven, the beginners of the group can usually rely upon the fact that the High Priest or High Priestess is experienced enough to be able to perform the casting efficiently, effectively and safely. When a circle of art is created it regulates what energy is risen and filters out anything negative which may have been created or evoked; a badly cast circle is not only weak, but is also dangerous to those within, as it does not offer this protection. Therefore, for the purposes of this portion of the book, I will instruct you on casting the 'Psychic Circle' from my coven's *Book of Ways*. The Psychic Circle differs from the full circle casting technique in two ways; the first is that the psychic method is less involved, requiring less knowledge than the traditional casting (which makes it perfect for the beginner). The second is that it creates a *high protection* but *low energy* space, eliminating the risk involved in casting a full magical circle. The third is that it will help improve your visualisation techniques, which are so important when calling the directions. Use this method for the following exercise, and whenever you perform any ritual or working, until instructions on the traditional circle cast are given further on in this book. You will be ready to perform the full circle casting once you have completed the reading and exercises which follow in this book, and which are required to ensure that your circle will be safe and its magic effective.

Put a candle in each of the four quarters of your magical space and switch off any electric lights. Sit comfortably – cross-legged with your back straight if possible – in the middle of your sacred space, and facing the east. If it helps, light a stick of incense and hold it between your palms; you can breathe in this incense to improve your concentration, and also use it to scribe the symbols which will instructed during this rite in the air.

Close your eyes and take a few deep breaths. Focus on your breathing – in, and out, in an out. With every breath in, feel yourself calm, and at peace. With every breath out, feel the tension of the day drain away. Your heartbeat becomes slower, your body becomes heavier. Breathe in peace, breathe out tension. All thoughts of the day and other distractions leave your mind as you become completely relaxed and focused. There is no rush. When you feel completely calm and relaxed, you can begin.

Feel the ground beneath you; the power of the rocks, and the minerals which support all life. Breathe in the strength of the earth, the place of rest and also rebirth. Smell the soil and feel it between your fingertips: soft and damp like fresh, black compost. Feel yourself grounded, solid and rooted like the mighty oak, or the ancient yew. Draw this energy up into your body, feel it reach up your spine as it refreshes and empowers you with emerald green energy.

Now focus your consciousness upon the sky above you: the purity of the air, the wisdom of the universe, the place of the Gods. Draw this golden energy down into your body; it passes through your crown chakra and fills your body with shining, divine light. It mingles with the green energy of the earth, making you feel pure, and complete. As Above, So Below.

Now open your eyes and stand up, continuing to face the <u>East</u>.

See in your mind's eye the colours of pale yellow and dusty white: the colours of the element of air, and the east. Begin to visualise the element of east: white clouds, gentle breezes and powerful storms. Now invite the powers of east into your circle:

Draw the elemental symbol of east purposefully in the air in front of you, either with your fingertips or with the tip of the stick incense. See the symbol remain there, a smoky image left by the incense.

Now turn to the South.

See in your mind's eye the colours of fiery red and luminescent yellow: the colours of the element of fire and the south. Begin to visualise the element of south: roaring flames, volcanoes, the gentle warmth of the hearth. Now invite the powers of south into your circle:

 *Draw the elemental symbol of south purposefully in the air in front of you, either with your fingertips or with the tip of the stick incense. See the symbol remain there, like the glowing path left by the tip of a lit sparkler.*

Now turn to the West.

See in your mind's eye the colours of deep blue and sea greens: the colours of the element of water, and the west. Begin to visualise the element of water: thundering waves, tranquil pools and the unexplored depths of the ocean. Now invite the powers of west into your circle:

 *Draw the elemental symbol of west purposefully in the air in front of you, either with your fingertips or with the tip of the stick incense. See the symbol remain there, rippling and bubbling like a deep pool of water.*

Now turn to the North.

See in your mind's eye the colours of deep browns, dark greens and black: the colours of the element of earth, and the north. Begin to visualise the element of earth: lush green forests, dark mountains and shady caves. Now invite the powers of north into your circle:

 *Draw the elemental symbol of north purposefully in the air in front of you, either with your fingertips or with the tip of the stick incense. See the symbol remain there, green and lush.*

Now, continuing to face the north, stand in the Pentacle Position (legs spread, with arms up and outwards).

Visualise the four elements around you, the powers of the universe above you and the powers of the earth beneath you. Feel the completeness of your magical space, a circle of elements and a balance of nature which reflects the macrocosm of life. When you are ready, draw a circle about you in a clockwise motion from north back to north to encompass your working space, again using your fingertips or the tip of the incense.

When you have finished, tap purposefully three times upon the floor and the psychic circle is now justly cast. It is then ready to be used for whatever workings you may have planned.

TASK: Cleansing and Consecration of the Instruments of Art

Now that you have learnt about the magical tools and the part they play in ritual, you may have managed to get hold of some of your own. The consecration of the tools should be performed to prepare any new tool for magical workings; it can also be used to re-consecrate an existing tool, if the need occurs.

The following rite should be performed within the psychic circle. It can be used to consecrate the pentacle disc, the chalice, the wand, the athame and any other magical tool and is adapted from the coven copy of the *Liber Umbrarum*. You should prepare a small dish of salt, a white candle, a stick of incense, and a bowl of water in which you have cast a sprig of rosemary, or hyssop. Use the Psychic Circle casting method outlined above to prepare the magic circle. When you are ready, hold the tool aloft above your altar, saying:

> *I consecrate this* (tool) *in the names of the Ancient Ones.*

Take a drop of water and anoint the tool, saying: *I cleanse you by Water.*

Take a pinch of salt and anoint the tool, saying: *I consecrate you by Earth.*

Pass the tool through the incense, saying: *I purify you by Air.*

Pass the tool above the candle flame, saying: *I warm you by Fire.*

Now to make the item truly yours breathe on it three times and then draw three 'x's with your own saliva on the tool. Now holding the item aloft in the centre again say:

> *In the name of the powers of light and life*
> *may all evil influences depart hence – now!!*

Visualise bright white light shining around the tool. Then say:

> *This* (tool) *is cleansed, consecrated and purified and is ready for magical workings.*
> *As above, So Below. As Without, So Within; As my mind wills; So mote it be!*

Closing the Circle

To close a psychic circle, simply imagine the elements fading away back into nature and then draw the circle up widdershins (anti-clockwise) with your fingertip or stick of incense. As the psychic circle casting is done completely with visualisation and movement, there is not need for any elaborate circle closing.

Chapter Five

Giving the Gods a Name

O thou, who givest sustenance to the universe, from who all things
proceed, and from whom all things return; unveil to us the face of
the true spiritual sun, hidden by a disc of golden light, that we may
know the truth, and do our whole duty, as we journey to thy sacred
feet.
    'The Gayatri Mantra', author unknown

Throughout history, mankind has been aware of an omnipotent
higher force. This higher being or deity was accredited with the
turn of the seasons, the gift of life and even the creation of the
universe. However, because our ancestry encompasses such a
variety of traditions and cultures it is not surprising that there
were, and still are, many different ways to interpret the
Godhead.

For instance, the Egyptians believed in many personified
Gods and Goddesses, whilst the earliest Romans saw their
deities not as individuals but as different aspects of nature and
home. Many cultures declared their Priests, Kings and Queens as
human incarnations of the Divine, whilst to others this form of
idolatry was seen as heresy. God and Goddess aspects have even
been shared by different societies, with the same deity being
worshiped in different places under different names.

These different theological views have been inherited though
tradition and on the whole, these belief systems can be broken
down into three theological views: Polytheism, Pantheism, and
Animism.

Polytheism:

The Association of Polytheist Traditions (www.many gods.org.uk) indicates that polytheists understand and relate to divinity or godhead as 'individual deities' and contrasts this understanding with the 'aspects of the divine' or 'avatars of the Godhead'. The APT states, 'We see our Gods as having independent existences outside of our own psyches, rather than being unconscious archetypes'. Polytheism was a view shared by some of the most advanced Pagan civilisations such as the Egyptians and the Greeks.

Pantheism:

Pantheists believe that deity and the universe are as one. The Gods are not viewed as separate individual deities but as different aspects of one divine power or one uniting God, a view which allows the idea of archetypes into its belief system. As humans are part of the universe, we are also considered as part of divinity. Many modern witches consider themselves as Pantheists, or indeed Duotheists, who recognise transcendent male and female aspects of deity.

Animism:

Animism was probably the earliest religious philosophy employed by our ancestors. Animism does not personify the Gods with human characteristics, names or myths. Instead, everything in nature is ascribed a spirit and an energy, and the Wheel of the Year and the cycles of life are seen as divine in their own right. Traditions such as European Cunning Craft often follow this form of belief system.

A fourth religious philosophy, Monotheism, is the belief in one God only. Although Monotheism is one of the most popular theological views and followed by mainstream religions, such as Christianity and Islam, I have not covered it in detail here as it is a very rare to find it practiced in Paganism.

Of course, belief systems are not a science and therefore defining your own view is not always going to be as easy as a, b, or c. In addition, it is very difficult to attribute modern witchcraft to just one of these three main theologies, as it is a composite and eclectic practice built upon many different traditions. My own coven identifies most closely with Pantheism; yet, we also believe that the Gods reside in the rocks, the trees, the animals and the spirit of nature: the belief of Animism. We visualise the God and the Goddess in personified forms, such as the Horned Lord, the Goddess Dame, Aphrodite the Goddess of Love, Hermes the God of Wisdom, Artemis the Goddess of the Hunt, and Anubis the God of Death: the belief of Polytheism. We also identify deities as a particular season, or seasons' change; traditionally, their myths were designed to be read and re-enacted at certain times of the year, in order to help our inner-selves become more connected to the Wheel of the Year and the cycles of life.

It must not be thought that the Gods and Goddesses are simply allegories of the seasonal cycles of the earth and the sun. Far more importantly their story can depict the seasonal fluctuations of the Life Force, the mysterious power that makes things grow and, when it wanes, causes them to die. For the witch, the life force is an expression of the divine power that moves all creation.

Maxine Sanders, 'Fire Child: The Life and Magic of Maxine Sanders'

Whilst different systems of belief are interesting to study, it is not necessary to limit yourself to one way of interpreting the divine; an open mind will allow you to experience divine power in many forms. Ultimately, this is a decision that you as a Craft practitioner will have to make for yourself.

The Goddess and the Feminine Spirit of Nature

Our Mother is the earth that brings forth birth. She feeds us and gives us water and takes us back when our time comes. The circle she is, with the spear that joins the universe, the never ending cycle.
'The Charge of the Mother',
written by Ron 'SilverEagleSpirit'

The cycles of nature and the turn of the year were of utmost importance to our ancestors, as they relied on the abundance of the earth and the favour of the seasons for their survival. Three major aspects of the Goddess in ancient belief were the 'Fertility Giver' (usually depicted as a pregnant woman as a sign of abundance) 'Birth Giver' (a woman portrayed in the birth giving pose) and 'Death Wielder' (a woman usually depicted in sculptures of bone: stiff and skeletal, who was the keeper of wisdom). The Goddess is 'The Lasting One' who never dies but simply changes between these three faces. She is the sustainer of all life, Lady of both the living and the dead, and the world moves in harmony with her phases.

Today, these three cycles of the Goddess are most commonly recognised as the Maiden, the Mother and the Crone. Although the popularity of the triple aspect is largely attributed to the poet Robert Graves, it cannot be denied that they hold a startling resemblance to the aspects of the Goddess that appear to have been worshiped by our ancestors. These three phases also appear in European Cunning Craft and folklore as the Three Sisters, the Three Fates, or the Wyrd Sisters who hold the Spindle of Fate. The Maiden, Mother and Crone can also be recognised in the phases of the moon: the Waxing, the Full and the Waning.

There has always been a special importance given to the number three, and in Craft we often do things by three to ensure a positive outcome to our workings. Many witches cast the circle by three, called the 'Three Times Pass' and also bless and consecrate the symbolic elements three times. Many old customs and traditions also adhere to the power of three, such as turning three times widdershins (anti-clockwise) on the spot if we walk across a bridge or a covered well to protect against bad luck, breathing three times onto a dice before we roll, and collecting three-leafed clovers.

> *O' old Fate, Queen of Asgardr, weaving wife of Woden*
> *Lady of two halves, bringer of life, and death, equal*
> *Lady Aulraune, Queen of witches, keeper of Wyrd*
> *Your call to hunt is heeded, sheild maiden of Asgardr*
> *O' old Fate, Beloved Lady, Mistress of Alfheimr*
> *Perfect one, whose name echoes down ancient halls...*
> 'The Poem of Asgardr', written by Rune and from the Coven Book of Ways

The female body brought forth life; it held within it the power to swell and give birth to new members of the community, and it was synonymous to the swelling grain and the abundance of the crop. As the sun shone, so the land prospered. These beliefs combined caused a strong reverence of the female and led to thousands of years of Goddess worship which associated the birthing rites of the female with the prosperity of the land. In associated mythology, the Goddess in her role of the Mother gives birth to the young Horned or Sun God at Yule, who will rule the land until the harvest time when the Goddess becomes Death Wielder and sacrifices him to ensure a good harvest.

The afterlife was another religious interest for ancient people. In Europe, our ancestors observed the crops in the fields as the corn was cut down and harvested. They saw that from this sacrifice came new seeds, which once buried in Mother Earth would grow and provide even more crops – new life from the death of the old - and people began to wonder whether they too could be reborn. The Goddess worship that ancient people developed combined the concepts of birth, death and rebirth and passage graves and burial chambers were all built with this in mind. Early tumuli (large mounds of earth and rock in which a person was buried) represented the swollen belly of the female: the Earth Mother whom would give birth to new life. In the same way, passage graves and burial chambers, such as West Kennet Long Barrow in Wiltshire, were built in the shape of the woman's cervix, uterus and womb.

This cycle also brought about the belief in the Crone Goddess, and sculptures of 'the stiff white woman' have been found in many graves along with the dead. It was believed that the Death Wielder, keeper of wisdom and the mysteries and a mediator between the worlds, would help carry the soul into its new life. As a Crone deity she was usually revered at the dark side of the year, a time for reflection, inner journeys and funerary rites. One such dark Goddess is Frau Holda or 'Dame Fate', the Germanic Underworld Earth Mother who rules over the realm of 'Hel' – the place of the dead. She is also remembered at Yule, as Mother Goose. However, the Death Wielder, usually depicted as skeletal and lifeless, was sometimes also portrayed as Birth Giver (completion of cycle) and depicted in squatted birthing positions as a symbol of rebirth, with half her face dark and half her face light to symbolise the two sides of her nature.

These images may be far from what we first imagine when we hear the word 'Goddess'. We may even find the symbology fetishistic, but we must remember that we view them from a very different perspective than that of the artists who created them. To our ancestors the fuller body of the female was seen as a sign of abundance and depictions of the female genitalia were not pornographic but images of sexuality and the power of new life. It is only the modern perception of what is 'right' and what is 'wrong' that causes us to find these images repulsive. We are conditioned from an early age to be ashamed of our bodies, that a plumper form is not acceptable, and that sex is taboo; these are limitations which ancient people simply did not have. In modern eclectic Paganism, we can learn to appreciate all of these different aspects of the Goddess and invoke their particular energies in order to enhance our own lives. Ultimately, the Goddess is the keeper of the mysteries, and her women are the mistresses of natural magic.

The Goddess Archetypes

Archetypes as a concept are deep enduring patterns of thought and behaviour laid down in the human psyche, which remain powerful over long periods of time and transcend cultures and generations. Archetypes form the basis for all instinctive patterns of behaviour that all of humankind shares in common.

The Goddess archetypes represent all aspects the divine female and we can recognise these archetypal characters both in mythological characters and within ourselves. The myths of both the Goddess and the God should be read holistically in order to recognise both the spiritual and psychological meanings behind the stories.

The Goddess archetype represents a model of a way of being and behaving, which all women share and recognise. In fairy tales, this archetype may be revealed to us as a queen, a princess or an evil witch. In our night time dreams we tap into the collective unconscious whereby we access the common pool of archetypal images.

Not only do the Goddess archetypes represent the Triple Aspect of Maiden, Mother and Crone but also every other part of life: education, intellect, sensuality, the arts, rulership, healing, hunting, knowledge and magic. Each Goddess represents a particular archetypal energy and we can use specific Goddesses in our rituals and magic in order to apply their energy to enhance and empower our rites.

Goddesses, as feminine archetypes, remain alive to this day in the psychology of women. So how can we recognise the Goddess archetypes within ourselves? Let's look at the Greek Goddess Demeter, a Mother archetype. Her myths weave a tale of motherhood: the joy of being a mother and the inevitable loss of a child when they grow up and move on. Her daugher Kore represents the virginal, carefree, child-like innocence of the Maiden. In addition, the journey Kore takes to the Underworld, her marriage to Hades and her name change to Persephone all represent the transformation from childhood to womanhood, as well as from one season to another. Hecate, the Greek Crone Goddess, represents the grandmother, old and wise from many years of life experience (although, she is also seen under many other guises). Her myths weave tales of wisdom, knowledge and power. So, the phases of Maiden Mother and Crone not only represent the feminine journey through life, but also different aspects of ourselves. And these archetypes are not limited to age – a ten year old child who is concentrating on her studies is expressing her wise Crone archetype, and the old lady who gets up to dance at a disco is expressing her Maiden.

Like Kore, the Norse Goddess Frigg also makes her journey between the worlds on the Yggdrasill, symbolising the journey of womanhood and the inherent power which is collected along the way. Both Frigg, and her later guise Frau Holda, are associated with witchcraft and magic.

Nor are the Goddess archetypes limited to gender. Just as the divine masculine can be found within the female, so too can the divine feminine be found in the male. We all have both a feminine side and a masculine side to us, and this balance of male and female makes us whole. In Jungian psychology, they are the Anima and Animus; the male has an inner feminine, whilst the female has an inner masculine. This makes total sense, as we all come from the masculine and the feminine: a mother and a father: an egg and a sperm. Neither is more or less important than the other, they simply offer us different, and very necessary, parts of our being. For instance, if a man denies his inner feminine self he will most likely find it difficult to be in touch with his feelings. This can lead to problems in relationships, not to mention his relationship with himself. He may also substitute the lack of warmth that he feels within himself with high ambition or ego, and live an emotionally unfulfilling life. Without heart he becomes hard and cold, judgemental, critical, egocentric and aloof. In the same way, a woman who denies her inner masculine self becomes too soft, too passive and may be unable to make decisions, inevitably becoming over-dependent upon others.

In a coven, the High Priestess epitomises the Goddess in all her archetypal forms; through invocation she communicates the wisdom of the feminine spirit of nature, whilst encouraging the archetypal aspects of the Goddess to manifest within others.

TASK: Embracing the Inner Goddess

Everyone has an inner Goddess, a divine female aspect, and no matter whether you are male or female it is important to recognise this inner Goddess; in men, she is the Anima, the inner female personality. Through the following exercise, you will be asking a Goddess to work with you.

Although you will be learning about and working with many different Goddesses, it is often the case that a particular Goddess stays with you throughout your whole life. This Goddess is usually the one with whom you associate with the best, and who will always be with you, regardless of what path you travel through life and what magical tradition you are following. When I first began on the path of Paganism, I felt an affinity with the Goddess Cerridwyn, a Celtic deity and Mistress of magic and rebirth whose symbol is the cauldron: the sign of transformation and change. I always used Cerridwyn within my rituals, but never really knew why. It was only several years later when I decided to fully research Cerridywn that I discovered her links to the Welsh town Carmarthen incidentally, my birthplace. It was there that Cerridwyn lived, and gave birth to Taliesin the gifted bard who, according to some legends, was the father of Merlin. In Welsh, Carmarthen is 'Caerfyrddin' which literally means 'Merlin's Fort'. My path has always embraced Cerridwyn in her different guises, from Ker to Frige.

She is Isis veiled, clad in the robes of nature. Then she is Isis unveiled, revealing her mysteries as we are ready to understand them.
    Dion Fortune

Take a look at the eight Goddess names listed below. Which one speaks to you the most? Is there one that particularly catches your eye, or one that you find particularly intriguing? Try not to rationalise your decision, and intuitively choose one name. Now do some very brief research on the chosen Goddess, and once you have done so, you can begin the meditation.

- Isis
- Rhiannon
- Hecate
- Gaia
- Artemis
- Aphrodite
- Eostre
- Brigid

Close your eyes and take a few deep breaths. Focus on your breathing, in and out, in and out. With every breath in, feel yourself calm, and at peace. With every breath out, you feel the tension of the day drain away. Your heartbeat becomes slower, your body becomes heavier. Breathe in peace, breathe out tension. All the thoughts of the day and other distractions leave your mind as you focus on this one task, breathing in ... and out, in … and out. Give this process as much time as you need to allow yourself to become completely relaxed and focused. There is no rush. Now close your eyes and we will begin the journey to meet this Goddess in a meditation.

You sit by the edge of a stream beneath the low hanging branches of a willow tree. It is almost dawn; the dew is still wet upon the grass and the night still eagerly holds its grip over the last of the shadows.

The quiet of the morning is broken by the faint calls of the earliest birds; they chirp and argue in the branches above you as they greet the approaching light. In the distance, the gentle rays of the sun begin to creep across the boughs of the trees illuminating the beauty of the forest before you. The new light reflects upon the surface of the bubbling stream and shimmers on the glistening fish and smooth pebbles beneath the surface. You scry into the clear water of the stream, focusing on the mysteries of the depths and concentrating upon the nurturing and purifying qualities of water. The water symbolises the womb of the Goddess and the primordial waters from which we all came and, in time, to whom we shall all return. Watch the ripples upon the surface; see how they subtly change.

Now you see a reflection upon the water. It is faint at first, but now it becomes clearer, and you begin to make out the shape of the Goddess who you chose at the beginning of the meditation. You look up at the riverbank opposite where she stands, solid and whole, looking at you with loving eyes. You sit in this place and feel the spirit of her, you feel the power of the feminine deity fill your very soul: The Goddess, divine spirit of nature – Maiden, Mother and Crone, Keeper of Wisdom and Mother of Rebirth.

She holds her hand out to you and you take it, and in that moment you feel at one with the energy of this Goddess. She now speaks to you, and gives you a message. Take your time to speak with her; there is no rush.

When you are finished, you glance back at her reflection in the water where she begins to fade and her image is nothing more but the bubbling stream. You thank the Goddess for her words and reflect on the power of the Goddess, the Mother, the Maiden and the Crone.

When you are ready, begin to feel yourself become more aware of your surroundings and when you are ready open your eyes and find yourself fully awake.

Once you have finished the meditation with your selected Goddess, write about your experience. What happened in the meditation? What sort of feelings did you get from the Goddess? Was she trying to tell you anything, and did she offer you any gifts?

TASK: Working with feminine magic - Poppets

A Poppet, also known as a 'Fetish', a 'Mommet' or a 'Bud-Will' is a doll created in the likeness of another person which is used to cause change. Poppets are particularly connected with Goddess magic, because of the creative and intuitive expression in the act of creating, and then breathing life into, the Poppet.

The Poppet is normally made during a Waxing or a Full Moon (for positive magic) out of wax, cloth, paper, wood or clay, or a plant root such as Mandrake or the 'Alraune'. After being decorated and stuffed with items connected with the person, the Poppet is then associated with the aim of the spell. Traditionally a lock of hair, a trimming of fingernail or a small amount of bodily fluid (such as spittle) of the person would then be incorporated into the Poppet along with herbs, crystals and talismans corresponding to the aim of the magic. The Poppet is then infused with life force by a concentrated effort and a psychic link created between the Poppet and the person who is being worked upon. The Poppet is then named.

Poppets have been used for thousands of years and have historically been feared by society. They have an unfortunate reputation as being evil, 'a tool of the devil' due to their ability to manipulate and cause harm. This reputation has lead to the popular image of the Poppet as the 'Voodoo Doll' and the practice of sticking pins into the effigy to cause harm to the person intended. However 'Vodou', is a syncretic religion that originated in Haiti (in the Caribbean) and a relative of the West African 'Vodun'. It is based on the worship of Gods and the ancestors, a diverse religion that has been misunderstood by modern society. Vodou dolls were primarily used for benevolent rites such as healing, protection against evil spirits and enemies, and for contacting the otherworlds.

It would be incorrect however to say that Poppets have never been used for evil. Early curse Poppets (Roman 'Defixiones', and Greek 'Katadesmoi') were often used for many immoral aims, from affecting the outcome of a chariot race to the more ominous intentions of lust and murder. These dolls were pierced with nails and buried along with a binding tablet made of leather, papyrus or lead and inscribed with a spell. The Poppet itself would normally be bound around the arms and the legs and there was sometimes a collar around the neck and a binding around the mouth. As with all magic, the power and the outcome of the spell lay in the hands of the witch.

So, although there *is* a history of Poppets being used for negative purposes, as a rule this is not the case. Although they have been used to *curse* throughout history, they have also been used to *cure*, and on the whole they were used for positive magic such as protection spells, healing and fertility. One must, of course, also take into account the element of Karma and the Law of Return when considering the use of a Poppet for evil ends. So then, it is much better to turn an ill-wisher's harm back on them (see Psychic Defence, Chapter 14) than to create new ill intent towards them.

The doll itself is often regarded as the 'little life' or the 'magical child', and its creation is, symbolically its birth; you are its parent. The more intent you are on birthing the Poppet, the more effective the link will be; some witches even act out the 'birth' of the poppet to bring it more fully to life. As Poppet magic is a form of 'Sympathetic Magic' - it is a lot easier and beneficial to cause positive change with the Poppet than it is to cause negative. Maxine Sanders puts this well as she describes the method of sympathetic magic in her book, *Maxine: Witch Queen*:

> *Sympathetic magic means 'working in entire sympathy with' and very often this involves the use of images. Sympathy with the image created is absolutely necessary if you are to hope for any success in this form of magic. Perhaps it isn't realised how absolute this love, this sympathy, must be. This is what makes things so difficult for the witch who may be working* (for evil). *You must love the image as much as you would your own child, and if this love isn't there you are wasting your time. The black witch is caught between this clash of emotions – love for what she has created, coupled with a death-wish. Not easy!*

In essence, whether we are using the poppet for healing, protection or love, we are effectively 'giving birth' to the representation of the person we are working for and the image we create is as our own child. We must care for it as we would a real child and, when the purpose of the Poppet has been fulfilled, the link must be broken between the person and the Poppet, and it must then be disposed of carefully and with respect.

More recently, Poppets have begun to be known as 'Fith-Faths' (pronounced 'fee-fa') although this term is slightly more obscure as its original Gaelic meaning was to 'shape shift' – to transform and take on the appearance of an animal. It can also mean to become invisible. However, it most likely became a term for Poppets in more modern times due to the transformation of one thing to another: from an inanimate doll to a symbol of a living being. Poppets are sometimes (although more rarely) known as a 'Pippies', and some believe that the fictional, witch-like character 'Pippi Longstocking' was named after the ancient art of Poppet magic.

A healing Poppet also appears in the 2006 Spanish movie, *Pan's Labyrinth*, in the form of a Mandrake root, in which the poppet is fed with milk to keep it alive. There is some truth in the tale; soaking a mandrake root with a mixture of milk, water and blood is an old tradition which is used to empower the Mandrake root before it is used within ritual.

Blessed be this Earth, this Root, this Night.
'On finding and uprooting a mandrake', author unknown

Anyone who decides to research the Mandrake will also discover the cautionary legends regarding digging one up – the Mandrake is said to give a most fearful scream if pulled from the ground, and much instruction is given on the correct way to remove the root in order to avoid the scream.

Creating the Poppet

In order to create an effective Poppet, one must first have a sufficient cause to do so and the desire for the purpose to manifest must be sufficiently strong in order for this to work. You may have someone in mind that you would like to heal of a wound of the body or of the mind, or someone who you would like to protect or empower.

We will be covering ethics in magic in more detail later in the book (Chapter 16) but for now look again at this quick check-list to see that you are not breaking any ethical rules:

Never work to influence any other persons will or freedom of choice
Never work to cause harm to others
Never work for ego or unreasonable financial gain

If there isn't anyone you can think of to help, choose a cause which is close to your heart such as healing of the earth or another current world issue. In this case, the Poppet will be created with the whole issue in mind and a figure designed to represent the issue in a personified form. For instance, if you choose to work on the healing of the earth, the figure may be a well-rounded female, dressed in green, much like the 'Gaia' Mother Goddess image. If you were working to aid a settlement of a national dispute, the figure may be a wise-looking figure, in a posture which conveys balance and justice.

Write your aim down on a piece of paper and then design your figure out of the chosen material. Remember it is not the aesthetics that matter; it's whether the figure represents that person or issue to *you*. Focus on the purpose of the Poppet as you make it.

You can design a Poppet out of almost any natural material, including wax, clay, cloth, paper, roots and wood. If using Wax or Clay, mould the Poppet into shape, leaving a hollow space in which to place items associated with the person and the aim of the spell such as a lock of hair, various herbs and crystals or rock or metal such as loadstone, and a small talisman. Once they are inside, fill in the hollow with spare wax/clay. When using cloth, cut two pieces of cloth out into the shape of your poppet, then place them together with the best side of the cloth facing in and stitch all the way round except for the top of the head. It is best to hand-stitch rather than machine stitch. Once stitched, turn the poppet through so that the best side of the cloth is now facing out and the stitches are hidden inside. Now the Poppet can be filled with items associated with the person and the aim of the spell. Once they are inside, sew up the remainder of the Poppet. If using paper, you can draw the shape of your Poppet and use your creative skills to make the image reflect the person as much as possible. Do they have a moustache? Do they have long hair or short hair? Do they wear certain items? Draw on these simple things which in your mind associate the image with the person. Again, it's not your drawing skill that matters; it is the intent, so don't be put off trying this method just because you are not an artist! If you have a photograph, you may choose to stick the picture onto the face of the Poppet.

If you want to get really traditional, you might choose to use plant roots or root vegetables. Many plant roots can be used to carve into Poppet figures such as potatoes, carrots and the very popular Mandrake or Ginseng which grow naturally in the shape of a body and require no carving at all. You should be aware that these Poppets will not last very long as they will perish, so they should only be for the short term or for a spell that you intend to manifest very quickly. Wood can also be carved into a figure and decorated with colours, paints and fabrics. You may choose to ask for a piece of the person's own clothing (unwashed) to add to the poppet. Once you have created the Poppet and you are happy with the end result, it is time to bless the Poppet and then infuse it with life force.

The Rite

Perform the Psychic Circle Casting from Chapter Four to prepare the sacred space for the spell, and then the Cleansing and Consecration of the Instruments of Art rite which will prepare the Poppet to be used for magical workings and cast out any negativity or ill intent. This, in itself, will ensure that the magic worked with the Poppet is for the good of all. If the magic were to cause any harm in the long run, this rite will 'cancel out' the spell and the magic will simply not work.

Now take a single white candle and place it into a secure candlestick. This candle represents the life-force of the Poppet, and as you light it you affirm the Poppet's connection to the person involved. Light the candle now, and then pick up the Poppet between your palms. See the Poppet as the person involved; feel as a mother feels to her child – protective, loving

and supportive. Say these words, replacing the name written here
with the name of your subject:

> *Little one, I made you and now I give you life*
> *I name you (John Doe)*
> *As life was breathed into us*
> *So shall life be breathed into you.*
> 'To Breathe Life into a Poppet', author unknown

Now cup your hands around the Poppet and blow three times
into your palms, to breathe life into the Poppet. At this point, you
can use the Poppet to help the cause you have chosen. Hands on
healing can be employed: a method of placing your hands upon
the Poppet and channelling healing energy into the Poppet. If the
issue is orientated upon wisdom and learning, you might choose
to create a talisman to reflect the qualities that you wish to be
endowed upon the person, and place the Poppet upon it. Talk to
the Poppet; instruct it on how best to move forward. If the aim is
protection, you might surround the poppet with holly or thorn to
represent their safeguard. You might choose rocks, metals,
colours, planetary symbols and elemental symbols to accompany
the Poppet.

When you have done all you can, raise the Poppet up and affirm,
As above, So Below. As Without, So Within, As my mind wills; So mote
it be!

Once you have completed the rest of your ritual you can leave the
white candle to safely burn down. Leave the Poppet on your altar
for the coming weeks whilst the magic is working; you may
decide to repeat the spellwork on the Poppet now and again
(always within the psychic circle) until the magic has manifested.
Take good care of the Poppet – remember that it is psychically
linked to the person it represents.

When you feel the magic has manifested and the Poppet has fulfilled its reason for being, it is time to dispose of the Poppet. This should be done carefully; the Poppet's link to the person involved should be severed and the Poppet should be affirmed as an inanimate object once again. Janet and Stewart Farrar recommend the following in their book, *Spells and How They Work:*

> *When the aim has been achieved or the period of working is over, no image which is identified with a person should be allowed to linger. It must be broken up into pieces, which are taken to naturally flowing water and thrown in, with the instruction "Return to the elements from which thou came".*

Keep in mind during this exercise that you are responsible for the person for whom you have chosen to work for. Care for the Poppet as you would for your own child. If you are in any doubt of your own intentions, this work should not be undertaken. This is a great responsibility for each of us to bear. Think wisely, act wiser.

The God and the Masculine Spirit of Nature

> *I ride the earth on cloven feet, or on wings of air. I am the hunter, I am the hunted. Stag and horse, bird and beast are mine. I am named Herne or Pan, Cernunnos or the Horned One.'*
> Janet Farrar, 'The Witches Way'

Witchcraft is often thought of as a Goddess path, the popular image of the witch being female. However, although there are some feminist paths of Paganism such as Dianic Wicca, in usual Craft practice the God is worshiped in equality alongside the Goddess.

Some of the first images of the God were created thousands of years ago in ancient cave paintings which depicted the Horned God in therianthrope form; such as part man-part Goat, part man-part Bison and part man-part Stag. One of the most famous therianthrope Gods is that of 'The Sorcerer' from Les Trois Freres caves, France. He was the animal master, who controlled the hunt. The image is outlined in black charcoal and is a composite creature of part owl, part wolf 'Con al Cernac', part stag, part horse and part lion. Images like 'The Sorcerer' are commonly associated with Pagan deities today, such as the Gods Cernunnos and Herne who to many veteran Pagans is fondly known as 'Old Hornie'.

However, there are many lesser known therianthrope God forms, such as the San creator God 'Kaggen' who is a composite deity of part man-part-preying mantis. Kaggen is a shape shifting God, and images have been found of this God transforming from man to mantis.

In the communities of our ancestors, men held important posts such as hunters, warriors and traders. Primitive man travelled much further than we might first imagine, and with trading came an exchange of culture and language between tribes and other societies.

The benefits of man in society were evident, but his role in the most important part of life, reproduction, was not. The role of the female in reproductive context was obvious; whilst the male's part to play was a hidden power. No wonder the Goddess was the primary deity worshiped by ancient people. Although a masculine deity *was* recognised at this time, he played a relatively small part in religion.

Worship of the God developed as mankind became aware that both male and female parties were required to create new life. Before this, our species only observed the female - swelling, gestating and giving forth life. It was a divine birth; the female who brought new life to the world was synonymous with the Goddess of the earth who provided the abundant harvest.

In popular Wicca, the male force is generally associated with the sun (the active force) and the female force with the moon (the passive force) just as the sun encourages growth and the moon nurtures in tune with the cycles of the land and the sea. However, this rule does not always apply due to the Anima (feminine side of the male) and Animus (masculine side of the female) which is present in the Gods and Goddesses as well as within ourselves. Throughout much of history, the two polar energies of masculine and feminine have ruled equally and the God was considered as having many feminine aspects, just as the Goddess had many masculine. For example, Thoth the Egyptian God of Wisdom is often pictured wearing a moon crescent upon his head – a sign usually associated with the Goddess. Therefore not only does he encompasses earthly knowledge such as literature, record keeping and mathematics, but also deep into the realms of psychic understanding. The Greek God Asclepius was a God of Healing, another trait that is usually associated with the Goddess. Even the raucous Greek God Dionysus had a more feminine side, in the form of the righteous Apollo – two sides of one God, played under different names. For this reason, our Initiatory Craft coven considers the sun and the moon as interchangeable symbols of the God and the Goddess.

The God of Passage

Whereas the Goddess never dies (but simply changes) the God must pass through a series of initiatory stages to aid the passage of life and death and the turn of the seasons. For instance, the British Vegetation Gods the Holly King and the Oak King are twin opposites of one another. They do battle twice a year for the possession of the land and together they lead a timeless war between darkness and light, and the two sides of the year. Osiris, the Egyptian Vegetation God, was murdered by his evil brother Set, the God of infertility and evil. Set then began to take hold over the cities of Egypt, turning it from a fertile land into a place of chaos, torment, disease and death. However, Osiris was brought back to life by his consort, the Goddess Isis, and soon after left to become God of the Dead and psychopomp of the Underworld.

This connection with initiation, transition and the Underworld also made the God the Great Initiator: the Guardian at the door through which all must pass. He was revered as the Great God of Judgement, as well as the dealer of punishment; old Hobb Lord of Initiation, holly trees, stags and death.

I am darkness and the Lord of Night;
to know me is terror, but also rebirth.
Without me I am divided,
and the light turns its face from me.
Will you come to me, O' Lady, and heal me,
even though it is death to thee?
Vivianne Crowley, 'Wicca'

Many God names developed due to the personification of the earth's natural rhythms and nature. The seasons, the weather, the sun, the moon, the stars, the darkness and the light were all attributed to certain Gods and Goddesses and as civilisation advanced further, people began recording the planets and their influences on daily life. These too were given God names, the characters of these deities reflecting the effect that their presence had on the people at various times of the year. The Sun, Saturn, Jupiter, Mars and Mercury were all worshiped as deities that ruled over specific days of the week and times of the year. Two feminine planets, Venus and the moon, joined the five masculine, which made up what was to be known as the 'Seven Heavenly Gods'.

When the Ice Age came to an end, the larger animals which had been hunted previously began to die out. People began to rely upon agriculture much more, and this sudden transition was highly disruptive to their culture. Agriculture was unpredictable;

the crops success relied upon so many more variables than hunting ever had. As a result the Sun God became the primary deity worshiped in an attempt to appease the God and encourage the crops.

Because of the agricultural struggle people began to dispute over crops and this eventually lead to segregation and ownership of land. With the coming of the age of Bronze, more advanced weaponry was being created and this led to more dispute and conflict over land and ownership. and as our ancestor's society developed, so did the character and diversity of the God. He became the Lord of War and death as well as rebirth – the Old Dark Lord, and the Gods of the Underworld.

The Gods of the Underworld are the opposites of their brothers the Solar Gods. Osiris is the Lord of the Underworld in Egyptian mythology who aids the deceased in their quest to reach the afterlife. Hades is the Greek God of the Underworld; he is well known because of the part he plays in transforming the Earth Maiden, Kore, into the Queen of the Underworld, Persephone. In Europe, the Stag God Cernunnos was the Great Hunter, whilst more recently the Horned Herne became a God of transition and death.

Gods from many different cultures are often depicted accompanied by a serpent, or as a serpent God, because of the regenerative properties of the snake. A snake can discard its old skin and be born again fresh and new, therefore symbolising new beginnings and rebirth. Cernunnos is usually depicted holding a snake in his left hand, and the Egyptian Osiris and the Greek Dionysus are often seen accompanied by a serpent, all symbols of the coiled serpent power within all living things and the earth.

The ancient Horned Gods such as Cernunnos and Pan are strong, powerful energies. Even though other Gods emerged, the archetypal Horned God continued to be the primary male deity worshiped in many different cultures and horns were often worn by Priests as a sign of divinity and power in Europe, Babylon,

India and Egypt, a tradition which is continued in the Craft today.

> I call strong Pan, the substance of the whole,
> Ethereal, marine, earthly, general soul,
> Undying fire; for all the world is thine,
> And all are parts of thee, O pow'r divine ...
> 'The Orphic Hymn to Pan'

There are many sites worth visiting which radiate strong God energy. In the village of Cerne Abbas in Dorset a colossal image of the God is carved into the chalk landscape, and it is customary for women to lie upon the giants' phallus in order to assure fertility and conception. Singular standing stones called 'God Stones' were also used throughout Europe as phallic representations of the Pagan God. When Christianity arrived, many of these phallic standing stones had crosses carved into them to aid the conversion of local people; however, untouched examples do still exist in certain places, such as Bodmin Moor in Cornwall which is dotted with these phallic places of pilgrimage.

Other images of the God, such as his Vegetation guise, can be seen in the architecture of many old churches and cathedrals in the British Isles and in Europe; the 'Green Man' face, made up of leaves, vines and fruit.

The Vegetation God

The Vegetation God's journey begins when the Goddess gives birth to the 'Child of Promise,' at the Winter Solstice. With his birth, light begins to return to the earth after the dark of the winter. During the start of the year, he grows to an adolescent, the 'Young Phallic God' of fertility. By late spring – the sabbat of Eostara – the God has become the consort of the Goddess and by Beltane he has become an equal partner with her and assumes responsibility for the land, the animals and vegetation. Late summertime, between Litha and Lughnassadh, the God becomes the 'Sacrificial King'. The Goddess cuts him down, synonymous to the crops being harvested, in order to provide for the inhabitants of the land. Thereafter, he retreats to the underworld and the Goddesses womb at Samhaine, where he awaits to be born again at the Winter Solstice.

By following the God's mythos and rites of passage we activate a change within ourselves which is in keeping with the seasons and the Wheel of the Year. This aids us in our lives as we begin to understand the lessons of life, death and rebirth on both physical and spiritual levels. Many of the Pagan Gods were also absorbed into mythology, with several of them becoming synonymous with archetypal heroes such as Hercules and Robin Hood, and folklore characters like Jack in the Green. Renewed though his own rebirth, the God embodies life potential and under this guise he is known as the Child of Promise, Lord of Fertility, fires, goats, horses, oak trees, and the Blackmiths' trade.

In a coven, the High Priest epitomises the God in all his archetypal forms; through invocation he communicates the wisdom of the masculine spirit of nature, whilst encouraging the archetypal aspects of the God to manifest within others.

The Pagan God is strong and powerful, a hunter and protector, a lover, a father, a tyrant and a hero. He is the ever renewing, ever growing lord of the dance. He invites us with open arms and warmly embraces us all.

TASK: Embracing the Inner God

Everyone has an inner God: a Divine male aspect. Male or female, it is important to recognise this inner God; in women, he is the Animus, the inner male personality. Through the following exercise, we will be asking a God to work with you.

Although you will be working with many different Gods, it is often the case that a particular God stays with you throughout your whole life. This Patron God is usually the one with whom you associate the best and who will always be with you regardless of what path you travel through life and which magical tradition you are following at the time.

I am a stag of seven tines, I am a wide flood on a plain, I am a wind on the deep waters, I am a shining tear of the sun, I am a hawk on a cliff, I am fair among flowers, I am a god who sets the head afire with smoke. I am a battle waging spear, I am a salmon in the pool, I am a hill of poetry, I am a ruthless boar, I am a threatening noise of the sea, I am a wave of the sea, Who but I knows the secrets of the unhewn dolmen?

'Song of Amergin', author unknown

Take a look at the eight Gods listed below. Which one speaks to you the most? Is there one which particularly catches your eye, or one that you find particularly intriguing? Try not to rationalise your decision and intuitively choose one name. Now do some very brief research on the chosen God. Once you have done so, you can begin the meditation.

- Poseidon
- Thoth
- Cernunnos
- Dionysus
- Herne
- Osiris
- Lugh
- Bel

Close your eyes and take a few deep breaths. Focus on your breathing, in and out, in and out. With every breath in, feel yourself calm, and at peace. With every breath out, you feel the tension of the day drain away. Your heartbeat becomes slower; your body becomes heavier. Breathe in peace, breathe out tension. All the thoughts of the day and other distractions leave your mind as you focus on this one task, breathing in ... and out, in … and out. Give this process as much time as you need to allow yourself to become completely relaxed and focused. There is no rush. Now close your eyes and we will begin the journey to meet this God in a meditation.

You see yourself standing alone on a wild grassy plain. The long grass is moist with dew, gently swaying as the breeze whispers across the wild expanse.

You look across the plain and you see a herd of deer grazing the tender grasses near the edge of a deep forest. The herd looks up all at once and observe you. They realise that you are there, but choose to ignore your presence and now begin to continue eating. You watch them for a while.

Now you look past the deer into the deep, lush forest. It seems to be bidding you; some ancient calling that asks you to explore the forest and the ancient spirits that live within. You walk through the grazing deer to the edge of the forest and look into its dark yet inviting folds.

A cool wind caresses your skin and you breathe deeply to smell the sweet scent of the leaf mulch beneath your feet. You step into the forest.

You follow a tiny track through the forest; an ancient path, that has never been trod by man - a path of the forest animals. You look around the forest and feel enveloped in its spirit; you listen to the call of tiny birds high up in the treetops, and the rustling of hedgehogs beneath the leaves. You see the soft bodies of mushrooms and other fungi, which have pushed their way up through the damp soil and display beautiful colours as they glisten with dew.

Now you smell the scent of a wood fire; you look for the source and see curling smoke billowing through the tree branches. You follow the smoke until you come across a tiny stone building in a clearing, deep in the centre of the forest.

You walk to the door of the building and study the magical symbols carved around the door frame. They may be Celtic,

Egyptian or Greek, depending on which God you chose at the beginning of the meditation. You realise that this tiny stone building is a temple to your chosen God, and you place your hand on the door handle and enter the temple.

Heavy incense fills the temple and you feel content, happy and in awe of this place. The temple is decorated with items of adornment and statues to your specific God, with wall hangings, carvings and images of this deity.

Now the incense begins to curl about in front of you, and transforms into the God whom you chose at the beginning of the meditation. Now he is solid and whole, and stands in front of you, looking at you with loving eyes. You sit in this place and feel the power of the masculine deity fill your very soul: the God – protector of the wilds, master of the underworld, keeper of wisdom and intellect. He holds his hand out and you take it, and in that moment you feel at one with the energy of this God. Now he speaks to you, and gives you a message. Take your time to speak with him; there is no rush.

When you are finished, he begins to fade and transforms back into the smoke that curls about you. You thank the God for his words and you leave the temple.

As you follow the tiny path back to the open plain, you reflect on the power of the God, the Protector, the Father, the Hunter.

When you are back to the open grass plain, feel yourself become more aware of your surroundings and when you are ready, open your eyes and find yourself fully awake.

Once you have finished the meditation with your selected God, write about your experience. What happened in the meditation? What sort of feelings did you get from the God? Was he trying to tell you anything? Did he offer you any gifts?

TASK: Working with Masculine Magic - Sigaldry
Whereas feminine magic is predominantly psychically and

intuitively led, masculine magic tends to lean toward the more calculated systems such as numerical amulets, (i.e. magical squares) and planetary magic (i.e. seals). This is a powerful way of using the masculine energy. The other side of masculine energy is raw emotion, and basic human instincts, such as impulsive and primal actions and magic within ritual, phallic fertility, the arts, the hunt, anger and passion. For this stage of the chapter, we will be focusing on the God energy of such deities as Thoth, Hermes and Odin – Gods of the intellect and mind – as we create a magical Sigil.

A Sigil is a magical symbol created to represent the desire of the witch, and is used to condense your intent into direct symbolism. They are made up of letters, which are rearranged into a design and reworked until a pleasing design is created, which ends up as a symbol and has no direct resemblance to the original power phrase. Although primarily made up of letters, other relevant symbols can also be added to the Sigil. Sigils use the power of the unconscious mind, taking an intellectual idea and communicating it to the part of the mind that relates to images and symbolism.

Creating a Sigil

When creating a Sigil, the following method is used:

1. Concentrate on the intention
   Decide what it is that you would like to bring into your life

2. Create a power phrase for the intention
   The sentence you decide on should be concise, using just enough words to express the meaning and no more – such as 'Intellect and Wisdom' or 'New Home'

3. Cross out all of the repeated letters

Remove letters which appear twice in the phase, i.e.

INTELLECT / WISDOM = 'INTELCWSDOM'

4. Arrange into a design within a box
   The letters can then be arranged into a design of your
   choice – you can join letters, turn letters upside down and
   back to front, and make letters larger or smaller. Use your
   artistic side to transform the letters into a symbol. The box
   helps structure your Sigil.

5. Reduce the design
   Use your creative side to reduce the design down as you
   wish to create a symbol that represents your intention. Re-
   draw the simplified version, this time without the guide
   box if you wish.

You can also add symbols or pictures that represent your
intention to the design. We will be going into more talismanic
symbology later in the book, but for now here are some traditional symbols which can be combined with the letters in your
Sigil.

COSMIC SPHERE   MANIFESTATION   DIVINE ORDER   DESTINY

Once you are happy with your design, light a candle and focus on
the design. Visualise your intention beginning to take form, and
see yourself achieving the goal. When you are ready, pass the

Sigil through the flames, and drop it into a bowl of sand to burn out. Fire, also a masculine principle, contains the powers of transformation and burning the paper will send the desire onto the astral plane where it will transform. Be careful with the candle and the flames – always have water nearby.

Chapter Six

Creation and Manifestation

In the Beginning, There was the One
And from the One, Came the Three... So mote it be!
'The Opening Chant', from the Coven Book of Ways

Who are we, where did we come from, and how was the universe created? This is a question that has puzzled mankind since time began. In this age of science we consider that we are more enlightened as to the origins of our universe; for instance, there is good evidence to suggest that creation occurred by way of a primeval explosion, which started from a single point and has been expanding ever since, aptly named 'The Big Bang'. But if the real question is why the Big Bang happened in the first place, then that becomes a religious question rather than an astronomical one.

The creation myths of our ancestors attempted to answer the question of where the earth and its inhabitants came from. The true nature of the universe was not as clear to our forefathers as it is to us today, and so the creation of the universe as a whole was rarely mentioned. Even in the Bible, God does not will his creation out of nothing – what exists before he begins his work is explained in Genesis 1: 1-3 as *'a formless waste, with darkness over the seas and only an awesome wind sweeping over the water'*.

This concept of primordial water is very similar to many other creation myths from around the world which also began their tales with a primordial sea or dark chaos. Our ancestors observed the movements of the planets, the stars, the tides and the seasons and began to realise nature's powerful influence upon their lives; it was these natural elements that gave our ancestors their inspiration. They tried to reflect what they saw happening in nature by recreating it in their myths, religious beliefs, ritual and culture and they personified the deities, giving them names and telling their stories. As time progressed these simple stories developed and become more elaborate. Creation myths do differ from one culture to another, but more than often they share one or more of these common factors:

- Darkness 'Nun' or chaos
- One Divine spark
- Mother and Father Figures
- Primordial Water
- Birth
- Eggs
- The Serpent
- Earth and Mud
- Joining or splitting of the Earth and the Sky
- The Active and The Passive Principle
- A fall from paradise, a war or some other tragedy

Many Pagan creation myths also explain the origins of the four elements, earth, air, fire and water, and the relationship between the male and female. In general, more developed societies such as Greece, Egypt and Rome had more complex creation myths solely due to their developed ability to communicate by the written word; however, all myths appear to share a particular common aspect – one divine spark, one source of creation which divides into two complimentary halves. It is this divine spark of creation that then fuels the rest of the creation story.

The cosmology followed by my own coven is a balance between our acceptance of the big bang theory and a recognition of this divine spark which acted as an ignition and brought about each aspect of primordial creation and evolution. Native to Europe, this spark is known as Dame Fate, who in her Earth

Mother aspect gave birth to all creatures, whilst the God breathed spirit into them to provide them with a soul.

The World Egg

The World Egg is a symbol that was used within mythology to explain the beginnings of the universe. In many myths, the egg was the outer shell inside of which the whole universe was created. This egg then either shattered (creating the sun, the moon and the stars) separated (creating the sky and the earth) or hatched (revealing a God or Goddess, who would then go on to design the rest of creation).

The mysteries of the egg spoke deeply to our ancestors; they observed life being conceived, the embryo growing in the darkness, and then life coming forth and hatching from the confines of the womb-like shell. In the Greek myths, the great Serpent Ophion coiled around and incubated the World Egg, which had been laid by his mother and lover Eurynone. From this egg hatched the rest of the world, the sun, the moon and the stars. Similarly in Nordic myths, the Goddess Luonnotar (whose name means daughter of nature) upset a nest of eggs and accidentally broke one egg into two pieces. The two haves of its shell became heaven and the earth, the yolk became the sun, the white became the moon, and the scattered fragments of shell became the stars.

Eggs were also of solar significance to our ancestors; the bright and round surface of the shell in contrast to the dark womb of the inner egg was seen as a parody to the bright sun in the sky and the darkness of night. Eggs would be coloured gold, red, yellow or orange to represent the sun, and then exchanged to offer fertility and prosperity; a tradition which is echoed today in modern Easter celebrations.

The concept of the World Egg has now been applied to modern science and is known as the 'Cosmic Egg' a term used to describe the notion that the universe is constantly expanding, but is also eternally old. The term 'The Cosmic Egg' is also sometimes used to describe the process of the Big Bang.

Cosmology, Magic and The Triangle

All Gods are one God and all Goddesses are one Goddess, and there is but one initiator.
Dion Fortune, 'The Sea Priestess'

The simple shape of the triangle has been used for thousands of years to communicate the way we believe our universe and our magic works. Our coven uses a hypothesis called The *Triangle of Manifestation*, which acts as a template for Initiatory Craft cosmology and indicates that many deities manifested from one Divine creative source whilst also existing independently. In the same way, all acts of magic must come from one point of creative intent.

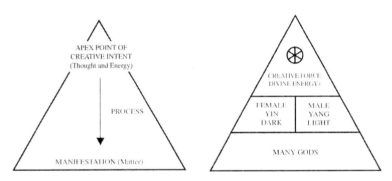

Imagine that you turn a spotlight on. The source of the light is strong, powerful and intense. It is almost impossible to stare at the source of the light, or comprehend shapes and images on or around the bulb. Now notice how the light naturally expands out and illuminates the surrounding area. The light now becomes something that helps our sight, rather than hinders it. This is similar to the source of Divine power, the tip of the pyramid. In Qabalah, this apex point is called the 'Ein Sof' which emanates other levels of existence and finally material form. In itself, it is an omnipotent, incomprehensible power, impossible for us to understand. But with the dilution of its energy, the variations of its power and the humanisation of deities, we can better understand the Divine godhead.

Modern scientific theories tell us that the universe is forever expanding, moving out from one single point of creation, so it makes sense that the subtle energies which we work with on a magical level should act in the same way. As we create images and intent on the astral plane, so they grow into form on the physical.

The triangle or pyramid has been used in many magical operations to both create and destroy, and the infamous Triangle of Art from the Lesser Key of Solomon is a perfect example. The Triangle of Art is a triangle that encloses a circle, and is surrounded by words of power and sacred God names. The triangle works by calling and containing certain spirits to do the magicians' bidding, and sigils and spells may be placed within the centre of the triangle to be manifested.

Another method which is more common among modern Craft is the Pyramid Spell. The Pyramid Spell is carried out by writing out a phrase in full, and then repeating the phrase above the original line but omitting one letter from the beginning and the end of the phrase. The pyramid can be built in either an upwards or downwards direction, depending on whether the aim of the spell is to gain or to banish, and can also be enclosed by God names in a similar way to the Triangle of Art.

PE
SPER
OSPERI
ROSPERIT
PROSPERITY

Although the methods of the Lesser Key of Solomon are largely Medieval, the belief in the power of the triangle or pyramid has existed for thousands of years.

The Egyptians buried their dead within the pyramid because they believed that the magical properties of the shape would aid them to journey into the afterlife, and allow their soul to be reborn. The four sides of the pyramid symbolise the extremes of each element; dark and light (west and east) and cold and heat (north and south). The triangular face of the pyramid symbolises the power of the trinity within both nature and divinity, and the total number of lines and sides of the pyramid correspond with the twelve signs of the zodiac.

Another triangle of power is the All-Seeing Eye, the image of the eye of God within a triangle or pyramid which has been used within Freemasonry and Rosicrucian traditions as a symbol of protection and power. Its origins can also be traced back to the Eye of Horus of Egyptian mythology.

Physicist and Alchemist Robert Fludd wrote several papers communicating the sacred geometry of the triangle. In his paper, *Utriusque Cosmi*, he included two diagrams illustrating his concept. The first diagram, *Divine and Mundane Triangles*, showed the world as a mirror image of deity. Just as deity was symbolically represented by an upper equilateral triangle, so a second triangle was reflected below which represented the world. In essence, Fludd was communicating that deity creates physical form by mirroring itself. And if we invert and lay these two triangles over one another we create a new shape: the 'Seal of Solomon', 'Hexagram', or 'Star of David'. In the centre of this new shape we also find a common ground where the two triangles cross – a union of spirit and matter, and a place of creation.

In his second diagram, *Interpretation of the material and formal pyramids*, Fludd again demonstrates the union of two triangles: one representing light and 'spirit' and the other representing dark and 'matter'. The 'matter' triangle reaches up, crossing with the 'spirit' triangle which is reaching down. In the middle, these two opposing principles counterbalance each other, and a point of creation is made.

Creation, the Triangle and the Building Blocks of Life

All of these accounts of the sacred shape of the triangle within mythology, architecture and alchemy are attributed to the power of the triangle to manifest and create. If at this point we begin to question the validity of this belief, we need only look to modern scientific concepts. The superstring theory, for instance, proposes that strings of energy vibrate out to form a sphere and then vibrate back in on themselves again, and form geometric patterns. Within the sphere, all line lengths and angles are the same as one another, and there are five possible triangular patterns which can be created.

One of these patterns is the Tetrahedron, which clearly depicts within its form the triangular elemental symbols of earth/north, air/east, fire/south and water/west: the building blocks of life.

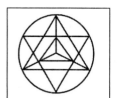

The Tetrahedron, depicting the four elemental symbols

Another pattern, the Octahedron, illustrates the foundations of our three-dimensional universe and also corresponds to the coordinates for our earth and the solar system. The Octahedron is also reflected in the measurements and angles of the Great Pyramid of Giza.

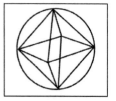

The Octahedron, depicting the foundations of our 3D universe

In the Craft, we learn that all things are sacred; our Gods, our beliefs and our magic are all able to be both symbolic and literal – one of the same, and all things can embody the Divine. Perhaps science can explain some of the mechanics behind magic - but it could never explain magic in its entirety. Magic is a part of nature; a living force which changes, transforms, and moves with the web of Wyrd. There are some secrets which science will never be able to truly explain, and magic is one of them.

TASK: The Pyramid of Manifestation
This meditation will enhance your visualisation skills and develop your understanding of the Gods and Goddesses and their various guises.

Close your eyes and take a few deep breaths. Focus on your breathing, in and out, in and out. With every breath in, feel yourself calm, and at peace. With every breath out, you feel the tension of the day drain away. Your heartbeat becomes slower, your body becomes heavier. Breathe in peace, breathe out tension. All the thoughts of the day and other distractions leave your mind as you focus on this one task, breathing in ... and out, in ... and out. Give this process as much time as you need, to allow yourself to become completely relaxed and focused. There is no rush. When you feel completely calm and relaxed, you can begin.

Imagine yourself in complete and utter nothingness. You float in space; it is pitch black, silent, and cold. Yet there is nothing to fear, because this is nothing. You are witnessing the universe before time began.

Now you look up, to see a tiny light appear above you. Like a star in the sky, it shines out of the dark, piercing through the gloom. And now it grows larger. It towers above you, a bright, radiant, shining light. This is the One Divine Source, the all omnipotent power. All seeing, all knowing. It has no form or gender. It is all, yet it is nothing. It is a single nucleus of divine energy.

Suddenly, the light splits into two - creating male and female, light and dark. They are the opposite polarities of one another, yet one of the same. They dance in perfect balance, like the Yin and Yang, and one cannot exist without the other. They are male and female in perfect union, a divine marriage.

Now, from these two polarities, burst forth three more – three forces of the feminine & three forces of the masculine. The feminine are the Maiden, the Mother and the Crone, the 'Three Fates', and the masculine are the Page, the Father and the Sage, Light God, Vegetation God and Dark God.

And now bursts forth four new forces; Earth, Air, Fire and Water. These elements hold the powers of Spring, Summer, Autumn and Winter, and give life to deities related to those seasons.

Now at the bottom of the pyramid bursts forth new rays of light, creating hundreds of different variations of Gods and Goddesses of all of different religions, archetypes, traditions, seasons and phases of life. Stay in this place observing this pyramid of manifestation for as long as you wish.

When you are ready, begin to feel yourself returning to this place and open your eyes. Have something to eat, and a glass of water to ground yourself afterwards.

'The Pyramid Meditation', from the Coven Book of Ways

Chapter Seven

Energy

Energy and Magic

The word 'energy' comes from the Greek 'ενέργεια' which means *'divine action'* or *'magical operation'* and the universal term for energy is *'the potential for causing change'* or *'the power to move things'*. Energy comes in many forms: electrical, gravitational, magnetic, kinetic, thermal and chemical, to name just a few. All matter is made of atoms: electrons circling around a nucleus of neutrons and protons, orbs of energy and force. Science has allowed us to master the creative power of energy and manipulate it to run our computers, our televisions, our heating and our hospital equipment, and using energy to our advantage has transformed our lives.

In nature, energy is the power behind the weather systems, the warmth of the sun, and the changes within the earth. Our entire world is constructed with, and maintained by, energy; it is the life force that creates, drives and nourishes all living matter. In European Craft it is symbolised by the spirit of the serpent, the spiral earth force which connects all things, and within ourselves, the serpent is the current of energy which makes a connection between the astral planes and the realms of the unconscious.

I cast the circle round about
Three times to seal it well
Three times to raise the power up
Three times to send the spell

I raise the powers of this place

145

I stir the serpent of this space...
Masters of the compass all
Guard this circle true
Send our magic forth we say
And to our power renew

I raise the powers of this place
I stir the serpent of this space...

Cerridwyn and Cernunnos
Green Goddess and Pan
We dedicate this place to you
And your ever changing plan...

'The Energy Chant', from the Coven Book of Ways

Einstein once said,

> *Up to the twentieth century, reality was everything humans could*
> *touch, smell, see and hear. Since the initial publication of the chart*
> *of the electromagnetic spectrum, humans have learnt that what they*
> *can touch, smell, see and hear is less than one millionth of reality.*

Einstein's equation, $E=mc^2$, showed that energy and matter can be transformed into the other, back and forth. The art of manipulating energy within a belief system or a magical operation is not 'new age' as it is often described by sceptics, but has been recognised as a valid and powerful practice for thousands of years. The eastern mystic cultures, such as Taoism and Zen, have historically recognised the innate power of energy and welcomed it into their belief systems. It is only relatively recently, as mankind has entered the era of 'rational thought' that the two have become divided – even though on further inspection, we see that the belief in spiritual energy and physics are not so different.

146

In most eastern philosophies, life force energy is recognised and called 'Tao', 'Chi' or 'Prana' ('absolute energy'), and practices such as Feng Shui, eastern Alchemy, Chi Jung, Astrology and the Martial Arts are all built around the belief system of raising, manipulating and working in harmony with nature's energy. Prana is in the atmospheric air, but it also has a distinct part to play in life in general, both physically and psychologically. It is from these eastern cultures that we borrow our practices of meditation, our understanding of the Chakras and the Aura, special breathing exercises and the importance of balancing energy within ourselves, in order to ensure a happy and healthy existence. Many eastern mystics developed spiritual concepts which were essentially scientific, but it was only their distrust in analytical methods and their commitment to traditional ways which prevented them from developing those concepts into scientific theories.

So we see that science is not so far from magic. But what makes the practicing witch, magician or eastern mystic different is the ability to transcend what is considered as 'reality' and summon, raise, and send these untapped currents of energy – forces that most people cannot normally detect. Leo Rutherford, founder of the Eagle Wing Centre for Contemporary Shamanism writes in his book *Principles of Shamanism,*

> *Normal waking consciousness is a 'trance' state which is governed by the culture that (we) are brought up in and live in. It is the way that we are taught to describe 'reality,' and the way that (we) have become accustomed to describing it and sharing with others. It is not the only reality.*

European Alchemy has also expressed a belief in life force energy, and the principle that all material processes are metaphors for spiritual processes. Established Alchemist Baron Carl Reichenbach called this vital energy the 'Odic Force', a spiritual power that permeates all living things. He also believed that the Odic force had a positive and negative flux, just like the flow of electricity, or the poles of a magnet.

The convictions of the Alchemist are given further credibility by modern scientific concepts such as Quantum Physics which has proven our universe to be able to perform the 'impossible' and contradict all laws of logic. It speculates that time and space can be distorted, and that many other dimensions exist. If the Superstring theory is correct, then at least 10 hidden dimensions should exist; at present, we only acknowledge 3. This is mirrored in the mythology of many ancient religions, including northern traditions which embrace the nine or more otherworldly dimensions within their belief systems.

Modern science also supports the microcosm and the macrocosm concept: a theory which describes the macrocosm (the universe as a whole) and the microcosm (the tiny parts that make up the universe) and confirms their inseparable bond. In turn, since time memorable, the magician and witch have created a miniature cosmos within their circle, surrounding themselves with the four elements of the universe, the planets and the zodiac, and have endeavoured to make changes on a small scale to make a change on the large scale.

Even in our day to day lives, we are encircled by energy: the forces of sacred sites or ley lines, the seasons, the elements and the heavenly bodies. We are surrounded by radio signals, power lines, heat produced by our homes. We feel the energy of other people's emotions, the anger of some and the love of others. We can imbue energy into amulets and talismans; we can use it to heal; we can use it to empower. Energy is universal, and like magic, it is impartial to consequence; therefore, it should be used with care.

The Chakras and the Astral Body
The chakras are vortex energy points of the body where the

physical, spiritual and psychological wellbeing is concentrated, and the central elements where energy is received, contained and transmitted. There are many energy points all over your body, but the seven main chakras are:

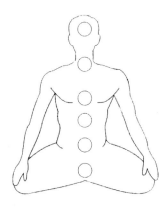

- Crown (just above the top of your head) – colour violet
- Third Eye (forehead) – colour indigo
- Throat – colour blue
- Heart (centre of the chest) – colour green
- Solar Plexus (centre of the abdomen) – colour yellow
- Sacral (Just below the belly button) – colour orange
- Base (the base of the spine) – colour red

Although the word 'chakra' is of eastern origin, the belief in vortexes of energy on the body is shared by many cultures - even as far west as northern Europe, where these vortexes were described as the 'sacred wells' within the body.

Each chakra is also associated with certain functions within your life, such as compassion, power, creativity, intellect, and spirituality. The Third Eye is of particular interest to the witch, as it is the place where psychic abilities and wisdom are collected. The Solar Plexus and the Crown are also of importance, as they are both associated with clairvoyance.

The chakra points also have an effect on the physical condition of your body, and if energy becomes blocked in one of these points then it can have an adverse effect on our health, spirituality and magical ability.

In addition to the seven main chakras, two other important

vortexes on the body for the witch are the energy points of the 'sun' or 'the future' in the right eye, and the 'moon' or 'the past' in the left eye. Remember here the associations between right and left and male and female, which we discussed earlier in the book.

In addition to the chakras, the whole person is surrounded by a field of energy called the aura, within which lies the 'Astral' or 'Etheric' body. The astral body is an energy blueprint of oneself, which lays the pattern to be followed by the physical body. Many occultists and mystics also believe that the astral body can leave the physical body and journey through the other planes; a method known as astral travel, or 'Lifting'.

TASK: A Chakra Cleansing

This Chakra Cleansing is used to open up each chakra and fill it with fresh energy, and is often used before or during healing. Research the seven major chakras of the body and their corresponding colours and functions, both physically and spiritually.

To prepare for the cleansing, either sit on the floor against a wall or in a high backed chair with your spine perfectly straight, and your legs uncrossed. This is to keep your your seven main chakras in line and uncramped. When you feel calm and grounded, light some candles and some incense and relax into the exercise.

Close your eyes and take three deep breaths. Now visualise a ball of bright violet light just above your head, the crown, spinning and sparkling. This is a ball of universal energy, the power of the universe itself. Visualise it spinning there. Feel the fresh, pure energy filling the top of your head, cleansing and invigorating that part of you.

Now, slowly it descends to your forehead. Visualise it spinning there – a deep indigo glow. Feel the fresh, pure energy cleansing and invigorating that part of you. Continue to visualise the previous chakra shining with bright light.

Now, slowly it descends to your throat. Visualise it spinning there as it begins to glow blue. Feel the fresh, pure energy filling your throat area, cleansing and invigorating that part of you. Continue to visualise the previous chakras shining.

Now, slowly it descends to your heart. Visualise it spinning there – a rich green glow. Feel the fresh, pure energy filling your heart area, cleansing and invigorating that part of you. Continue to visualise the previous chakras shining.

Now, slowly it descends to your solar plexus. Visualise it spinning there – a golden yellow glow. Feel the fresh, pure energy filling your chest area, cleansing and invigorating that part of you. Continue to visualise the previous chakras shining.

Now, slowly it descends to your sacral. Visualise it spinning there as it begins to glow orange. Feel the fresh, pure energy filling your lower abdomen area, cleansing and invigorating that part of you. Continue to visualise the previous chakras shining.

Now, slowly it descends down to your base chakra. Visualise it spinning there – a deep red glow. Feel the fresh, pure energy filling your base chakra area, cleansing and invigorating that part of you. Continue to visualise the previous chakras shining.

Now all the seven chakras are glowing with bright purifying light and your whole body shines. Visualise those balls of energy at each chakra point, spinning, filling your entire body, healing you, and purifying you.

Now slowly visualise this energy fading as the chakras begin to close slightly, and your body retains the energy you have gathered.

Visualise closing all the chakras, sealing the light away within your body except for your crown chakra (your connection to the universe and the divine) your heart chakra (your compassion) and your base chakra (your connection to the earth)
The other chakras should be closed, as leaving them open can allow negative energy enter your body and leave you vulnerable.
'Chakra Meditation', from the Coven Book of Ways

When you are ready feel the excess energy drop back into the earth and gradually come back into the room, feeling refreshed and revived. Stand up, stretch, and stamp your feet to ground yourself.

The Serpent Technique

The following method is designed to open up the energy centres in your body and allow creative energy to flow from the very top of your head to the soles of your feet. In order to perform magic, we must be efficient vessels to channel and direct creative energy, and the Serpent Technique allows us to awake the primal powers within.

If you would like to use the powers of herbs to help you with this, you could gather mugwort, yarrow, acacia and honeysuckle and keep those near to you whilst performing the Serpent Technique, perhaps in a fabric bag around your neck. All these herbs are known for their ability to open the chakras, the psychic senses and third eye.

Close your eyes and take a few deep breaths. Focus on your breathing – in, and out, in an out. With every breath in, feel yourself calm and at peace. With every breath out, feel the tension of the day drain away. Your heartbeat becomes slower, your body becomes heavier. Breathe in peace, breathe out tension. All thoughts of the day and other distractions leave your mind as you become completely relaxed and focused. There is no rush. When you feel completely calm and relaxed, you can begin.

With every breath in, visualise energy being drawn up from the ground, from the base of your spine, to your abdomen, up through your chest, to your heart and to the crown of your head. As you exhale, release any tension within you. Still keeping your eyelids closed, allow your eyes to look up towards your forehead, and focus on your third eye, the place where witch wisdom is collected. Repeat the exercise until you feel you are able to draw the energy up with ease. This technique can make you feel tingly and a little dizzy, so be careful; however it is extremely powerful.

Now feel it travel up and down your spine as it creates a circuit of energy around your body. Feel your whole body filling with energy; keep it flowing, from chakra to chakra, up and down the spine, cleaning, healing and empowering. Visualise the serpent energy of the earth as it flows around your body and your ritual space.

Each part of your body that the energy moves to becomes refreshed, revived, and re-energised. This energy is part of the power behind magic. It is this energy that we can move and manipulate in order to create. Feel it moving around your body, tingling, energising and empowering you.

When you are ready, feel the excess energy drop back into the earth, and gradually come back into the room, feeling refreshed and revived. Stand up, stretch, and stamp your feet to ground yourself.

'The Serpent Energy Technique', from the Coven Book of Ways

Chapter Eight

Ritual Components

What is Ritual?

Humans are ritualistic animals by nature. Since the dawn of time mankind has been creating habits and ritual both within their mundane lives and their spiritual. The *Oxford Dictionary* describes ritual as,

> 1. *a religious or solemn ceremony involving a series of actions performed according to a set order. 2. a set order of performing such a ceremony. 3. a series of actions habitually and invariably followed by someone.*

Have a quick look at your life. Maybe you always get out of bed from the same side or maybe journey to work by the same route every day. Maybe Monday is always your evening in, but you can always be found in the pub on a Thursday. Maybe you always use the same coffee cup. Maybe you always brush your hair before brushing your teeth in the morning, or maybe you brush your teeth and only then will you brush your hair. These are all forms of mundane ritual.

Ritual sometimes grows from convenience; we might travel a certain way to work everyday because it is the quickest route, or there is less traffic. However, some things are grown purely from habit, things that either consciously or sub-consciously we choose to do for no particular reason, except that we feel comfortable with them. But what about religious ritual?

Forms of ritual can be found in all religions and cultures. Within a religious ceremony, ritual acts as a trigger to let our subconscious know that something special is about to happen; it is a mental reminder of where we are, what we are about to do, and why. It also gives the celebrants a framework around which they can design and perform the rest of the ceremony.

The word 'ritual' encompasses the entire experience of a rite, from the place and time, to the layout of the altar, to the order of the rite, and even to the libation afterwards. When specific sacred acts are repeated, it imprints those actions within our minds and many sacred acts contain deeper mysteries than they first appear to, such as the Symbolic Great Rite. For those witnessing the rites, the repetitive nature of these actions start to allow a greater understanding of the mysteries behind them.

Ritual Framework

In eclectic witchcraft, we believe that we should not be limited to any particular form of ceremony. It is this appreciation and incorporation of all available ceremonial methods and ritual that makes eclectic Initiatory Witchcraft and Paganism so diverse and interesting. However, we do use a set of pre-determined ritual methods, giving us a framework around which we can build the rest of the rite. The ritual framework given here is based on the works of Gerald Gardner, as printed in *Eight Sabbats for Witches* by the Farrars. However other ritual acts are often incorporated within the framework, such as *The Eye of Horus* litany, which my coven likes to perform at the beginning of every ceremony.

- The Sweeping of the circle
- The Blessing and Consecration of the elements
- The use of these elements to Cleanse, Consecrate, Purify and Warm the circle
- The Casting of the Circle
- Calling the Quarters of the Compass
- Evocation/Invocation of Deities
- The Charge is read
- Energy and magic is risen

- The reason for the ritual, or the magical workings, performed
- Energy grounded
- Libation
- Quarters and other energies farewelled
- Circle closed

In the following short descriptions I have referred to a traditional ritual framework, in which at least three or four participants are involved including the High Priestess, the High Priest and the Maiden (assistant to the High Priestess). However, for the Solitary witch all of these actions can easily be performed on your own, with very little adaptation. I have presented the ritual outline and wording for each component, for your use within the rituals and magic throughout this book.

The Sweeping of the Circle

Horse and Hattock! Horse and Go!
Horse and Pellatis, Ho Ho!
Isobel Gowdie, tried as a witch in 1662

The sweeping of the circle is usually the first sign that a ritual is about to start. It also symbolises the first act of purification, as negative energy is swept out of the sacred space. The sweeping is usually performed by the Maiden using the Besom (the witches broom) whilst the rest of the coven wait outside the temple or sacred space. The traditional Besom is made out of three woods; the handle is made of ashwood (representing the phallus, and the Yggdrasill or 'Steed of Woden') the brush is made of Birch (purification and rebirth) and the branch that binds the handle to the brush is made of Willow, which represents water and the moon. Sweeping with the ashwood besom has an additional use however; Ash makes the first exchange between this world and the other realities, and designates the space which will become a 'place out of time'.

Sweep thrice deosil (clockwise) round the circle, visualise brushing any negative energy up and then sweep it out of the door or circle, preferably at the north-east. The Besom can then be left either beside or across the threshold of door, or if it is to be used somewhere within the ritual brought back inside the sacred space.

Besoms have other uses in the Craft besides just sweeping; they are often used as symbols of protection and placed above the door frame, built into walls or hung in the rafters for good luck. They are also used in astral travel or 'Lifting' rites whereby they are known as the 'Riding Pole' or 'Flying Steed'. The Egyptians also used brooms to sweep the sacred space. Folklore says however that the broom should not be used for sweeping during the month of May, for it will bring bad luck.

The Blessing and Consecration of the Elements

We have already discussed the properties of the four elements in previous chapters; now we will begin to use them within ritual. Our coven uses a slightly different blessing and consecration method than those you may have seen elsewhere. We designed it to suit our own coven, but it does, however, follow the same basic structure as the traditional methods. For this process you should have upon your altar:

- A dish of Salt (representing the element of Earth)
- A dish of Water (representing the element of Water)
- A candle (representing the element of Fire)
- A censor or stick of incense (representing Air)

These elements are blessed and consecrated as follows and then the elements are taken around the circle to cleanse and purify the sacred space, and the members of the coven themselves.

Holding your palms above the dish of salt (representing earth) say:

> *May blessings be upon this creature of salt. May all malignity and hindrance be cast out herefrom, so that only good may enter herein. Therefore do I bless thee and consecrate thee, in the names of* [chosen Goddess] *and* [chosen God]. *As I do will, so mote it be.*

Now hold your palms above the dish of water and say:

> *May blessings be upon this creature of water. May all malignity and hindrance be cast out herefrom, so that only good may enter herein. Therefore do I bless thee, that thou mayest aid me, in the names of* [chosen Goddess] *and* [chosen God]. *As I do will, so mote it be.*

Now add three pinches of salt to the water:

> *To this Water, I give blessings of earth.*
> (First pinch): *One for the mind....*
> (Next pinch): *One for the body...*
> (Next pinch): *And one for the spirit. So mote it be.*

By mixing water and salt you are mingling the magical energies represented by water with the physical world represented by the salt (earth).

See the water shining with a bright light. Stir the water three times and walk deosil (clockwise) around your magical space and back round to the altar sprinkling the water upon the ground as you go, saying:

> *I cleanse this circle with water, I consecrate this circle by salt.*

Now hold your palms above the candle flame and say:

May blessings be upon this creature of fire. May all malignity and hindrance be cast out herefrom, so that only good may enter herein. Therefore do I bless thee, that thou mayest aid me, in the names of [chosen Goddess] *and* [chosen God]. *As I do will, so mote it be.*

Now hold your palms above the curling incense and say:

May blessings be upon this creature of air. May all malignity and hindrance be cast out herefrom, so that only good may enter herein. Therefore do I bless thee, that thou mayest aid me, in the names of [chosen Goddess] *and* [chosen God]. *As do will, so mote it be.*

By mixing the smoke with the fire, you are representing the ever present relationship between fire and air. Now pass the incense through the flame three times, saying:

To this incense, I give blessings of fire.
(First pass): *One for the mind….*
(Next pass): *One for the body…*
(Next pass): *And one for the Spirit. So mote it be.*

See the incense as it shines with a bright light. Walk deosil with the incense and candle around your magical space and back round to the altar, saying:

I warm this circle with fire, I purify this circle by air.

Casting the Circle

This is the advanced circle casting, which can be used once you have thoroughly studied and practiced the work in the previous chapters of this book. If you would like to cast a circle but have not yet completed the previous chapters, follow the Psychic Circle Casting at the end of Chapter Four instead.

If it is possible, the circle should be marked with chalk, and measure 9ft in diameter. Gerald Garner outlines the following method for scribing the circle in the *Gardnerian Book of Shadows, 1949:*

> *Having chosen a place proper, take the sickle or scimitar of Art or a witch's athame, if thou mayest obtain it, and stick it into the centre, then take a cord, and 'twere well to use the Cable Tow for this, and loop it over the Instrument, four and one half feet, and so trace out the circumference of the circle.*
>
> Sourced from the works of Aidan A Kelley

However, depending on how many people will be working within the circle or the limited space available, it may be necessary to change the size. If working outdoors, the circle can be marked at the four quarters of the compass with tea-lights, contained in safe candle jars or lanterns.

The circle is cast deosil (clockwise) around the sacred space, starting at north (the altar) and returning to north. As you become more experienced, you will be able to say the words and perform the casting at the same time, but for now it is acceptable to perform the casting first and then read the words out loud afterwards once you have returned to the altar. The most important thing in the circle casting is your intent.

The circle is traditionally cast with the athame, sword or wand, but can also be cast by the hand. Raise your hand up high toward the north and begin drawing a circle in the air. Visualise a bright white or electric blue light coming from the tip of your athame, creating the circle as you draw it round clockwise. Try to maintain the visualisation of the energy that is being created as you complete the circle, saying:

> *I conjure thee, O' circle of power, that thou be a meeting place of love, joy and truth. A shield against all wickedness and evil. A boundary between the worlds of men, and the realms of the Mighty*

Ones. A rampart and a protection that shall preserve and contain the power that (I/we) shall raise within thee. Wherefore do I bless thee and raise thee. As above, So Below. As Without, So Within, As I do will; So mote it be! * Adapted from 'Eight Sabbats for Witches', by Janet and Stewart Farrar

* A note on circle casting alternatives

There are other versions of the circle casting which you can use if you prefer. The most important thing in my opinion is that you choose a circle casting that you like and stick with it. Eventually, the words will flow off your tongue without effort, and you will be able to focus all your attention on the casting itself.

The 'Three Times Pass' should then be performed by circling the space three times:

First Pass: *This circle is cleansed;*
Second Pass: *This circle is consecrated;*
Third Pass: *And this circle is sealed, and ready for magical workings. As my mind wills; so mote it be!*

You may tap the altar or floor three times at the end, to indicate that the circle is sealed.

You can also add a verse such as one of these to the Three Times Pass to seal the circle, such as the following rhyme published by Sorita D'Este and David Rankine in their book, *Circle of Fire*:

By fertile Earth and whirling Air
By rushing Fire and Water fair
By Spirit joined and all held fast
This sacred circle now is cast!'

A note on cutting doorways in the circle

Although we try to avoid it, sometimes it is necessary to leave the circle mid-ritual while the circle is still cast. This could be because we have forgotten something we need, or someone needs the toilet, or because the smoke alarm goes off from using too much incense! Cutting a doorway is a quick and simple way of leaving the circle without having to close it down, and also allows us to return and finish the ritual afterwards. The doorway is cut with the athame at northeast (this is just to the right of the altar).

I usually start on the bottom left hand side of the 'door' and draw up the athame from the floor, across the top and then back down to the bottom right hand corner. You should visualise blue light coming out of the athame like a blowtorch, cutting through the boundaries of the circle. When you are done, step through the circle and close it up again from the outside. When you seal the doorway, visualise the same blue light sealing the gap in the circle. Do the same method in reverse to re-enter the circle.

Calling the Quarters of the Compass

The quarters or directions are called directly after the circle has been cast. As we discussed in 'Ritual Components', calling the quarters allows us to evoke all of the associated energies of those compass directions. It may be an idea to read Chapter Four on each element again and re-familiarise yourself with the colours and the associations of each quarter before you start. The actual process and wording for calling the quarters is common knowledge nowadays and can be found in most books which discuss witchcraft; however I have given them here once, as reference.

You should start at the east, and work your way deosil back round to the north. The evoking pentagrams should be drawn at each quarter as you go:

These pentagrams should be drawn as one continuous line, starting at the point indicated above and finishing at the same point.

East

Stand facing the east. Try to visualise the attributes of air: the spring breeze, a bird on the wing, new beginnings, and fresh and purifying energy. Visualise the colour of east – yellow. Then say:

Lords of the East, Element of Air
Winds of Inspiration and Intelligence
I invite you to join me in this rite tonight
To guard and guide the circle.
I bid you, Hail, and Welcome!

Draw the evoking pentagram of east. >> IMAGE 23 HERE<<

South

Stand facing the south. Try to visualise the attributes of fire: the summers' heat, the rutting stag, and passion and fertility. Visualise the colour of south – red. Then say:

Lords of the South, Element of Fire
Flames of Passion and Creativity
I invite you to join me in this rite tonight
To guard and guide the circle.
I bid you, Hail, and Welcome!

Draw the evoking pentagram of south.

West

Stand facing the west. Try to visualise the attributes of water: the autumn rain, the creatures of the sea, and the mysteries of death and rebirth. Visualise the colour of west – blue. Then say:

> *Lords of the West, Element of Water*
> *Waves of emotional balance and healing*
> *I invite you to join me in this rite tonight*
> *To guard and guide the circle.*
> *I bid you, Hail, and Welcome!*

Draw the evoking pentagram of west.

North

Stand facing the north. Try to visualise the attributes of earth: the winters chill, dark fertile forests, and growth and protection. Visualise the colour of north – green or black. Then say:

> *Lords of the North, Element of Earth*
> *Stones of Stability and Grounding*
> *I invite you to join me in this rite tonight*
> *To guard and guide the circle.*
> *I bid you, Hail, and Welcome!*

Draw the evoking pentagram of north.

Spirit

Come into the centre of the circle, and say:

> *'Spirit, all encompassing element that binds the other elements into one, that connects us with the powers of unity, the God and Goddess and the web of Wyrd, join me this night. I bid you, Hail!'*

Evocation or Invocation of Deities

A full *Invocation* of deities or other spirits is usually practiced in an established Coven and under the training of an experienced High Priest and High Priestess. However, *Evocation* can be performed within a circle by almost anyone. I recommend that you start Evocations with generic deities, such as the Lunar Goddess and the Solar God, as evocation of more complex deities can often be overwhelming for the beginner. The God and Goddess are usually evoked at the north towards the altar, and it is customary to call the Goddess first and then the God. As well as being a process for communicating with the Gods, Evocation and Invocation are also listed as one of the eight ways of raising power. *For more information on the methods of Evocation and Invocation see Chapter 13.*

The Charge is Read

The most popular Charge of the Goddess that is used today was written by Doreen Valiente with the help of Gerald Gardner in the 1950's, and came from a collection of sources. The most prominent source is 'The Charge of Aradia' translated by Charles Leyland and published in his book, *Aradia: Gospel of the Witches*, a work based on his research of Italian witchcraft. There are also several references within the modern charge that can be attributed to the infamous author and occultist, Aleister Crowley who wrote the first version. A similar verse now known as *The Charge of Isis* can also be read in the eleventh chapter of *The Golden Ass* written by Greco-Roman author Apuleius. Any of these Charges can be used within ritual, and whilst the modern 'Charge of the Goddess' can be found in many books on Wicca today, some of the more ancient Charges can be equally as powerful.

The Charge of the Goddess is usually performed just after the Evocation or Invocation of the Goddess. In *Invocations*, the Charge is often recited by the High Priestess, who represents and speaks for the Goddess herself. In *Evocations*, the Charge acts as an offering to the Goddess just after the Evocations have been performed. Although it is not as common, the Charge of the God can also be read once the Evocation or Invocation of the God has been completed, in order to maintain a balance of the sexes within the circle. Again, in the case of *Invocation*, the Change is recited by the High Priest who at that point represents, and speaks for, the God.

The Charge of Aradia: translated by Charles Leland in 'Aradia: Gospel of the Witches'

> *Whenever ye have need of anything,*
> *Once in the month, and when the moon is full,*
> *Ye shall assemble in some desert place,*
> *Or in a forest all together join*
> *To adore the potent spirit of your queen,*
> *My mother, great Diana. She who fain*
> *Would learn all sorcery yet has not won*
> *Its deepest secrets, then my mother will*
> *Teach her, in truth all things as yet unknown.*
> *And ye shall all be freed from slavery,*
> *And so ye shall be free in everything;*
> *And as the sign that ye are truly free,*
> *Ye shall be naked in your rites, both men*
> *And women also; this shall last until*
> *The last of your oppressors be dead*
> *And ye shall make the game of Benevento*
> *Extinguishing the lights and after that*
> *Shall hold your supper thus...*

The Charge of Isis: Apuleius, 'The Golden Ass'

> *'Behold; I am come, thy weeping and prayers hath moved me to succor thee. I am She that is the natural mother of all things,*

mistress and governess of all the Elements, the initial progeny of worlds, chief of powers divine, Queene of heaven, the principal of the Gods celestial, the light of the goddesses: at my will the planets of the air, the wholesome winds of the Seas, and the silences of hell be disposed. My name and my Divinity is adored throughout all the world in diverse manners, in variable customs and in many names, for the Phrygians call me the Mother of the Gods: the Athenians, Minerva: the Cyprians, Venus: the Candians, Diana: the Sicilians Proserpina: the Eleusians, Ceres: some Juno, other Bellona, other Hecate: and principally those who dwell in the Orient and the Egyptians, who are excellent in all kinds of ancient doctrine, and by their proper ceremonies accustome to worship me, and do call me Queene Isis'.

The Charge of the Mother

Our Mother is the earth that brings forth birth. She feeds us and gives us water and takes us back when our time comes. The circle She is, with the spear that joins the universe, the never ending cycle, that goes round from Imbolc to Eostara to Beltane, to Summer Solstice to Lughnassadh to Mabon to Samhaine, to Yule, and round again; death and rebirth. The Sun, the great God, gives light and fertility to her. We are her children and we must care for her as she does for us; if we treat her wrongly she gives us punishments by her elements, who are her family. So remember, she is in all that you see around you, and in yourself. Now my message has been given; so keep the knowledge of our Mother of all.
Written by Ron 'SilverEagleSpirit'

Energy and Magic is risen

There are many ways to raise energy. Raising power in one or more of these forms has been used by many different traditions from all around the world, including the Shamans, Greeks, Egyptians, Buddhists and Voodoo practitioners. Ancient Hindu tradition also speaks of the 'Eight Siddhis' the psychic and magical powers obtained through meditation and concentration.

The practices of modern initiatory witches are reminiscent of these ancient cultures. Within Initiatory Craft, some forms of raising energy must be performed within a magical circle for safety and effectiveness; however, others are suitable for using within your generic sacred space. The eight accepted ways of raising power are:

- Meditation/Concentration
- Trance/Astral Projection/Pathworking
- Herbal knowledge/Incense
- Evocation/Invocation
- Dance/Music/Movement
- Chanting
- Scourge/Body and Blood Control
- The Great Rite (symbolic or actual)

Meditation and Concentration

Meditation and concentration allows us to discover the mysteries by quieting our mind and focusing our thoughts. Through mediation, we can raise subtle energy within ourselves and then, through concentration, we can focus this energy and our intent by way of Spellwork. *For more information on Spellwork see Chapter 16.*

Trace/Astral Projection/Pathworking

Trance describes the method of altering our consciousness and is often induced by employing a repetitive rhythm, such as a continuous drumbeat or another persistent sound. Through trance, we can access the otherworlds and embark on spiritual journeys through Astral Projection or 'Lifting'. Shamanic tribes in particular employ the use of 'Spirit Masks' to change their state of consciousness; masks work well to change how others see you, as well as how you feel within yourself.

Herbal Knowledge/Incense
This form of raising power traditionally incorporated the 'use of drugs and alcohol' in the *Book of Shadows*. However, we do not feel that this is a safe way to raise energy, and we choose to limit our use of this practice to legal herbs and incense, which can have similar effects when used correctly. We do not permit our coven to partake in the use of non-prescribed drugs within ritual, although in some cultures the use of drugs is a common part of their ritual, magic and initiation ceremonies.

Knowledge of standard, non-toxic herbs allows us to evoke the individual energies of the plants by using them safely within ritual and magic. Incense is a very common aid; the scent of the incense changes our consciousness and acts as a trigger to our minds that something special is about to happen. If incense is made out of pure herbal and resin ingredients, we also evoke the energy of the ingredients when we burn it. *For more information on herbal knowledge see Chapter 11.*

Evocation and Invocation
Although Evocation and Invocation are accepted parts of the circle casting framework itself (as above), they are also one of the eight ways of raising power. Therefore Evocation or Invocations can also be carried out further into a ritual in order to raise more energy within the circle. *For more information on the methods of Evocation and Invocation see Chapter 13.*

Dance, Music and Movement
Dance works directly with our physical bodies. Just as exercise enriches our blood and strengthens our tissue, so it empowers the etheric energy that resonates within us. As you may have started to realise, witchcraft is a very holistic belief system; we believe that both mind and body are important factors within

spirituality. With movements, stretches, postures and exercise we empower our bodies and therefore empower our spiritual selves and evoke the powers of the earth energy around us. In the same way that any piece of music has the power to fill us with joy or fill us with sorrow, so too can music empower us and add certain energies to our ritual. Gerald Gardner gives the following 'Meeting Dance' from the *Gardnerian Book of Shadows 1953*; this particular excerpt is sourced from *The Witches Way* by Janet and Stewart Farrar:

The Maiden should lead. A man should place both hands on her waist, standing behind her, and alternate men and women should do the same, the Maiden leading and they dance following her. She at last leads them into a right-hand spiral. When the centre is reached (and this had better be marked by a stone), she suddenly turns and dances back, kissing each man as she comes to. All men and women turn likewise and dance back, men kissing girls and girls kissing men. All in time to music, it is a merry game, but must be practised to be done well. Note, the musicians should watch the dancers and make the music fast or slow as is best. For the beginners it should be slow, or there will be confusion. It is most excellent to get people to know each other at big gatherings.

We have already covered the use of drums to induce a trance state previously in this chapter. Perhaps we could listen to very upbeat music to fill us with bright, cheery energy, or instead listen to something more solemn and meaningful to evoke a more profound energy. Remember that it doesn't matter what music we use – the important thing is what that piece of music means to us.

Circular movement is often used within the circle, to raise energy and make contact with the earth and the underworld. It also a fantastic way for us to enter an altered state of consciousness and connect with our higher selves. In European Craft, the art of walking the circle to alter the consciousness is called 'Treading the Mill'.

Chanting

Chanting is a very old, and a very effective, way of raising power. Chanting is the method of rhythmically repeating any phrase or word over and over, usually (although not always) getting faster and faster until the person leading the chant indicates that the energy has been gathered and can be released in a crescendo.

There are many complicated chants; however, it is important to remember that often the simplest of chants are the most effective – for example, repeating just a single word – and although there are chants that can be found that are specifically written to evoke certain types of energy, chants can also be made up on the spot.

The aim to the chant is to focus on that one goal, the thing that you are chanting to achieve; all other things are pushed to the back of your mind whilst you focus on that one, single thing. God and Goddess names made very effective chants, and often other magical methods are used alongside chanting, such as movement or dance.

One of the most popular chants to raise power in a circle which incorporates movement is *The Witch's Chant*, originally written by Gardner in 1957. He later rewrote the chant into a new rhyme with the help of Doreen Valiente, and they renamed it *'The Witch's Rune'*. The *Witch's Chant*, or *Rune*, is usually combined with a deosil movement around the circle, which becomes faster and faster until the chant comes to a climax.

The method is usually performed with two or more people, who all join their right hands in the middle of the circle and race clockwise around the centre of the space. However, it can be done by a solitary witch by circling the cauldron or chalice (with care). In this method, you should extend your right hand over the cauldron in the centre of your circle, again moving clockwise.

There are different versions of *The Witches Chant* which have been adapted by various authors, but this is the one that we use in our coven which is sourced from *Eight Sabbats for Witches* by Janet and Stewart Farrar:

> *Darksome night and shining moon*
> *East, then South, then West, then North;*
> *Hearken to the Witches' Rune -*
> *Here we come to call ye forth!*
> *Earth, Air, Fire, Water,*
> *Wand, Pentacle and Sword,*
> *Work ye unto our desire,*
> *And hearken to our word!*
> *Cords and censer scourge and knife,*
> *Powers of the witch's blade -*
> *Waken all ye into life,*
> *Come ye as the charm is made!*
> *Queen of heaven, Queen of hell ***
> *Horned hunter of the night*
> *Lend your power unto this spell*
> *And work our will by magic rite!*
> *By all the powers of land and sea*
> *By all the might of moon and sun*
> *As we will so mote it be*
> *Chant the spell and be it done!*
> *Eko Eko Azarak **
> *Eko Eko Zamilak **
> *Eko Eko Cernunnos ***
> *Eko Eko Aradia!' ***

This last part of the chant should be repeated, faster and faster until you decide that enough energy has been risen. At this point, within a Coven setting, the High Priestess monitors the energy and when she feels the time is right will shout *'DOWN!'* at which point everyone drops to the ground to bring the energy into the circle. When done properly, *The Witch's Rune* can be very effective. Care should be taken though, as it can make you feel very dizzy or light-headed. Starting off slowly is recommended.

* A note on Eko Eko Azarak Eko Eko Zamilak

Some say that the chant 'Eko Eko Azarak, Eko Eko Zamilak Eko Eko Cernunnos Eko Eko Aradia' translates to 'Hail Hail force of fire, Hail Hail to the glory, Hail Hail Cernunnos Hail Hail Aradia'.

** A note on Heaven and Hell and the Gods and Goddess of the Rune

'Queen of Heaven' and 'Queen of Hell' can appear to be a somewhat derogative and Christianised in such a Pagan chant. However, the Pagan view of Heaven and Hell are very different to the Christian. The word Hell or Hel comes from an old Goddess name which means Hill, Hollow or Barrow, associating it with the underworld, death and rebirth. Researching the Pagan origins of Heaven and Hell may be rewarding if you feel uncomfortable with these words. Aradia and Cernunnos are most commonly used within *The Witch's Rune*; however, the names can be replaced with whichever God and Goddess you happen to be using in the ritual that night.

Scourge and Body/Blood Control

This method should only be attempted within a magical circle. In today's society, the scourge (or flail) has acquired an unfortunate reputation as a symbol of sex, domination and corruption. Its partnership with modern Craft can sometimes appear confusing, and many critics have claimed that it is an unnecessary tool introduced by Gerald Gardner, along with the rule of working scyclad, to 'spice up' his rituals. Consequently, opinions are divided within the Craft community regarding the use of the scourge. However, when used correctly, scourging does allow the consciousness to be altered and energy to be risen, by causing changes within the body.

Some of the oldest evidence of the scourge is depicted in the artwork of the ancient Egyptians. In Egypt and other mystery religions, the scourge was a sign of fertility rather than as a scourging tool, because it was used in agriculture for thrashing wheat in order to separate the corn from the chaff. Consequently, the scourge was often depicted in the hands of fertility Gods such as Osiris as well as the hands of Kings, to demonstrate their power and wealth during their reign.

The scourge or flail was also associated with the power of the Gods. During the 'Mysteries of Bacchus' (God of Wine) in ancient Greece, the scourge was used together with the partaking of alcohol to change the consciousness and encourage trance-like chants and dance. The use of the scourge was used to represent the dedication of the temple initiate, and this continues symbolically in modern Craft initiations today to test the commitment of the person and confirm their willingness to 'suffer to learn'.

As time passed, the meaning behind the scourge as a symbol of power and fertility began to change and it started to become more associated with sexual virility, depicted with such deities as the Egyptian Phallic God, Min. It is important to remember that the fertility of the fields and the fertility of the people was seen as synonymous; an important balance between nature and mankind.

The agricultural flail did not look the same as the scourge we know today. Rather than a handle with rope or leather thongs, the farming flail was made of a wooden club chained to a handle which swung freely to thrash the corn. Later in history people began to recognise that this was also a very effective and very deadly weapon.

So, the combination of fertility, power, abundance and eventually punishment led to the scourge becoming associated with dominance, but it was only with the coming of Christianity, that it became known for its role in chastisement as part of religious discipline, within the practice of 'flagellation', or scourging as part of self-dicipline.

In Initiatory Craft, the scourge represents the authority of the Priestess and the Goddess, together with the willingness of the trainees and initiates to learn. It is used symbolically only, and is never used to inflict harm.

The Great Rite/Sex Magic

This method should only be attempted within a magical circle. The Great Rite is a form of raising power which makes use of the energy produced by sexual union. Again, this form of raising energy should only be performed in a situation of perfect trust between a loving couple who are also magical working partners, and in private, or in exceptional circumstances with the rest of the covens backs turned.

However a symbolic Great Rite can be performed instead, usually by conjoining the athame representing the phallus, and the chalice representing the womb. Another way of staging the symbolic Great Rite is for the High Priest and the High Priestess to face one another and join foot to foot, knee to knee, hip to hip, chest to chest, palms to palms and lips to lips.

Reasons for the Ritual are performed ('workings'):

Once we have raised energy, how might we send it to do our bidding? At this point in the ritual, the circle is fully prepared and we are ready to begin any magical 'workings' that have been planned for the evening. One of the many forms of sending energy is spellwork – releasing the energy raised in the ritual by certain magical methods, such as burning a candle, or creating a sigil or talisman. In the event of psychic protection, energy is often sent via mirrors and other reflective surfaces. Energy can also be released by a shout at the end of chanting, or a gesture with the athame, wand or hand.

Energy Grounded

When we are raising energy in any form, we must also know how to ground it. This allows us to raise the energy that we require and once we are finished, 'earth' the residual energy that we do not need. Grounding energy is also recommended after any ritual or meditation to bring you 'back down to earth'. We ground energy for two reasons; the first being that if residual energy is left within your body it can leave you dizzy, confused and unable to competently perform tasks, such as driving. The second is that natural energy, just like energy in the form of electricity, must be directed somewhere or it can become dangerous. Residual energy can cause problems such as negativity and so-called 'poltergeist' activity and other unwanted side effects.

In order to ground energy, you can put two simple methods into practice. First, as you end your meditation or ritual visualise the residual energy draining down through the bottom of your feet and out of the sacred space through the ground. If it helps, crouch down and place your palms to the floor to increase your contact with the earth. Occult writers Sorita d'Este and David Rankine also suggest stamping your feet to shake off residual energy and encourage the mind to get back in touch with the physical world.

Grounding energy should not cause any loss of energy in your body or from any spellwork you have performed. If you have done the ritual properly then you will have contained the energy that you require within the working, and all that will be left is what is no longer needed. See that energy leaving your physical body and your sacred space and being absorbed into the ground, where it will be recycled by the earth. The second method is to have something to eat and drink once you have closed the circle.

This will ground your body, and bring you back into a normal state of consciousness. The Libation (see below) does not count as food for grounding, as the act of Libation is part of the ritual itself.

Libation/Sacrament

The Libation, or Sacrament, is the act of partaking of food and drink after the main part of the ritual has been completed and the circle is about to be closed. The food and drink is usually blessed by the High Priest and the High Priestess, representing Divine Union and the Sacred Marriage of the male and the female.

The libation is first taken by the High Priestess, then the High Priest, and then passed clockwise around the circle for everyone else. When outdoors, it is customary for some of the libation to be spilt on the ground as an offering to the Gods and the Old Ones, but when indoors the High Priestess and the High Priest may eat the portion of the libation offered to the Gods, as they represent the God and Goddess within the circle.

The event of Libation within the ritual is normally when the mood becomes lighter and everyone starts having some fun. Drums may be played and stories told. The energy usually becomes more playful – whether you intend it to or not!

In coven ritual, the libation rite is performed by both the High Priest and High Priestess. For your rituals, I have simplified the rite into a method suitable for the solitary witch, but the structure is very similar to the original:

The Wine

Take the chalice of wine or juice and place it in the centre of the altar. The chalice represents the Goddess, the feminine force of nature. Take the athame or wand and bring its point down into the chalice. The athame or wand represents the God, the masculine force of nature. Say:

As the athame is to the male, so the cup is to the female. And together, they bring blessedness. So mote it be!
'Gardnerian Book of Shadows' 1957
Sourced from the works of Aidan A Kelley

You can now drink the wine.

The Cakes

Place the dish of cakes in the centre of the altar, and cast your athame over them in the shape of the earth pentagram, saying:

O Queen most secret, bless this food unto my body, bestowing health, wealth , strength, joy and peace, and that fulfilment of love that is perfect happiness.
'Gardnerian Book of Shadows' 1957
Sourced from 'Eight Sabbats for Witches', by J&S Farrar

You can then eat the cakes. We like to think that any food that is eaten within the magic circle has no calories!

Quarters of the Compass and other Energies Farewelled

We must now farewell the quarters and their associated corre-spondences. In our coven, the quarters are normally farewelled in the same direction in which they were called (clockwise – east, south, west, north, spirit) but with closing pentagrams used instead of invoking. You may notice that this is different from the practices of most covens, who usually farewell the quarters in the opposite direction to which they were called (anti–clockwise - north, west, south, east). Our coven differs because we carry out our rituals within a permanent ritual area, and we do not wish to completely *banish* the sacred space but simply to *close* it. This is not a new practice - the Egyptians always moved clockwise (sunwise) around their permanent temple spaces; they considered that to move against the course of the sun would be disorderly and against the natural laws of the universe.

For simplicities sake, I have given our coven's version here; however if a ritual is being performed in a public area or somewhere which will be a 'one-off ' working space, then the quarters should be farewelled in an anti-clockwise manner to completely dissipate all ritual and magical energy.

The closing pentagrams should be drawn at each quarter as you go:

These pentagrams should be drawn as one continuous line, starting at the point indicated above and finishing at the same point.

East
Stand facing the east. Try to visualise the attributes of air: the spring breeze, a bird on the wing, new beginnings, and fresh and purifying energy. Visualise the colour of east – yellow. Then say:

> *Lords of the East, Element of Air*
> *Winds of Inspiration and Intelligence*
> *I thank you for attending this, my rite tonight*
> *And I bid you, Hail, and Farewell!*

Draw the closing pentagram of east.

South
Stand facing the south. Try to visualise the attributes of fire: the summers' heat, the rutting stag, and passion and fertility.

Visualise the colour of south – red. Then say:

> *Lords of the South, Element of Fire*
> *Flames of Passion and Creativity*
> *I thank you for attending this, my rite tonight*
> *And I bid you, Hail, and Farewell!*

Draw the closing pentagram of south.

West

Stand facing the west. Try to visualise the attributes of water: the autumn rain, the creatures of the sea, and the mysteries of death and rebirth. Visualise the colour of west – blue. Then say:

> *Lords of the West, Element of Water*
> *Waves of emotional balance and healing*
> *I thank you for attending this, my rite tonight*
> *And I bid you, Hail, and Farewell!*

Draw the closing pentagram of west.

North

Stand facing the north. Try to visualise the attributes of earth: the winters chill, the dark fertile forests, and growth and protection. Visualise the colour of north – green or black. Then say:

> *Lords of the North, Element of Earth*
> *Stones of Stability and Grounding*
> *I thank you for attending this, my rite tonight*
> *And I bid you, Hail, and Farewell!*

Draw the closing pentagram of north.

Spirit

Come into the centre of the circle, and say:

> *Spirit, all encompassing element that binds the other elements into one, that connects us with the powers of unity, the God and Goddess and the web of Wyrd, I thank you for joining me here this night and ask that you remain with me always.*

Circle closed

It is our coven's belief that the circle should be closed in balance, in a similar way as it is opened, and so the 'Three Times Pass' is used once again, to 'cleanse' and 'consecrate' the circle and this time to 'release' the magic. Our coven performs the 'Three Times Pass' with these words:

First Pass: *This circle is cleansed*
Second Pass: *This circle is consecrated*
Third Pass: *And this circle and its magic is released. So mote it be!*

Chapter Nine

Ritual Practices

So far throughout this book we have discussed the history and origins of witchcraft, the cycles of the earth that witches follow, the components of ritual, safe and correct practice, and have also introduced ourselves to some simple, yet effective, rituals and traditions. There is so much more that we could discuss on just these initial subjects alone that I would need to write another book to cover it all; however, background and introduction to the Craft is essential if you are to work effectively within magic. The introductory subjects which we have covered so far will be strong foundations on which I hope you will continue your learning and practice.

So, now we have learnt about the core beliefs and practices behind the Craft, how can we put this to use in ritual? What sorts of practices are common among witches and the rest of the Pagan community?

Anthropologist Margaret Murray identified common practices of witches from her research, many which reflect modern Craft today. These included *seasonal and fertility rites, feasting and dancing, renewing vows, adoration* and *chanting and turning in circles*, the latter which could be interpreted as an older version of our cones of power and *'Witch's Chant'* or *'Rune'* today.

I have outlined some modern practices, within some of which I have given tasks so that you can start these practices now. Others are too advanced to cover in this portion of the book, and some are coven work only. However, if you do decide to join a group in the future these practices will probably be used at some time during your time with the coven, with a High Priestess or Priest guiding you. These sorts of more advanced practices *can* be found in books; however, I would not recommend attempting them until you are in an established group, or have been working solitary for some time and feel confident in your ability to control the forces that are used within the rituals.

Ritual Practices: The Esbats – Rituals of the Moon

'The tide will be rising now,' she said. The man roused himself and looked at her. 'The moon will be rising too,' she added. 'The power is beginning to gather,' said Lilith Le Fay. 'Shall we go and robe?'
Dion Fortune, 'Moon Magic'

The esbats are rituals performed on the New and the Full Moons, which honour the moon and make use of its energy. The structure of the Full and the New Moon esbats are fairly similar, although the magical working of the ritual often changes depending on the phase of the moon. It is normal for the members of the coven to bring along requests for the evening esbat: spells, chants, healing and so on which they would like the coven to carry out, and the High Priest and High Priestess may also plan a specific praxis or workings for that night.

It is worth pointing out at this stage a difference between modern Craft views and Traditional Craft views. Many Traditional witches believe that magic should not be performed during a Full Moon; like the tides, at a Full Moon it appears that the moon is neither coming nor going; it seems static in the sky, and so whereas many modern witches consider the Full Moon a time where magic is at its fullest, many Traditional witches see it a time of rest. Again, the decision is entirely up to you.

Most covens get together on both the New and Full Moon esbats, with a meeting before hand to discuss any business. Some covens have a feast on the evening (traditionally, rituals would start at 9pm, so the feast would be before the ritual. Personally, we find that having dinner is very grounding experience and best done *after* the ritual, so we start earlier and eat afterwards).

A cone of power is usually raised during the esbat, either by using *The Witch's Rune* (as outlined in Chapter Eight). Another witches chant, 'Io! Evohe!' can also be used.

Invocations (when a God or Goddess enters the body of the Priest or Priestess) are also more common on the Full Moon, and the 'Drawing down the Moon' is performed as a ritualised way of invoking the Goddess into the body of the Priestess. Contrary to belief, 'Drawing down the Moon' is not a modern rite, neither is its name; illustrations of female magicians performing this rite can be found depicted on old carved reliefs from Greece. The 'Drawing down the Sun' is performed in a similar way to invoke the God into the body of the Priest, although this is more likely to be performed sabbats (festivals of the Sun) in most covens.

The Witches Tides

For each moon phase, season and hour there is an associated tide. Tides are created because the earth and the moon are attracted to one another other by a magnetic pull and since water is a fluid, the gravity of the earth cannot hold it still and so the water flows in harmony with the movements of the moon. As the earth moves and the moon pulls, the ocean is constantly moving from high tide to low tide, with about twelve hours between two high tides.

The sun also omits a gravitational pull, although its force is much less powerful. However, when both moon and sun are combined (i.e. on New and Full Moons) the gravitational pull is more, and this is called a Spring Tide (note, this has nothing to do with the season of spring). This causes tidal variations such as very high tides and very low tides. When the sun and moon are not working together, the gravitational pull is less, and the tides are not as extreme. These are called Neap Tides.

Witches use the tides by taking advantage of the natural energy flow available to them. Just like the tides of the sea, it is easier to go with the natural flow than against it; so taking notice of tide times and consequently the biorhythms of the planet can make ritual and spellwork much more successful.

For instance, a Full Moon usually indicates to modern witches that energy is at its peak. However, if we also work at a High Tide during that Full Moon, then the results will be even more effective. Additionally, if we were working to banish, using a Dark Moon at Low Tide would be the best time for that particular spell.

You can usually find out about your local tides by checking the Shipping Forecasts and Tide Tables, which are easy to get hold of on the internet and are usually updated every day. As well as the daily and monthly tidal variations, witches also attribute a tide to each season of the year, and parts of nature. These are called the Elemental Tides.

Earth Tide: Begins at Yule > Peaks at Imbolc > Ends at Eostara
Fire Tide: Begins at Eostara > Peaks at Beltane > Ends at Litha
Air Tide: Begins at Litha > Peaks at Lughnassadh > Ends at Hærfest
Water Tide: Begins at Hærfest > Peaks at Samhaine > Ends at Yule

The elemental tides allow us to use the power of the tides together with the Wheel of the Year, and our journey through own lives. The tides of earth relate to matters of the body; tides of fire relate to matters of the spirit; tides of air relate to matters of the mind and the tides of water relate to matters of the emotions. So for instance, to hold a rite at Lughnassadh, on a Full Moon and at a High Tide, is sure to be the most effective time to work towards your mental abilities or studying. And a ritual held at Yule, on a Dark Moon and at a Low Tide, is likely to be a most effective time of working towards releasing ties to an old relationship and making way for the new.

Moon Worship

Moon worship is as old as mankind itself. Our ancestors witnessed the moon as it reflected the rhythms of life, the cycles of the seasons and the tides of the seas. They watched the moon move across the sky, transforming and changing – a beacon of light that shone through the darkness of night. In short, it seemed to our ancestors that the moon caused the rhythms of life that they relied on so very heavily.

The gravitational pull of the moon moved bodies of water, causing fluctuations in fishing, travel, and flooding. The weather, too, was affected by the changes in the moon and this also had a direct effect on mankind. Bad weather and storms were more likely around the time of the full moon, and rings around the moon predicted rain. A red moon signified the time for harvest or impending death, 'blood on the moon', whilst a lunar eclipse meant a time to perform magic to appease the moon and ask it to return its light to the earth.

The moon's relationship with water was of particular interest to the ancient people. Our ancestors observed how the moon affected the tides, and how it reflected upon the waters, shining and bright. The power of moonlight and Moon Water (water that was exposed to the light of the Full Moon) was seen as being especially magical, and was gathered for use in healing, magic and childbirth. Children were sometimes laid out in the light of the Full Moon to cure disease and affliction, and nowadays, witches leave their magical tools and talismans out in the light of the Full Moon, mimicking this ancient rite.

But sometimes the moon hides its face suddenly, and without warning. This event – a Lunar Eclipse – was described as a time of 'pre-creation chaos,' and fantastic and elaborate rituals were performed in an effort to bring the moon back. Sir James Frazer writes in his book, *The Golden Bough*, that the tribes of Orinoco in Venezuela believed that if the light of the moon was extinguished then all light in the world would go out, except what was hidden from the moons' sight. So at the time of an Eclipse, they would take their lighted torches underground, bringing them out after the eclipse so that they might relight their fires.

The Egyptians were more educated in astronomy and knew that the moon shone because the light of the sun was illuminating it. They described the moon as the 'Eye of the Sun' and attributed it with the power to see through the dark. The moon also became associated with the hare, Egyptian 'Un' which means 'eyes open' and the cat – the eyes of the night.

The moon also works with the zodiac, as it moves in and out of astrological signs throughout the month. Depending on the astrological position of the moon, the energies that are exposed to the earth differ and cause changes to the results of our magic - and even our daily lives.

Women, the Goddess and the Moon

Xquic... Isis... Luna... Hecate... Astarte... Nuit... Selene...

Women and the Goddess have long been associated with the powers of the moon, and for our ancestors their mysteries lay in womanhood and menstruation. Because of the moon's effect on bodily fluids, the flow of women's menstrual cycles were (and often still are) in tune with the phases of the moon. This timely bleeding usually occurred at the Full or the New Moon, when the moon had its ultimate hold on the earth.

Menstruation was a form of bleeding which did not exist naturally anywhere else; it was bleeding that did not lead to illness or death. This led our ancestors to associate the event of menstruation with the symbolism of the 'Womb to Tomb' (life and death hand in hand). This supported what the ancients saw occurring in the sky: the moon transforming, disappearing for three days, and then suddenly reappearing again. So, Moon Goddesses also became associated with the Underworld, death, and ultimately rebirth.

The power of the moon was sometimes described as the 'Elixir' of the Moon Mother, and menstrual blood was seen as one of the most powerful magical ingredients available. Xquic, a Mayan Goddess, was a Goddess of the moon and of the Underworld and was also known as the Blood Maiden, or Blood Girl. In certain menstrual cults, red ochre body and face paint was used to evoke the energies of life blood, and the natural magic of womanhood.

A Temple dedicated to the moon was built in Caucasian Albania, where women were held in high regard and many women were great warriors who evoked the powers of the moon at every opportunity to ensure a fortuitous outcome in battle. The women warriors carried crescent-headed arrows, mystical weapons of great magical power, and blades that could cast a wicked blow at short range. They wore blood-red woollen material into battle, along with beautifully cast armour and décor. They also made use of the bow, the crescent axe, and a light buckler (a shield worn on the arm). Early versions of the Goddess Ishtar were also worshiped at the moon temple of Caucasus, who was depicted with a moon upon her brow.

The Sumerian Goddess Innana was often depicted with the symbol of the crescent moon, and it is believed that it was at the height of her worship that the model for the sickle and the boat axe were crafted, both in the image of her sacred symbol.

Man, the God and the Moon

Mani … Yah'la … Sin … Thoth … Nanna … Osiris … Annigon

The moon is often seen as an exclusively female deity in modern Wicca, but this was not a belief shared by all of our ancestors. Many cultures associated the moon with man just as women and some societies even associated the moon *solely* with a masculine force. Within our coven we do not limit the moon solely to its feminine or masculine aspect. Instead, we try to embrace its totality and balance, which is offered by the powers of the Goddess and the God, and both the masculine and the feminine.

As agriculture became more important to our ancestors, the Sun God and Dying and Rising Vegetation Gods began to appear more and more in the sacred lore of the land, particularly in the part that they played by impregnating the womb of the Earth Mother. In fact, the time of the Dark Moon, (when the moon could not be seen for three days), was often described as 'a cave-like time', or 'mother's womb', where all was in darkness ready for the God to be reborn.

This three-day, tomb-womb process was also reflected in the later stories of Jesus who dies, withdraws into a tomb for three days and then rises again. In a similar way, Osiris, the prede-cessor of the modern Jesus, was killed by his brother Set on the 28th day (28 days per moon phase) of the 3rd month (3 days of Dark Moon).

But the Gods were not only associated with the moon for their powers of fertility and self-sacrifice. There were many moon Gods who ruled over different aspects of the moon as a symbol of mystery and divination, and the moon soon became synonymous with the Gods of intellect such as the ibis-headed Thoth - the Egyptian God of writing and the mind. There were also Gods who were involved in the movement of the moon, such as the Norse God Mani who dragged the moon across the sky every night. And Annigan, an obscure Inuit moon God who chased his sister, the sun, across the sky. In the heat of the chase he would forget to eat, and so would get thinner and thinner. Realising he could not go on, he would rest for three days, feasting only to return to the chase again once the three days were up.

The Moon and the Lunar Calendar
The moon makes a complete orbit around the earth in approxi-

mately 28 days. As it makes this orbit, it stabilises earth's rotation, makes changes in the subtle energy of the planet and guides the ebb and flow of the tides. In the same way, the moon's energy affects all liquid on the earth. The liquid within our bodies and the sap within plants and trees both react to the changes of the moon. Because of its biorhythmic effects on the human body, the Full Moon is often blamed for increases in crime, suicide and accidents, as well as more positive changes such as birth rates and fertility. The words 'Lunatic' and 'Lunacy' both come from the word Luna (the Roman word for the moon, named after the Goddess Luna) due to the strange effects the Full Moon has on the human body. Folklore weaves tales of werewolves and other monsters that are said to walk the earth at the Full Moon, also empowered by this auspicious time.

The first farmers of ancient times kept a record of the moon's phases and carved them into stone, wood or bone. They realised the relationship between the moon phases and the progress of the crops. In general, the Waxing Moon was the time to planet fruit and vegetables, the Full Moon to gather berries and spread fertiliser, and the Waning Moon to harvest, preserve and store.

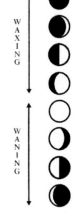

The Phases of the Moon
NEW MOON 0º – 44º **Associated Sabbat: Yule**
At the beginning of the moon's cycle it emerges from the dark where it has been resting and gathering energy. The New Moon marks the rebirth of light and as the moon begins to appear out of the shadow of darkness it is fresh and revitalised. This is a time for planning new projects and establishing new relationships and goals.

CRESCENT MOON 45º – 89º **Associated Sabbat: Imbolc**
In the Crescent Moon phase the moon appears in the sky like a

harvest sickle. The Crescent Moon marks the energising of your new projects and at this time, there is fresh power available for the new challenges ahead. This is the time to put your ideas into action, and make a positive step towards your goals.

FIRST QUARTER 90º – 134º **Associated Sabbat: Eostara**
Seven days after the New Moon the First Quarter Moon occurs. Half the moon is still dark and half is light. The First Quarter Moon marks the time of balance and it is now that we can perform magic to do with choice and decision.

GIBBOUS MOON 135º – 179º **Associated Sabbat: Beltane**
The word 'Gibbous' describes the swell of the moon. The moon prepares for its most powerful phase, the Full Moon. The Gibbous Moon marks new growth, and indicates that the most powerful time is about to peak - the Full Moon. Now is the time to prepare workings and magic.

FULL MOON 180º – 224º **Associated Sabbat: Summer Solstice**
For modern witches, magic is at its most powerful at this time. The Full Moon marks the height of the lunar month, and it is at this time that magic comes to its fullness. The Full Moon is also a time when we can perform any type of magic that we want strengthened and empowered; put ritual items, magical talismans and water in the moonlight to cleanse and empower them.

DISSEMINATING MOON 225º – 269º **Associated Sabbat: Lughnassadh**
As the darkness starts to crawl round the opposite side of the moon, its light side starts to shrink. The Disseminating Moon marks the start of the Waning Moon phase. The projects started in the Waxing Moon have now been set in motion, and now it is time to let things take their course as the lunar month progresses.

THIRD QUARTER 270º – 314º **Associated Sabbat: Hærfest**
Once again, the dark and the light of the moon are in balance and energy is equal at this time. The Third Quarter Moon marks a time for winding down and removing the things that may be weighing you down. It's also a time for harvesting the things that you have manifested from magic in the Waxing Phase.

BALSAMIC MOON 315º – 360º **Associated Sabbat: Samhaine**
The moon prepares to rest and regenerate as it becomes enveloped in darkness. As we approach the Dark Moon, the Balsamic Moon marks a time for turning within, and looking within ourselves. It is a time for considering what has occurred over the past moon cycle and beginning to plan for the next. It is also ideal for prophesy and divination.

DARK MOON **Associated Sabbat: Yule**
Now, the moon rests for three days whilst it gathers energy for the next cycle. This part of the cycle, like the Full Moon, is steeped in mystery and folklore. The Dark Moon of the three 'moonless' days signifies a time of inner searching, contemplation and psychological work. It is also a time for rest and recuperation before the next cycle begins. Moon energy is low at this time and, except for magic that honours and works with the ideals of introspection and rest, it is not usually worth performing magic at this time. However, the time of the Dark Moon is used by Second Degree witches, as they work through the inner mysteries.

The Waxing and Waning of the Moon and Magic
The 'Waxing Moon' describes the period of time between the New Moon and the Full Moon. It is at this time that the moon is growing, and we reflect this in our magic. The Waxing Moon marks a time for spells involved with growth, fertility, healing, new projects, new jobs and new relationships and covers the

New, Crescent, First Quarter and Gibbous phases of the moon.

The 'Waning Moon' describes the period of time between the Full Moon and the Dark Moon. It is at this time that the moon is decreasing, marking a time for spells involved with banishing, divination and endings. The Waning Moon covers the Disseminating, Third Quarter, Balsamic Moon and Dark phases of the moon.

Void of Course Moons

A Void of Course moon marks the period between the moon's final aspect (angle) in an astrological sign and its entry into the next sign. Depending on the position and the speed of the moon, a void of course can last for minutes, hours or even days. A void of course moon sits in 'empty space' between two astrological signs, and therefore has no planetary influences. At the time of the void of course, it is unproductive to start any new projects or long lasting commitments, and it is best to relax and put magical work aside during this time. Anything of any importance is best left until the moon enters a new sign, where any work will be more fruitful.

Meditation and divination can be performed during this time, however the results cannot always be relied upon and should be checked later when the moon is no longer void. Magical work should also be avoided in this way if the ruling planet is in Retrograde – when a planet appears to be moving in the opposite direction to its normal course.

The Moons of the Year

January	Snow Moon
February	Death Moon
March	Awakening Moon
April	Grass Moon
May	Planting Moon

June	Rose Moon
July	Lightening Moon
August	First Fruits Moon
September	Harvest Moon
October	Blood/Hunter Moon
November	Tree Moon
December	Long Night Moon

The Horseshoe, Iron Nails and the Moon

Although modern horseshoes are usually made of steel, in the past they were made of iron. The horseshoe has been a symbol of luck for hundreds of years, and iron horseshoe nails and iron filings were often an ingredient in spells and Witches Bottles. Even to this day, horseshoes and horse brasses are a popular symbol of luck for weddings, and worn on the person or used to decorate wedding cakes and cars.

To our forefathers, the crescent-shaped horseshoe was a perfect symbol of the moon. In addition, the properties of iron – its blood-like taste and red rust – became associated with life blood, and the power of the Moon Goddess. The horse was also associated with the Goddess, in particular Epona the Horse Goddess and the Celtic Goddess Rhiannon. For men, the horseshoe represented the power of the Farrier who was attributed with magical powers for his ability to shape iron with fire. The Farrier and the Blacksmith have long been associated with Craft and magic and many customs have been born from this belief, in particular the ritual properties of iron, and iron horseshoe nails. 'Firing the Anvil' was a custom created in honour of Wayland Smith, the Germanic God of Smithcraft, which demonstrated the power of smithcraft by lighting gunpowder beneath the anvil and shooting it up into the sky.

The lucky horseshoe we see today is usually hung upright, to contain good luck. However, it was traditional for witches to hang them upside down over the front door, as both a symbol of their Craft and to pour good luck over those who walked beneath it. To them, the horseshoe was a permanent symbol of the moon, a talisman which never ran out of fortune.

As with many Pagan customs during the Medieval era, the meaning of the horseshoe changed and it became considered a deterrent *against* witchcraft rather than a sign of its power.

TASK: A Full Moon Ritual

What phase of the moon is it right now? How can you use this time to aid both your magical and earthly life? Study the moon at this time; research how its energy can be used. Begin to make notes of the moon phases and how they affect your life over the coming month. I would recommend setting aside the New and Full Moons (esbats) for your own personal rituals. Use this time to practice the work that we have covered in the book so far, and make the best of the moon's energy. Keep in mind the associations relevant to specific moon phases, and tailor your work to suit. For instance, the New Moon esbat would be a good time to start practising new things and learning, and the Full Moon for advancing your studies and working on your personal power.

Carry out the following rite in accordance with the directions for ritual in Chapter Eight. Before the ritual begins, you should have a cleansing sea salt purification bath in preparation for the rite.

Directions: (as Chapter Eight)

- Sweep the circle
- Blessing and Consecration of the Elements
- Cast the Circle
- Call the Quarters of the Compass
- Evocation of the God and the Goddess
- Workings:

Once you have completed the Evocation of the God and the Goddess, pull the curtains open (if working indoors) so that the light of the moon can shine into the room. If you are outdoors, pause for a moment to look at the moon and contemplate her mysteries and beauty. When you are ready you can perform the dedication to the moon, as follows:

I stand within this circle of art
In the shining light of the moon above
Queen of magic, Queen of night
I have built this sacred space for you.

Queen of the waters, Queen of stars
Shine your wisdom down on me.
Bring your gifts of foresight and truth
Luna, moon, come to me. Io! Evo-he!

Stand silently for a while, meditating on the mysteries of the moon. Does Luna have anything to say to you? Does she impart any wisdom, or advice? Feel the power of the Full Moon filling you and empowering your mind, body and spirit. At this point, you may choose to prepare some Moon Water. Pour some water into a separate dish (a large shell is ideal, due to its connection with the sea and the tides) and leave the dish on a window ledge for three nights. The water can then be decanted into bottles when the three days are up.

At this point you can perform any other workings which you may have planned for the rite. Once you feel the ritual is finished, face the altar with palms raised again, and say:

O' gracious Luna moon
I give thanks for your presence in this rite
May your wisdom be with me always.

- Libation
- Quarters Farewelled
- Circle Closed.

Ritual Practices: The Sabbats – Rituals of the Sun

The sabbats are celebrated at eight points throughout the year and signify key changes within nature and within ourselves. *See Chapter Ten for more details on the Solar Sabbats.*

Ritual Practices: Rites of Passage and Celebration

The term 'Rite of Passage' describes any ceremony that an individual goes through which marks a turning point in their life, or causes a transition from one social role to another. These can include the following:

Wiccaning/Saining/Baby Naming

The word 'Wiccaning' is a very new word to describe a very old ceremony. The word 'Wiccaning' appears an obvious adaptation of the word 'Christening' which seems odd, as borrowing words from Christianity is not something that Paganism has ever needed to do. Our coven prefers to use the word 'Saining' (Old English/Scots Gaelic) which holds its roots in the word 'breast'. It translates as 'to bless and protect from evil.'

We like to combine the Saining together with a Baby Naming. Saining has been performed for thousands of years, with later Saining ceremonies using the symbol of the cross within the ritual. In our coven Sainings, we anoint the baby with oil, wine and consecrated salt water, as well as presenting the child to the God, the Goddess and the elements. Smudging with incense is also sometimes used, for older children.

Within a Saining it is understood that the child is only named, blessed and protected by the rite, and not bound to the religion. The child can then go on to select his or her own path when he or she is old enough.

There are some nice traditions accompanying the art of Saining, such as presenting the mother with an iron nail or iron filings at the birth of the child, which are said to protect the baby up until the Saining.

Sainings are usually performed by an established coven and lead by the High Priestess, but there is no harm in anyone performing their own baby naming for friends and family.

Coming of Age

'Coming of Age' is a loose term to describe a ritual that marks a young person's transition into maturity and is usually performed at the point of puberty around the early to mid teens. Many indigenous cultures still use a Coming of Age ceremony, in which it is seen as an initiation into adulthood. Often, there is a trial for the child to endure (usually boys) such as a sacred hunt, or exclusion from the tribe whilst they fend for themselves for a period of time. Some cultures use ritual circumcision and scarification (ritual cutting of the skin) on both boys and girls and the people of the Hamar Tribe in Ethiopia carry out a ceremony which consists of a scourging which is followed by running naked across the backs of ten or more cattle - a rite called the Cattle Leaping Ceremony.

All of these methods are fascinating, and worth researching, but not really suitable for use within a western society. We like to follow the origins of the Coming of Age by getting the child to do a certain task such as artwork, tapestry, or writing, which they must complete for presentation at the ritual. Then, depending on whether the child is male or female, a red bracelet or necklace is given to mark the day.

Initiations

The practice of initiation is important within our Craft. There are three Degrees of initiation, four if you count the initial Dedication, and each is given to mark a specific period of learning for the initiate. Usually, there is at least a period of a year and a day between each Initiation to ensure a standard of learning, and a new name is taken at each Degree.

Despite common opinion, initiation is not a status symbol. In true Initiatory Craft the witch is given an initiation to represent the hard work that he or she has undertaken in order to achieve a certain level of training.

In the second degree, this training involves learning how to control the ego. Within this training, the student shifts the ego in order to unite self with spirit, with the aim to achieve full consciousness and the ability to transform fate. So theoretically, there should never be a High Priest or High Priestess with an over-inflated ego. But unfortunately there are, and my advice would be to avoid ego lead covens at all costs, as it can indicate a lack of formal training at second degree - if indeed there has been any proper training at all.

In ancient cultures, part of the aim of the initiation was for the initiate to face a symbolic 'death' and in many Craft and mystery traditions a hood was used to cover the Initiate's head during the ceremony. Once the hood was removed and light was returned to the Initiate's eyes, it symbolised their rebirth. Nowadays, it is more common to use a blindfold; although the use of the hood has continued in some esoteric traditions.

In Egyptian rites the initiation gave instructions of how to navigate the afterlife once actual physical death occurred, a 'run-through', if you like, of the passage after death. It was necessary in Egypt for those who wished to enter the afterlife to learn the texts from the Book of the Dead, so that they could recite them when the Gods of the Underworld ordered them to do so.

Witches who associate themselves with Old Craft rather than modern Initiatory Craft rarely recognise initiation within their belief systems; however it is not unknown. Many covens who follow this type of Craft have embraced some sort of dedication, initiation or passing of power from the teacher to the student.

When moving between covens, Degrees can become tricky; some covens may ask you to repeat the period of learning that you have already done with a previous coven, and some may ask for a reference. This is not because they do not trust you – it is a way of gauging the standard of learning that you have achieved so far, and gives them an idea of what you may have missed, or may need to go over again.

The Dedicancy precedes the Degrees outlined below and encompasses much of what has been covered in this book, including the elements Within and Without, Ethics, origins of the Craft, the esbats, the sabbats, the Goddess and God, and basic ritual structure.

The First Degree

O thou who standeth on the threshold between the pleasant world of men and the domains of the dread lords of the Outer Spaces, hast thou the courage to make the assay?'
'Gardnerian Book of Shadows 1957' and sourced from 'The Witches Way', by J&S Farrar

The symbol of the First Degree is the inverted triangle.

The First Degree is given at least a year and a day after the initiate has been Dedicated into the Craft and the coven itself. Some of the tasks and training within the First Degree are:

- To act as support to the High Priest and the High Priestess
- To learn the Outer Mysteries
- To observe, learn and contribute 100%
- Drawing down the Moon
- Raising power

- Magic and divination
- A journey through the Goddesses
- The Fools Journey – an exploration of archetypes

The Second Degree

The symbol of the Second Degree is the inverted pentagram.

The Second Degree is given at least a year and a day after the First Degree. Some of the tasks and training within the Second Degree are:

- To oversee the First Degrees and act as mentor
- To become Deputy to the High Priest/ess
- To face and conquer your Inner Demons and Ego
- To learn the Inner Mysteries
- To take the title of Priest/ess
- To observe, learn and contribute 100%
- Drawing down the Sun
- Shadow work
- Advanced magic
- A journey through the Gods

The Second Degree marks the start of The Test, a period which tries your commitment to the Craft. It is also the period of the Dark Moons, the point during your training when you learn to overcome your inner demons and go through the process of rebirth. Much of the ethos of the Second Degree training is reflected in the mysteries of ancient Goddesses such as the Greek Persephone and the Babylonian Ishtar. More recently it was re-worked in Gerald Gardner's myth, 'Decent of the Goddess' which, like its predecessors, reflects the mysteries of life, death, rebirth and the values of suffering to learn.

In ancient times our Lord, the Horned One, was, as he still is, the Consoler, the Comforter, but men knew him as the Dread Lord of the Shadows – lonely, stern and hard. Now our Lady the Goddess had never loved, but she would solve all mysteries, even the mystery of death – and so she journeyed to the Nether Lands. The Guardians of the Portals challenged her. "Strip off thy garments, lay aside thy jewels, for nought may ye bring with ye into this our land." So, she lay down her garments and her jewels and was bound, as are all who enter the realms of Death the Mighty One.

The Decent of the Goddess, from the 'Gardnerian Book of Shadows 1957'

Sourced from 'The Witches Way', by Janet and Stewart Farrar

The Third Degree

The symbol of the Third Degree is the pentagram with a triangle at the top.

The Third Degree is the final Degree within our tradition. It is the Degree that marks that the initiate is ready to create a newly formed coven, and to begin training others. This Degree is given at least a year and a day after the Second Degree and although on the surface it appears that achieving the Third Degree can take as little as three years and three days, this is rarely the case; in a good coven you would expect to be involved in training for possibly six years or more before you reach this stage.

It is important to realise that the Degree system is not a way of achieving 'status' or a 'medal' – it is a structured programme of learning, which allows the initiate to go through a psychological re-birthing into the next stage of their education and spiritual development, and reaffirms their connection with the Gods. It's also important to remember that we NEVER stop learning, no matter what Degree or age we might be.

After the Third Degree, the witch may stay with the coven he or she has trained with, or 'hive off' to create a new coven of their own.

Handfasting

The practice of Handfasting is a pre-Christian ceremony of marriage. A Handfasting allows the couple to join for either a year and a day (a sort of trial period) or for their lifetime. If they wish, they can even Handfast for many lifetimes - although this should be approached with caution, as the rite ties the couple together for many, many lifetimes to come.

A Handfasting, usually performed by an experienced High Priest and Priestess, presents the couple to the five elements, the God and the Goddess and the ancestors, and employs a method of fastening the couple together by binding their wrists with red cord. Although not legally binding, the ceremony can always be officiated by a simple visit to the Registry Office afterwards.

Eldership

Despite its name, an Eldership is not given according to age. It is more a factor of maturity, responsibility and experience within the Craft and the community. An Elder is an individual who is deeply involved with the Craft and respected by others, and someone seen who is seen as a role model for the whole community. The community itself usually decides when it is time for an individual to receive an Eldership; what a lovely thing to receive. We only know one, maybe two elders in our wide Pagan community; they are a rare breed and that is what makes this Rite of Passage so very special.

Requiem

The Requiem is the last Rite of Passage – the last in this particular life, anyway. On the death of a member of the Craft, the whole community gets together and organises the Requiem. It is traditional for the *Book of Ways* and any other ritual documents owned by the witch to be destroyed. They are usually burnt, so that the element of fire may transfer them and the owner can take the knowledge with them into the next life. Death is seen as a transformation in itself, and the Requiem is both a farewell to the loved one and a celebration of their journey to the otherworld and into the next life.

Ritual Practices: Group Bonding

Group bonding is vitally important to build a Group Mind within the coven; with a strong group mind, a coven can work magic and ritual much more effectively. Some covens also assign roles to members of the coven to promote a feeling of belonging; our own coven includes the additional roles of Gatekeeper, Astrologer, Seer and Hand Maiden.

Group Bonding is a fun way to develop a coven, and is very effective when carried out as a ritual practice within the circle. With new members involved, it could be as simple as finding out about one another – all sitting in a circle and each person saying a little about themselves and answering questions from the others. Another idea for bonding, more suitable for more established groups, is the talking stick method - a chance for coveners to get anything off their chest that has been bothering them about the coven or somebody in it. Without complete honesty in a coven, magic can become misdirected and the harmony of the coven upset.

What about getting together to do something artistic, such as designing a coven emblem, or sewing a tapestry? The Bardic Arts is another idea for group bonding, a method borrowed from Druidry which consists of re-enacting mythos, reciting poems, singing, storytelling, ritual dances and making music.

Magically, group bonding can consist of working out new chants, group breathing exercises, and raising energy together, through such practices as Yoga and Tai Chi. Other ways of magical group bonding includes attuning the chakras, creating astral temples and passing energy around the circle of coveners to create a group mind.

One Mind, One Purpose

This meditation is designed to both connect the coveners within the circle and raise energy within the magical space. It is also the perfect way to begin a ritual.

All coveners should come into the centre of the circle and join hands, alternating male to female if possible, whilst one member recites this guided meditation.

Close your eyes and take a few deep breaths. Focus on your breathing – in, and out, in an out. With every breath in, feel yourself calm and at peace. With every breath out, feel the tension of the day drain away. Your heartbeat becomes slower, your body becomes heavier. Breathe in peace, breathe out tension. All thoughts of the day and other distractions leave your mind as you become completely relaxed and focused.

Now, begin to visualise tree roots reaching down from your feet and deep into the ground, connecting you to the earth. Imagine your roots descend into the soil; past the rocks, through underground streams, and deep into the heart of the earth.
Now begin to draw the energy of the earth up through your roots; a deep green light, which ascends to the soles of your feet. Now feel it as it travels up to your knees, then to your thighs, up to your abdomen and then to your heart. Keep breathing deeply, and repeat the process again as you continue drawing energy into your body.

Now when you are ready, visualise the energy you have collected **flow down your left arm, and into the palm of the person of your left.** *At the same time,* **collect energy from the palm of the person on** *your right. Imagine this energy as it starts to slowly move around the group in a clockwise direction, blending your energies into one. Whilst still drawing further energy up from the earth, keep this energy spinning around the coven ... faster and faster, and faster.*

Feel the group begin to sway as the energy passes from person to person. Rise ... rise ... rise ... we are One Body, One Mind, with One Purpose.

ALL: io! Evo-he!

At this point, the coven breaks hands and throw their arms into the air, releasing the energy that has been risen into the circle. Each person should then place their palms upon the floor to ground any residual energy still within their bodies.

Ritual Practices: Studying and Teaching

Teaching is a common practice within ritual. Doing training within the magical circle means that not only do you have the High Priest and Priestess to learn from, but you also have the influence of the elements, the energy of the land which you have risen, and even the Gods themselves, to tutor you. Training can become very psychically led, and you will find that learning becomes easier as you are guided by the energies which are present.

Teaching within a coven should cover everything: the origins of the Craft, the practices of magic, tools, herbs, trees, the powers of the mind, the sabbats, the esbats and ritual itself. The material in this book is based on the training structure for Dedicants and First Degrees of both our coven and our affiliated covens, who are all focused on mental training as well as spiritual training to develop the person as a whole.

When I train, I train. I teach herbs, how to make mixtures, how to make ointments; this is the Craft, this is what the old Craft was, and what it should be today. There should be training given in these covens, train them for God's sake; give them questions, ask for homework, make them work mentally, that's what it's all about. Anyone who doesn't go down that path, I'm sorry, but they are not Craft.

Maureen Wheeler, Craft Elder

Maureen teaches her students the power of visualisation by getting them to imagine different fruits; the texture of their skin, their different colours and smells. She often catches the odd student out by getting them to close their eyes and visualise a ripe lemon - and then asks them to cut it and take a big bite ... everyone tastes the bitter fruit in their mouths!

Studying and teaching as a coven is particularly effective, as there are many of you to discuss ideas and practice what is being taught. However if you are working on your own, I would suggest that you start studying within your sacred space and observe how it differs from working in an everyday space. When you next perform an esbat take some studying in with you, so that you can experience working within a magic circle. Next time you're lacking inspiration or you are finding it hard to study any sort subject, set up a circle, ask for help from the Gods and the elements and meditate on the work. Gather your answers, and go with your intuition.

Ritual Practices: Magical Work with Intent or Purpose

The art of spellcraft has been used by mankind for thousands of years, from the first hunting images sketched by our ancestors on cave walls right through to modern forms of ceremonial magic. It has been used across the world from the shamans of South America to the Shinto temples of Japan, and has become an important part of folklore and tradition in almost every culture.

Magic is a key element in Craft ritual, and the hard work that a witch has put into his or her Craft study and practice will pay off when a magical working is carried out. When used ethically and with care, it can be a very positive part of our spirituality and our religion. See Chapter 16 for more details on magic and spell-craft.

Ritual Practices: Exorcism of Unwanted Influences

'Exorcism' is a loose term to describe the banishing of any type of unwanted influence, which exists either inside or outside of the circle and can be a chance phenomenon or a magically conjured spirit. I give instruction on protection and defence from both types of entity in Chapter 14, 'Psychic Defence'.

Magically Conjured Entities

I have used this term loosely to describe a phenomenon which occurs directly because of something that we have done within the circle, or by our use of magic. These are our own responsibility, and must be dealt with. Sometimes, the energy has been conjured purposefully to carry out a task, or to aid the ritual in some way. A common spirit used for this purpose is the *Egregore*, an entity which is created by a group mind and sent to perform a specific task or purpose. However, these entities must always be ordered to dissipate once their task has been carried out; if left unchecked, they can get out of hand and begin to start working to their own agendas. Egregores can also be conjured accidentally, at times of extreme group-mind work. However, there are many other entities that may be called upon to perform tasks or influence magic, all of which have the potential to get out of hand.

In High Magic, the Magician will often call upon a Daemon or High Spirit to aid their ritual; however, these sorts of spirits can catch out even the most experienced Magician – as Aleister Crowley, 20th Century occultist, discovered after performing a magical rite called the 'Abramelin Operation'. The purpose of performing the lengthy Abramelin ritual was for the magician to communicate with his 'Holy Guardian Angel' or Higher Self. Unfortunately for Crowley, he succeeded only in summoning daemons, 'the Abramelin devils', as he called them. During Crowley's occupancy in his house, there were reports of a heavy, oppressive atmosphere and dark eerie shadows which filled the property. Fierce winds blew through the rooms despite calm weather outside, and strange figures were seen in the area. I would not recommend attempting to perform any sort of high magic by yourself, and certainly not without a teacher to guide you, so I hope you will never have to deal with this sort of event!!

For witches, magically conjured phenomena usually amounts to residual energy that has not been properly grounded, or the result of a circle being broken prematurely or not properly closed. It is usually down to an 'operator error'; however, even the most experienced witch can still make mistakes and find that a spirit has accidentally manifested as a result of his or her magical workings.

Chance Phenomena

'Chance Phenomena' describes entities and phenomena which are present through no direct result of our own magical workings. This could be a ghost who lives in your house, or a negative energy that inhabits part of your property, the spirit may have some link with the household and its surroundings, or perhaps hopes that we will notice them where others ignore them. Sometimes land is just 'bad' for no particular reason, and harbors negative energy or a feeling of foreboding. Whilst many spirits are friendly and can live in harmony with us, others can be more dangerous. In these cases, we may decide to do take action if we find them disruptive. Instructions on exorcism and clearing negative energy can be found in Chapter 14, but if you have any hesitation in your capabilities for dealing with a spirit, you should consult a Craft elder or a Priest of any religion.

Our coven has performed exorcisms at both local shops and in private homes. One spirit whom we helped pass over dwelt in a small gift shop by the seaside near Bournemouth. The ghost of a little girl who had become a vengeful spirit after being trapped within the shop for so many years, would hurl items off the shelves at the customers and the manager, and would generally make a nuisance of herself. Overnight, she would pull the stock off the shelves so the staff had to spend each morning putting it all back up. Further investigation found that the basement of the shop had been a home for working children in the Victorian times. A simple blessing for the child to move on to the next life in peace dealt with this problem.

Ritual Practices: Working through the Gods and Goddesses

As we start to advance magically, learning the myths of the Gods and the Goddesses becomes part of our practice. This is an important part of the First and Second Degree, when the witch may begin to follow the path of a particular deity. Often they will take on the name of the God or the Goddess for that period of time, and allow that deity to influence both their magical and their day to day lives. In this way, the witch's magical journey and the rituals that are performed in that period are all in parallel to the myths of that Goddess or God.

For instance, a witch who chooses the myths of Persephone will, for a year, follow Persephone within her rituals and re-enact the cycle of life as interpreted by the myths of Persephone, Demeter and Hades. This sort of work can also mark the beginning of the initiates journey through the Inner Mysteries. This practice is not something that can easily be done without the guidance of a High Priestess and Priest within a coven; however, you can certainly make the best your relationship with deities, and details on evoking their energies into your life can be found in Chapter 13.

Ritual Practices: Divination

Divination is a key practice within the Craft. Sometimes we have a specific question to ask, whilst other times we may ask for messages from the Gods, guidance in magic and other energies through Divination. Some forms of Divination include:

Cartomancy   (Sets of cards read with direct meanings and using the intuition, such as tarot)

Runes   (Prescribed set of symbols read with direct meanings and using the intuition)

Ogham   (Prescribed set of symbols read with direct meanings and using the intuition)

Scrying   (Observing water, fire, clouds, mirrors, smoke, etc and using the intuition)

Bibliomancy   (Opening a book at random to receive direct answers or inspiration)

Palmistry   (Reading of the palms)

Tealeaves   (Reading of tealeaves at the bottom of the cup with the intuition)

All of these forms of divination are wonderful aids for the working witch, and I cannot possibly cover them all in this one book. Instead, I have chosen to focus on the Ogham, an ancient set of symbols which allow the user to develop an understanding of both the symbols as a divinatory alphabet, whilst becoming more familiar with the natural world.

The Ogham

The Ogham is an ancient alphabet that was first used in Europe, and dates back to as early as 2200 BCE. It was used as a secret writing system, unintelligible but to those who knew the translation, and also for divination.

The word 'Ogham' comes from the Old Irish 'Ogam' named after Ogma, the brother of the Breass, the King of Ireland.

According to mythology, Ogma, otherwise known as 'sun face', was the inventor of the Irish Ogham.

The Ogham consists of 25 glyphs. The first 20 are divided into four sets, each named after the first glyph in its set – Aicme Beithe: 'the B Group', Aicme hÚatha: 'the H Group', Aicme Muine: 'the M Group', and Aicme Ailme: 'the A Group'.

TABLE 9.1

NAME	WELSH	TREE	MONTH	PLANET	LETTER / NUMBER	CORRESPONDENCES
Beith	Bedw	Birch	November	The Sun	B, 5	The Goddess, the pheasant, white
Luis	Criafol	Rowan	December	Venus	L, 14	Protection, prediction, the duck, red
Fearn	Gwernen	Alder	January	Mars	F, 8	Bran, building, the sea, the seagull, crimson
Saille	Helyen	Willow	February	The Moon	S, 16	Moon, protection, night, bright light, the hawk
Nion	Fuinnseog	Ash	March	Neptune	N, 13	Otherworlds, divination, green, the snipe
Huath	Ysbyddaden	Hawthorn	April	Vulcan	H, 0	Sexuality, Crone Goddess, purple, night crow
Duir	Derwen	Oak	May	The Earth	D, 12	Strength, invisibility, the Oak King, grey, the wren
Tinne	Celyn	Holly	June	Jupiter	T, 11	Boldness, the Holly King, black, the starling
Coll	Collen	Hazel	July	Mercury	K, 9	Magick, protection, discovery, brown, the crane
Quert	Afel	Apple	-	Saturn	Qu, -	Immortality, eternity, dark green, the hen
Muin	Gwinwydden	Vine	August	Venus	M, 6	Gathering, inner-development, variegated colours, the tit
Gort	Eiddew	Ivy	September	Jupiter	G, -	Famine, change, transformation, sky blue, mute swan
NGètal	Cawnen	Reed	October	Pluto	Ng, 1	Preserver, knowledge, communication, green, the goose
Straif	Draenenwen	Blackthorn	-	Neptune	St, -	Magical powers, witches, curses, purple, the thrush
Ruis	Ysgaw	Elder	October	Saturn	R, -	Protection, the fates, the Crone, red, the rook
Ailm	Ffynidwydden	White Fir	-	The Moon	A, -	Strength, divine capabilities, blue, the lapwing
Onn	Eithin	Gorse	-	Mercury	O, -	Fertility, longitivity, yellow, the Cormorant
Ur	Grug	Heather	-	Venus	U, -	Fresh, new, luck, healing, purple, the skylark
Eadhadh	Authnen	Aspen	-	Mars	E, -	Spirit, immortality, silvery white, the whistling swan
Iodhadh	Yw	Yew	-	Saturn	I, -	Death, rebirth, mysteries, blood, dark green, the eaglet

GLYPH	NAME	WELSH	TREE	MONTH	PLANET	LETTER / NUMBER	CORRESPONDENCES
	Koad	Aethnen	Aspen	-	-	K, or Ea, 13	Death, green
	Oi	Gwesberen	Gooseberry	-	-	Oi, or Th, -0	Childbirth, white
	Ui	Gwyddfid	Honeysuckle	-	-	Ui, or Ph, or F, -	Wisdom, intellect, light brown
	Peine	Ffynidwydden	Pine	-	-	Ia, -	Illumination, intellectual & spiritual. Dark green / black
	Emancoll	Dewines Collen	Witch Hazel	-	-	Ae, -	Cleansing, purification, green, white

The last five are later editions to the set, called diphthongs (single syllable vowel combinations which move smoothly from one vowel to another) and were added to the Ogham as language developed.

Each glyph represents a tree or plant, and although most of the trees and plants listed in the Ogham can be found in Britain today, this was not always the case; evidence points to the River Rhine in Switzerland as the place of origin for the very first Ogham, an area which naturally possesses tmore the trees listed in the Ogham than any other place in Europe. The shore of the River Rhine was home to the Iron Age 'La Tène' cultures, who are regarded to be the ancestors of the Celts.

The 25 glyphs are also divided into Chieftain, Peasant and Shrub trees. Some of the 'trees' listed in the Ogham are not actually trees at all (i.e. Vine, Reed, Heather). However before the official studies of botany, any plant to have a hardy or rough stem was usually referred to as a 'tree'. Much of the modern translation of the script comes from a 15th Century manuscript called The Book of Ballymote, the main source of information on traditional Oghams.

The list of traditional glyphs and the later editions my coven follows are taken from the work of Nigel Pennick, an authority and lecturer on ancient mysteries, whose work we relate to and often refer to for our own work. There are many variations to the Ogham (hundreds to be found on the Internet!), and in the Book of Ballymote it is stated that there are 150 kinds of the script – including all sorts of ingenious ways to present the Ogham, such as the Fionn's Sheild.

TASK: The Powers of the Ogham and Fionn's Shield

Research the mythological character and Celtic God, Fionn McCool (Mac Cumhaill) and his involvement with the Ogham – Fionn's Shield. Research the myth of Fionn and his wheel. What is the purpose of the shield/wheel? How could we use the Shield in our own magical and spiritual development? Practice scribing the Ogham glyphs on paper, and if you are handy with wood, try carving the individual Ogham into staves of wood.

Carving the Ogham on wood

Traditionally, the Ogham glyphs were cut into either wood or stone and carved from the bottom up, into the edge of the material. More recently the Ogham has been used as a divination tool and for this purpose each glyph is carved onto the face of a single stick of wood. A simple set of Ogham can be made from Birch.

After finding and cutting your birch*, take the branches home and strip the bark back, then sand down to a smooth surface. Cut the branches you collected up into 25 sticks, approximately 5-8cm long. If you wish, you can cut the branch in half to give a flat surface to carve or draw the Ogham glyphs onto. Draw or carve your Ogham onto the staves. If you can get hold of a pyrography set, you can burn the symbols into the wood. Pyrography sets are good for making wands and pentacle discs, too.

After they are decorated, you can rub in some linseed oil or

FOOTNOTE: *Andrew Chumbley (1967 - 2004) was an English practitioner of magic and the Magister of Cultus Sabbati, which practices a form Traditional Witchcraft that is not associated with the Garnderian or Alexandrian paths of Wicca.

wood oil into the Ogham sticks if you wish, but avoid varnishing the Ogham as this limits the natural energy of the wood itself.

* *When collecting wood, you should ALWAYS ask permission from both the landowner and the tree itself. Touch the tree gently and ask in your mind whether it is right to gather your wood from this specific tree. If you feel within you that it is right, then go ahead and collect your wood. If not, move onto another tree and ask again. When cutting the wood, you should take small branches, no more than a couple of centimetres in diameter – the size of your thumb or smaller – and always cut proud of the branch collar (the swollen area where one branch meets another). Correct pruning is actually beneficial for the tree, whereas incorrect pruning can result in disease and even the death of the tree.*

Chapter Ten

The Solar Year

*For even as the fire has burned brightly at the circle's centre, so we
and the circle must eternally turn around its axis through the many
seasons of Time and Fate; and through the sacred dimension of the
Arte, we are brought ever closer to the timeless centre amidst the
changing whirl of aeon and hour.*
Andrew D Chumbley, 'A Brief Discourse regarding the nature
of Traditional Witchcraft' *

The worship of the sun came into play with the rise in agriculture
that was employed by man when the climate began to change. Up
until then, their worship had primarily been that of the moon,
which illuminated their hunts and appeared in tune with the
tides and with women. People were nomadic, following their
prey and often hunting larger game by night; they were healthy,
fit, and well-nourished. But when the larger prey began to die
out, the supply of food was not so constant. People were forced
to begin practicing agriculture, which although constant often
yielded very little in relation to the amount of manpower
required. The people began to look to the sun, the source of light
that watched them as they worked throughout the day and made
their crops swell and grow and they believed they must appease
the sun and ask the solar deity to provide them with good crops.
The sun and its relationship with the farming year became of the
utmost importance to the ancient people and began to reshape
their religion.

The sabbats are the eight festivals which are celebrated during
the year and comprise of four 'Greater Sabbats' and four 'Lesser
Sabbats'. The practice of celebrating the eight festivals together as

one system is a relatively new idea which was designed by Gerald Gardner and Doreen Valiente in the 1950's who named the system 'The Wheel of the Year'.

However these sabbats are based on some very old festivals which, although not always practiced at the same time or by the same people, have been followed for thousands of years. Even today, outside of Pagan communities, these sabbats are celebrated in our bank holidays, village festivals, and culture.

A Solar Year is the period of time that the sun takes to travel across the heavens and back to the start of its journey. Along its path, the sun passes through four principal points – two Equinoxes, when both day and night are equal in length, and two Solstices, when either day or night is at its longest. These four festivals are of an astronomical significance and have much to do with the workings of the heavens and its effect on the earth. Astronomical reckoning says that these are the midpoints of the seasons, crossing quarter days. These festivals are called the Lesser Sabbats, or 'Solar Rites' (see table 10.1). The remaining four sabbats mark the start of the energy of that season. These four festivals are therefore usually seen as being of a more agricultural significance, as they mark the beginning of that particular farming period. These festivals are called the Greater Sabbats, or 'Nature Festivals'.

TABLE 10.1

Season	Sabbat	Lesser/Greater	Astronomical Event
START OF WINTER	SAMHAINE	GS	
MID WINTER	YULE	LS	(WINTER SOLSTICE, SHORTEST DAY)
START OF SPRING	IMBOLC	GS	
MID SPRING	EOSTARA	LS	(SPRING EQUINOX, DAY & NIGHT IN BALANCE)
START OF SUMMER	BELTANE	GS	
MID SUMMER	LITHA	LS	(SUMMER SOLSTICE, LONGEST DAY)
START OF AUTUMN	LUGHNASSADH	GS	
MID AUTUMN	HAERFEST	LS	(AUTUMN EQUINOX, DAY & NIGHT IN BALANCE)

The popular mythology of the eight sabbats can seem complicated, as they often appear to move independently of one another. The Greater Sabbats are more associated with the farming cycle and vegetation myths, whilst the Lesser Sabbat myths are more focused on the effect of astronomical events upon the land. However, they can work together, as I will show later in the book.

The Solar Festivals

The sabbats reflect the time of year, local mythology and the seasonal energy of the earth. Fire was an important part of sabbat ritual for our ancestors, and the themes of the rituals held often involved both the Inner and Outer Mysteries of the flame.

Although the term 'Wheel of the Year' was established to describe the practice of sun worship in modern terms, the connection between the Wheel and the movement of the sun is much older. For instance, the Greek Sun God Helios was often depicted moving across the heavens in a golden chariot with eight-spoked wheels, as was Shamash, a Babylonian God of the Sun. The Goddess Ishtar can also be associated with the Solar Wheel in relation to its effect on vegetation: the things grown upon and within the earth. Her symbol was the eight-spoked wheel or star.

Because the sabbats are based on astronomical rhythms and farming patterns during the year, countries which shared similar climates often shared similar solar astronomical and vegetation myths, and practiced celebrations which were very alike.

The sabbats also work within ourselves. The seasonal cycle is inherently sacred, and acts as a framework for celebrating the cycle of human life. Just as things change in nature, so changes take place within ourselves. The sabbats and the Wheel of the Year allow us to embrace the cycle of life and recognise our own inner connection and relationship with the land.

As I mentioned earlier, the myths can often appear confusing due to the Greater Sabbats and the Lesser Sabbats originating from separate sources. These two sources are the solar astronomical events (marked by the Equinoxes and Solstices and their relationship with what is occurring on earth at that time) and the vegetation year (often speaking of the two conflicting halves of the year – i.e. summer and winter, and dark and light). Both offer reasons for the seasons and the myths of the Gods, in different ways. For instance, the popular vegetation myth of the Holly King and the Oak King draws a story of two brothers, one representing the dark side of the year, and the other the light. The Summer and Winter Solstices mark the battle between them when the world is handed over to one of the brothers to reign for half a season.

However, the duality myth does not directly correspond with the common mythology of the Greater Sabbats, which mark the death of the God occurring later on in the year, at Lughnassadh. Both events mark the sacrifice of the God, but apparently at two separate times of the year. This is a direct result of solar astronomical myths and vegetation myths being woven into one system. So for clarity, I have arranged a popular astronomical myth and a popular vegetation myth together into one table (10.2) to help you begin to understand the two systems and how they can work together.

In the next portion of this chapter we will explore the myths and practices behind each festival, and I have given you ideas for activities to do for each one. Sometimes I have focused on the solar astronomical myths, and sometimes the vegetation duality myths. Ultimately, the decision of which sabbats you choose to follow is your own; many witches choose to celebrate them all.

TABLE 10.2

Time of year and Sabbat	Solar Astronomical Myth	Vegetation Myth	Associated Moon
02 February (Imbolc)	Sun/Corn God & The Goddess are courting. Stirrings in the Goddesses body.		Crescent Moon
21 March (Eostara) Spring Equinox	Sun/Corn God and The Goddess become lovers, and the God impregnates Her. Balance of male and female, light and dark.		First Quarter Moon
30 April (Beltane)	Sun/Corn God and The Goddess wed.	Oak King is at his strongest as he rules the land	Gibbous Moon
22 June (Litha) Summer Solstice	Sun/Corn God begins to turn into the Harvest God now that the Dark side of the year begins to return and the Goddess turns into the Dark Goddess.	Holly King returns and slays his brother the Oak King. Now he reigns, the Waning Year begins and darkness returns.	Full Moon
31 July (Lughnassadh)	The Dark Goddess sacrifices the Harvest God. The God descends into the Underworld becoming the Dark Lord. It is here that he begins the tomb-womb cycle.		Disseminating Moon
21 September (Haerfest) Autumn Equinox	Completion of the harvest as the Goddess drops the remainder of Her bounty. The Goddess prepares to leave the Earth and day and night become equal.		Third Quarter Moon
31 October (Samhaine)	The Dark Goddess, now The Crone, also descends into the Underworld to join the Dark Lord where she gestates in readiness to give birth.	Holly King is at his strongest as he rules the land	Balsamic Moon
22 December (Yule) Winter Solstice	The Goddess emerges from the Underworld and gives birth to the Child of Promise, the Sun/Corn God reborn, so that the cycle may begin again.	Oak King returns and slays his brother the Holly King. Now he reigns, the Waxing Year begins and light will return to the land.	New Moon

The Solar Year: The Sabbat of Yule

20th – 23rd December

Sun enters Capricorn

Festival of Rebirth

Shortest Day and Longest Night

Yule – From Indo-European meaning 'ghel' meaning 'to shine'
Deuoriuos – Celtic meaning 'great divine feast of frost'

The stang may be positioned in the north of the circle, and adorned with seasonal decorations.

Yule is one of the Minor Sabbats on the Wheel of the Year, and falls between December 20th and December 23rd. It marks the shortest day and the longest night.

Since the previous festival of Samhaine, very little outer growth has been visible in nature, as the plants have receded into the earth, and the trees have dropped their leaves to conserve their energy through the cold winter. Many animals have also gone underground to hibernate through this cold season; whilst under the surface the roots of the plants grow strong, and the animals are renewed by their period of rest and hibernation.

For many of us, the darkness of the short daylight hours since Samhaine has been reflected in our own lives and we have begun to inwardly reflect, choosing to study, read, stay indoors and 'hibernate' in our own way.

But now at this point of Yule we feel the return of the light as we become prepared for the return of the active principle of our lives as the days begin to lengthen. Megalithic monuments were made by our ancestors to mark this special occasion, such Newgrange, in Co.Meath, Ireland. On the morning of the solstice at Newgrange the position of the sun is such that the light is able to penetrate the angle of the roof-box and crawl down the passage, illuminating engraved patterns along the walls until it reaches the inner chamber.

Yule is sacred to the reborn Sun Child, who was sacrificed by the Goddess at Lughnassadh to bring harvest to the land. This festival of rebirth has been echoed in later Christian mythology, in which the Son (...sun?) of God is born at the very same time of year. The celebration of Christmas was moved forward a few days however to the 25th, which is odd as most of the other Christian holidays are still celebrated on the same days as the Pagan festivals from which they originate.

A Yule log made of oak would be burnt in the hearth to bring warmth and light into the home, and its ashes would be scattered on the fields to promote prosperous crops. In keeping with the return of prosperity, mistletoe would be hung inside the house for fertility. See the sabbat of 'Litha' later in this chapter for more information on the sacred mistletoe.

Another Pagan myth that is played out to reflect this sabbat is the story of the Holly King and the Oak King. The returning light is represented by the Oak King, the symbol of the light side of the year. A battle ensues between the Oak King and his brother the Holly King, the symbol of the dark side of the year. The Oak King triumphs, allowing light and warmth to return to the land for the coming half of the year, until the Summer Solstice, when his brother will return again to take the land back into winter. Although this particular myth was first suggested by the writer and poet Robert Graves and introduced to modern Craft to represent a duality within nature, Graves may have gathered his inspiration from the tales of Gwyn ap Nudd and Gwythyr fab Gredawl from the Welsh book of mythology 'The Mabinogion'. Just like the two Kings, these two characters are also condemned to continual annual combat, and Welsh custom re-enacts their fight on the Solstices and May Day as a parody to the balance between summer and winter.

The story of the Holly King and the Oak King and the battle between dark and light is also depicted in the old folk story of the Wren and the Robin, which sparked the custom of Wren Hunting. Janet and Stewart Farrar write in their book *Eight Sabbats for Witches*,

The wren, the King of the Waning Year (i.e. Holly King), is killed by it's Waxing Year counterpart, the robin redbreast (i.e. Oak King) who finds it hiding in an ivy bush (ivy representing the goddess). The robin's tree is birch, which follows the Winter Solstice in the Celtic Tree Calendar. In the acted out ritual the wren would be hunted and killed with birch rods.

TASK: Yule Activities
These are all optional activities, but will really help you feel in tune with this festive season. And remember, many of the

common customs of Christmas originate from the Pagan festival of Yule, so don't abandon decorated trees and present giving with your friends and family. Instead research these customs and see if you can find their Pagan roots. Even the common Christmas tree has a wealth of Pagan origins.

Decorate your home with Holly, Oak, Ivy and Mistletoe

We all know the custom of decorating our homes with Holly and Mistletoe; add Oak and Ivy as well this year. The Holly and Oak represent the dark and light sides of the year; the Ivy represents the Goddess, and the Mistletoe represents the return of prosperity and fertility. Go outdoors and cut your own boughs for your decorations, and avoid plastic imitations. Remember to ask permission from whoever owns the trees, as well as asking permission from the tree itself before you cut. If it doesn't feel right, find another tree.

Witches Ball for Protection

The Witches Ball is an inspiring and powerful tool: a spherical globe usually made out of glass which hangs aloft in the homes of many British witches. There they hang, dusty and still, yet they play an important role for the witch. Their main purpose is to deflect or trap negative energy that might enter the home, and depending on the type of the Witch Ball they can sometimes be opened and filled with herbs or other items to evoke protection. A similar globe is used in eastern mysticism called the Gazing Ball, which has a reflective surface to repel evil spirits and bring good fortune. The Witches Ball also acts as a symbol of the moon and all that it represents. It may also be hung in the window to indicate the services of the witch to anyone passing by who might need them.

Witches Balls can be hard to find, however other spherical items can be used instead, such as glass fishing floats, and even glass baubles.

Try making these protection balls for luck and prosperity; they make fantastic Yule presents for friends and family. Witches Balls are traditionally made of blown glass, however they are virtually impossible to find and expensive to buy. This is a home-made version, which works just as well.

Supplies:

Silver or glass baubles
Ribbons – colours of your choice
1 White Candle
Powdered Orange Peel
Crushed Ivy leaves
Crushed Holly leaves
Crushed Bergamot leaves
Wood Sorrel leaves
Powdered Orris Root
Pen and Paper

Crush the herbal ingredients, ideally with a mortar and pestle, and working in a clockwise direction. Try and focus your intent into the ingredients as you crush, creating a herbal mixture for protection, luck and prosperity. Pull out/unscrew the removable pin from the top of the bauble and tip the herbs inside.

On a small piece of paper write the words, *protection, luck* and *prosperity*. Fold the paper into four and place it inside the bauble, along with the herbs. Now replace the pin of the bauble.

Carefully turn the bauble in your hands and seal the bauble closed with a small amount of wax. Then tie the ribbon around the bauble like a parcel and tie it off, and thread a thin loop of ribbon through the pin of the bauble, so that it can be hung.

The protection ball should be hung high up in a window or over the front door all year long, to evoke the positive energy of the herbs and the moon.

The Solar Year: The Sabbat of Imbolc

31st January - 2nd February
Sun falls in Aquarius
Feast of Brigid
Festival of Lights
Fertility of the Earth
Fire of the Sun

Oimelc – M (B) LIG – Meaning 'ewes milk' and 'lactation'
Imbolg – Meaning 'in the belly'

The stang may be positioned between the northern and the eastern quarters of the circle, and adorned with seasonal decorations.

Imbolc is one of the Major Sabbats on the Witches Wheel of the Year, and falls between January 31st and February 2nd. Imbolc marks the first stirrings of spring: 'the strengthening spark of light, piercing the gloom of winter.' (Janet and Stewart Farrar).

This time of year symbolises the waxing of light since the previous festival of Yule. Yule marked the birth of the returning sun, which started the process of the days beginning to lengthen, and spring returning to the land. Agriculturally, as thawing begins the ploughing and sowing can commence. It is now that we begin to see the first signs of spring approaching as the life giving energy of the new light encourages bulbs to begin pushing their way up to the surface. The 31st of January also marked the beginning of the traditional lambing season and the time when ewes began to lactate; which links the origins of the name Imbolc or 'in the belly' most definitely with the start of this agricultural event.

A southerly sun

A full belly
Prepare for the spring.
Cornish saying, author unknown

It is at Imbolc that the Goddess begins to rise from the under-world to greet the Bright God of Promise. As she rises to the surface along with the snowdrops, she brings the potential of new life into the world, and prepares for spring. This is the Goddess Brigid - the lady of fire, smithcraft, pregnancy, warmth and new life. Yet, although this is a time of new beginnings, the climate is still very cold. The seeds within the earth, and the spark of potential within ourselves, lie beneath a mantle of ice and snow; changing and transforming, waiting to be reborn. Brigid's opposite, the Hag Goddess Callieach, still lingers over the land with her cold hand of Fate, and decides on the length of winter.

Imbolc also symbolises a change of relationship between the Sun God and the Goddess since she gave birth to the God at Yule; he has now become her consort and they rule the land hand in hand. They will come together in late February, when the Sun God will impregnate the Goddess and the cycle will begin again. At Imbolc, the Goddess has become aware of stirrings in her body (synonymous with the earth) and the God is aware of his growing potential power to fertilize (synonymous with the sun).

For ourselves, it is an opportunity to recognise the inner wisdom that we acquired during the winter months and start to bring this new wisdom out, allowing it to help us grow in the coming year. It is time to recognise this 'divine spark' within each of us, which grows and pushes to the surface of our uncon-sciousness. We begin to leave the past behind and recognise the potential in the future.

Imbolc was traditionally a time of purification, and it is customary to have a 'spring clean'. Clear out the clutter from winter, especially things left over from Yule, and get ready for the coming warmer months. Then take a look at your life – what can be swept away or purified in your own life to allow the progression of the new? Get rid of the past, and look to the future.

This time of year marks a delicate balance between winter and spring, death and new life, and it is this energy that we seek to rise within ourselves; the ancestral energy and wisdom of winter, and the fire breath of spring.

The Goddess Brigid and Imbolc

I call unto thee, Lady of golden hair
Bestow upon me the secrets
Of the sacred fires of creation.
'Brigid's Evocation', from the Coven Book of Ways

The Goddess Brigid is associated with the festival of Imbolc, and the unlimited potential of the womb and new life. Brigid is believed to be a *Triple Goddess* – that is, she can take on the guise of the Maiden, Mother or Crone, and as such, three is a sacred number to Brigid.

The name Brigid originates from Brighidh, a more ancient aspect of the Goddess and a deity of the sun, and the fiery aspect of Brigid makes her matroness of light, heat and hearth, warm motherly love and the perpetual flame. Brigid 'firey arrow' was also associated with smithcraft and the art of weapon making, and she was a battle Goddess for the armies of Kildare in Ireland.

The Christian festival Candlemass (February 2nd) is an adaptation of the more ancient festival of Imbolc and the word Candlemass comes from the Anglo-Saxon Candali, Kundali and Kundalini, an association with the sexual energy of the serpent which is heavily interwoven into the myths of the ancient Goddess Brighidh, and awakens from hibernation at Imbolc. Brigid was also amalgamated with the Christian Saint St Brigit, which allowed many of the Pagan Brigid customs to continue under the guise or misinterpretation of St Brigit.

Although Brigit is commonly associated with fire, she was also associated with water and purification. This can be seen by the many sacred wells which have been dedicated to Brigid/St Brigit and are decorated on Imbolc morning.

As things in nature appeared fresh and new, so too did the ancient people see this change in the Gods and themselves. Rites of Lustration were practised, which including the washing of the head, hands and feet with blessed water in sacred springs.

This is also a clue to the origins of the later myths of Christianity, which claimed Candlemass as the time of purification of the Virgin Mary after she had given birth to Jesus. Imbolc is the time when the God and the Goddess separate after the birth of the Sun God at Yule, and the Goddess becomes her own person again. The relationship between the God and the Goddess changes, and this separation allows change to occur in nature. The difference between the two traditions however is that to Christians the purification was not seen as a mark of the change, but a requirement to purify the mother after childbirth who had been 'made unclean'.

TASK: Imbolc Activities
Try the following Imbolc activities on the sacred day of the Goddess Brigid.

Making a Brigid's Cross 'cros-Bride'
Brigid's Cross – sometimes referred to as 'Bogha Bride' (Brigid's Brow) or 'crosog' (little cross) – was a talisman that granted Brigid's protection. The Brigid's Cross is another part of Pagan heritage which has been adopted by Christianity, and is now called the Saint Brigit's Cross. As well as being a symbol of protection and good luck, it also represented the Wheel of the Year and the four arms of the cross symbolised the four major

sabbats of Imbolc, Beltane, Lughnassadh and Samhaine. The original Brigid's Cross was made from plaited rushes, however it can be made with straw, sedge or vine. For a quick and easy Brigid's Cross, use pipe-cleaners in red, orange, yellow and white – Brigid's colours.

1. Loop a horizontal reed around a major vertical reed
2. Loop the next vertical reed around the horizontal reed
3. Now loop next horizontal reed around both vertical reeds
4. Then loop vertical reed around both horizontal reeds
5. Now loop a horizontal reed around both vertical reeds going down
6. You now repeat stages 1 - 5 approx. four times
7. Tie the ends and trim with a scissors.

The construction of the cross can be made simpler by replacing the reeds with dowling rods or lollypop sticks in the first three stages (the four-armed skeleton of the symbol). Hang the cross above your door to invoke the protection and power of Brigid.

Making a Brigid's Mantle 'Brat Bride'

The Brigid's Mantle is another important symbol of Imbolc. It is a length of cloth that is left outside overnight on Imbolc to absorb the powers of new beginnings, promise and fertility.

Choose a piece of white cloth (100% natural cotton) approximately 2 inches x 12 inches and knot it onto a small piece of rowan or birch. On Imbolc hang the Brat Bride outdoors, and leave it out all night. If it snows on your Brat Bride, you are doubly blessed.

Remove the cloth the next day; you can then wear the mantle on your person, hang it above your door for protection, or use it to decorate your altar. You may choose to simply offer it to Brigid by hanging it at a local wishing well or by your hearth.

Raising the Serpent of Spring: The Paper and Bulb Spell
From the Coven Book of Ways

This working is a symbolic act of raising the power of spring, which will come to fruition at the next festival of Eostara.

Supplies:

1 snowdrop bulb, fresh soil and a plant pot
Small piece of paper and pen
1 Floating Candle
1 Cauldron or scrying dish
Fresh water

Fill the cauldron or scrying dish with the water and place it in the centre of your working space, together with the bulb, the soil and the plant pot. Light one floating candle and place it on the surface of the water.

Sit by the cauldron and focus on the candle; become entranced by the light of the flame, which shines brightly against the dark water. Start by paying reverence to the ancestral energy which has taken you through winter, the dark side of the year. Think about what you have learnt, and how you have changed.

Now begin to acknowledge the coming season of spring, feel its abundance and new beginnings which it makes available to you. Look forward to the approaching sabbat of Eostara, when the abundance of spring will come to fruition.

Still focusing on the candle, visualise the energy of spring beneath you, curling about you like a mist. It brings new opportunities, fresh beginnings and new life.

Now take up the pen and write a wish on the paper. What new opportunity would you like to bring into your life? What are your aspirations or goals for the coming season? Once you have written the wish on the paper, fold the paper into two and push it deep into the soil. Now, take the bulb and also bury it in the pot.

Visualise energy rising up from the earth and coming into your body to the three sacred wells: the Base of your spine, which is the place of primal instinct, your Solar Plexus or abdomen which is your energy centre, and your Third Eye or forehead, the place of wisdom. Equally, it rises into the bulb which is nestled in the earth in the centre of the circle.

When you feel the energy starting to flow, begin a simple chant: Rise...Rise...Rise...

When you feel ready, you can stand up and start to circle the cauldron, still chanting, until you feel the energy is ready to be released. When you do, bring your palms down over the cauldron or dish of water. As you do this, acknowledge the rising power of spring within yourself and in nature, and contemplate what changes and opportunities may lie ahead for you this spring.

After the rite has ended, decant the water from the cauldron into a small watering-can and use it to water the bulb for the first 3 days of germination. Once the bulb has pushed its way to the surface and flowered, it is a sign that your wish has been granted.

The Solar Year: The Sabbat of Eostara

20th March - 22nd March
Sun enters Aries
Light and dark in equal measure
Lady Day

Ostara
Eostra
Eo'star
Easter
Spring/Vernal Equinox

The stang may be positioned in the east of the circle, and adorned with seasonal decorations.

Eostara is one of the Lesser Sabbats of the Witches' Wheel of the Year, and falls between March 20th and March 22nd.

During the previous festival of Imbolc, we greeted the lengthening of days with open arms. We also celebrated the spark of potential that returned with those longer days, and began to recognise the stirrings within the body of the earth which guided us towards movement and growth. It is now, at Eostara that we begin to see this inherent spark of potential manifesting itself all around us. Buds have begun to bloom, the first of the flowers have begun to push their way up through the soil, and birds have begun to collect material for their nests in readiness for their young.

The Spring Equinox also marks one of the two points during the year when both day and night are in equal measure, and dark and light are in perfect balance. The sun begins to rise closer to the east and set closer to the west, until we reach the equinox when it rises exactly east and sets exactly west. The Spring Equinox sits opposite the Autumn Equinox on the Witches Wheel of the Year, a festival that also marks a period of perfect balance between day and night, when this event will occur again.

The origins and celebrations of the Equinoxes are a little more obscure than that of the other sabbats, as there appears to be very little historical and written evidence regarding the celebration of these sabbats. There are also many different versions of the word Eostara, and therefore much debate regarding the true origins of the festival. However, this has not stopped this sabbat being a fun and rewarding celebration, full of culture and folklore. Besides, when we begin to connect to the land and the inherent Wheel of the Year, we can begin to feel the energies of the earth and reflect what we feel in our rituals and celebrations. The most important thing is to follow our intuition, and go with what feels right to us – here and now.

The Goddess Eostre and the Festival of Eostara

Popular tradition links the sabbat Eostara with the Germanic Goddess Eostre, whose name means 'east', 'shining', and 'glorious'. For our European ancestors, the end of the month of March marked the beginning of 'Eostur-monath,' the name for April in the Roman calendar that was used by Anglo-Saxons of England. The arrival of Eostur-monath was celebrated as a time of beginning and birth, and feasts to Eostre may have been held at this time.

On the surface, the only historical evidence behind this festival comes from just one source – a document called *The Reckoning of Time*, written by a monk and scholar named Bede (673-735). The original purpose of his work was to demonstrate the calculation of the Christian festivals. In his work, Bede included a chapter called *The English Months*, in which the worship of the Goddess Eostre was mentioned as part of the traditional Pagan customs for Eostur-monath. Bede writes,

Eosturmonath was once called after a goddess of theirs named

*Eostre, in whose honour feasts were celebrated in that month. Now
they designate that season by her name, calling the joys of the new
rite by the time-honoured name of the old observance.*

So it appears that we only have one reference to the Goddess
Eostre and her worship. However, as we discussed in the
previous chapters, there are many names for Gods and
Goddesses whom are essentially the same deity. So with further
research it becomes apparent that the Goddess Eostre can also be
considered as another form of the Semitic Goddess Astarte, and
also the Mesopotamian Goddess Ishtar, who were both revered
as deities of fertility, creation, returning light, the east, and the
spring, and were also celebrated at a similar time of year. Even
the names Astarte and Ishtar come from the same root word as
Eostre, meaning 'east', 'shining' and 'glorious'. As there is no
obvious reason to doubt Bede in his account of the worship of
Eostre, and there is evidence to prove that other, very similar
Goddesses were being worshiped in the same way, we feel that
this Goddess fits in perfectly to the Witches Wheel of the Year.

What is also certain is that the Christian word 'Easter' shares
the same root word as the older Pagan words Eostre and Eostara.
The Christian myth of Easter – that of death, resurrection and
rebirth – is also a similar theme to the ancient Pagan myths
surrounding Eostara.

The Embryonic Symbolism of the Egg

The egg is a powerful symbol of this time of year, and is used in
ritual and folklore to represent the changes occurring upon the
earth and within ourselves. Nowadays people give chocolate
eggs at Easter: an echo of older customs when boiled or blown
eggs were traditionally exchanged, often as symbols of
prosperity. Their shells were usually dyed red to represent the
sun and the returning light, which was in balance with the
womb-like darkness inside the egg. The egg is also interwoven

with many ancient myths and beliefs, and egg staves (a stang with an egg fixed between its fork) were used in magic as a symbol of protection and new life.

Outwardly, the egg symbolises new life, fertility and potential. The Goddess Eostre is a deity who represents rebirth and new life – the seed of potential and ultimate manifestation. The egg, too, represents these qualities and has been a part of Pagan symbolism long before Easter was conceived.

Now that the Sun God has impregnated the Goddess, the 'Child of Promise' begins to grow within her womb – a womb that is symbolised so very well by the embryonic egg. This is also reflected in later Christian mythology when Jesus (also a 'Child of Promise' and a Son) enters the tomb (earth womb) at Easter and is reborn. Jesus is an echo of earlier deities called the 'dying and rising gods' such as Attys and Osiris, who represented the death and rebirth of the vegetation and nature.

Many games were also devised to celebrate this time of year, including egg rolling (racing eggs by rolling them down slopes) and the egg and spoon race.

The Moon Hare

The hare is said to be the companion of the Goddess Eostre. The origin of this belief most likely began with the connection between the Goddess Eostre and the esbats (moon festivals) which were celebrated throughout the year. The hare was a sacred symbol of the moon; its activity was nocturnal, its gestation period was one month long, and the silhouette of the hare could be seen upon the face of the moon on clear evenings. There is a wealth of myth and folklore surrounding the hare. Research the hare, especially its connection to Eostara, the moon, and the season of spring. Some key words you might use in your research are 'Hare', 'Moon Hare', 'Eostara Hare', 'March Hare', 'Hare Totem' and 'Spring Hare'.

TASK: Eostara Activities

Try these activities on the sacred day of Eostara.

Decorating Eostara Eggs

Using a sharp pin make two holes in an egg, one in each end. When doing this it is best to either hold the egg in the palm of your hand or set it back in its carton, to limit the chance of breaking the shell.

Once the holes are made, try to break up the yolk by swirling a needle around inside the egg. Then, holding the egg over a bowl, blow through one hole. Try to blow at a constant pressure to rid the shell of all the contents. It will be difficult at first and will take a few tries – you may have to rest for a bit!

Once you have blown the egg and removed its insides, you will need to wash it out. To do this fill a small bowl with a 1/4 vinegar to 3/4 water solution. Dip the egg into the bowl and let it slowly fill. Give the egg a good shake and once again blow out the solution (don't worry; it should be a lot easier this time). Repeat the cleaning process until all of the liquid egg is removed. Allow the eggshell to dry out for a day, before decorating it with traditional colours – red, orange or yellow – to represent the sun.

For bright colours that last, you may want to use acrylic paint. However, if you are planning to leave the eggs outside as an offering or for egg rolling, you can boil the eggs in colouring, rather than blowing them. For bright yellow, boil the eggs in yellow onion skins for approximately 10/15 minutes. For red, boil eggs with a pack of raspberries for 45 minutes. For a much darker colour, let the eggs stand in the raspberries overnight.

A Rite of the Equinox – Recognising the Balance
From the Coven Book of Ways

Supplies:

1 White Candle
1 Black Candle
An boiled, unblown egg, plain or decorated (if decorated, it should be dyed with natural colouring for this ritual such as raspberries or yellow onion skins)

This is a rite to to mark the balance of the equinox from my coven's *Book of Ways*, and if possible this ritual should be performed at daybreak, just before the sun rises. Before you start the ritual, have a purification bath; you could put essential oils, herbs or sea salt in the water. Whilst in the bath, meditate on purifying your aura. See your aura as grey and dirty at first, but gradually becoming lighter and cleaner, until it is brilliant.

Find yourself somewhere to work where you will not be disturbed. By now, you probably already have somewhere that you regularly use to perform your meditations, rituals and spellwork. The room should be as dark as possible and the candles unlit.

Lay the candles out on the altar in front of you, with the black candle on your left and the white candle on your right. The black candle symbolises the night and the dark side of the year, and the white candle symbolises the day and the light side of the year. Finally, place the egg in the centre of the table between the two candles. Traditional craft suggests that the egg should be placed in a birds nest, but if you do, make sure the nest is abandoned before you take it, or even better, make your own.

Close your eyes and take a few deep breaths. Focus on your breathing, in and out, in and out. With every breath in, feel yourself calm, and at peace. With every breath out, you feel the tension of the day drain away. Your heartbeat becomes slower, your body becomes heavier. Breathe in peace, breathe out tension. All the thoughts of the day and other distractions leave your mind as you focus on this one task, breathing in ... and out, in ... and out. Give this process as much time as you need to allow yourself to become completely relaxed and focused. When you feel completely calm and relaxed, you can begin.

Now light the black candle, and say:

Powers of the night,
Energies of darkness
Symbolic womb and fertile soil
I recognise your silent wisdom.

Hidden potential of the dark
Powers of protection and growth,
Nurture me, contain me,
And grant me renewal.

Watch the black candle as it flickers and burns. Contemplate on what the darkness can teach you. Now light the white candle, and say:

Powers of the day
Energies of light
Beaming sun and blooming flower
I recognise your purity and wisdom.

Radiating powers of light
Gifts of potency, and intensity

Energise me, illuminate me
And grant me the strength of spring.

Watch the white candle as it flickers and burns, and contemplate on what the light can teach you. Now, focusing on the egg in front of the two candles, say out loud or read inwardly:

Eostara is the time of springs' return; when the promise of Imbolc comes to fruition and life bursts forth from the earth as the chains of winter are finally broken. This is a time of birth and of manifestation. The crocuses and daffodils have bloomed and trees have begun to blossom. The air smells of wet earth and flowers; it is a time of new life and the egg, the potent symbol of fertility: the glorious sun and the warm dark womb.

Focus on the two candles, one symbolising the dark and one symbolising the light. Together they represent the perfect balance of the Equinox. Meditate on honouring both of these sides of yourself, both the dark and the light.

When you are finished, take the egg outdoors and bury it in freshly turned soil, as an offering to the Goddess Eostara, the ancestors, and the fertile powers of spring. If you can, spend the rest of the day enjoying all that the spring has to offer.

The Solar Year: The Sabbat of Beltane

30th April - 1st May
Sun in Taurus
Bright Fire
Two Fires
May Day

Calan Mai
Welsh, meaning 'The Calends of May'

239

Belo-Tenia
Old Celtic, meaning 'Bon-Fire of Belos the Bright'
Walpurgis Night
'Witches Night', northern Europe

The stang may be positioned between the eastern and the southern quarters of the circle and adorned with seasonal decoration.

Beltane is one of the Major Sabbats on the Witches Wheel of the Year, and falls between April 30th and May 1st.

The solar God Bel, or Belos, lends his name to this sabbat. Also known as 'Belenos' (Bright One) and Ba'al (God of Fertility), Bel rules over this sabbat bringing the gifts of light, heat and fire to the festival. The lighting of the 'Need Fire' or 'Bale/Bel Fire' was common on the Eve of Beltane, and cattle were driven between two flames in a rite of purification to protect them from illness and mischievous faeries. Another fire was also lit on a high point at dawn, by nine men with nine different woods.

Nine has always been an auspicious number, as it is the sum of the sacred number three multiplied by itself. Nine is also the number of the Norse otherworlds on the Yggdrasill tree, itself sometimes known as the source of the 'Great Fire'.

In northern Europe, Betlane was celebrated as 'Walpurgis night', and shared with Samhaine marked one of the two points during the year when the veil between the worlds was at its thinnest. It was said that spirits of the dead could visit during the eve of Walpurgis, and so it was a time for commemorating the wisdom of our ancestors, followed by the celebration of the returning light of summer the next day.

This time of year symbolises the very start of the summer, the prosperity of warmth and the uninhibited sexuality of May. Marigolds, representing the sun and fire to be scattered on the floor of the home to bring prosperity to families, and Rowan, the tree of protection, was tied over the doorways with red ribbon.

Beltane is the time when the trees have begun to blossom and the flowers have started to bloom. The hawthorn is a tree of the Goddess, and the opening of its flowers was synonymous with the Goddess coming into her full sexual being. In fact, it is said that Beltane has not properly arrived until the hawthorn has flowered.

Traditionally, a 'Queen of the May' was chosen to represent the Goddess, and she was decorated with headdresses of flowers and hawthorn blossom. Boughs of hawthorn were also used to decorate the house at this time, with oak alongside it to represent the fertile young God who was also coming into his sexual power. In Ireland and parts of southern England, a 'Maybush' was constructed with hawthorn boughs and decorated with flowers, whilst whole hawthorn trees were dressed with ribbons in a ceremony called 'Bawming the Thorn'.

Other hawthorn games included the 'Planting of the May' which involved young men gathering hawthorn and creeping into the home of a young girl of their choice to place the boughs around her bed while she was asleep.

Mythologically, Beltane is portrayed as the height of the Sacred Marriage: the time when the God and the Goddess are in their full sexual being. In keeping with this sexual theme, Beltane became a time for 'Greenwood Marriages', a popular tradition in which young single people would go out overnight to celebrate the sabbat with unashamed sexuality.

The sexual nature of the Beltane rites and games are all in order to evoke the energies of fertility and summer into ourselves, and into the land. Other fun and carefree games of this sabbat included the 'Love Chase', the origin of the playground game of 'kiss chase'. Our coven performs this when we have enough people to play, by lining the men up on one side of a field and the women on the other. We then give each man a silk scarf and the chase begins, with the man seeking out his partner and catching her with the scarf.

Nowadays, the associated celebrations of Beltane have been dissolved into the modern Bank Holiday, 'May Day'. Many May Day celebrations, such as dancing round the Maypole, are reminders of our Pagan ancestry. In keeping with the sexual symbology of Beltane, some say that the erect Maypole symbolised the phallus, and by dancing about it, weaving the ribbons in and out, the people brought the magical properties of fertility under their control in a form of folk magic. In his book, *The Stations of the Sun*, Professor Ronald Hutton suggests another possible origin of the Maypole: the Irminsul or 'mighty pillar' of Odin.

A form of knot magic (a magic associated with the element of fire) was also performed at this time. Cow hairs, knotted with red string into a rope, were dragged through the morning dew to encourage good health and purification. Other customs included baking oatmeal cakes called Bannoch Bealltainn, which were rolled down slopes and used for divination.

TASK: Beltane Activities
Try these Beltane Activities on this sacred day.

Working with Flowers and Trees
Flowers are an important part of Beltane. The Welsh Goddess Blodeuwedd, the beautiful Maiden Goddess of this sabbat, was made entirely out of the flowers primrose, oak, broom, meadowsweet and hawthorn.

Become attuned to this sabbat by collecting flowers, decorating the house with them and giving them to others. Hawthorn, oak, rowan and marigolds are the ones I generally use (always check with the landowner before collecting flowers). If you have a garden, now is a good time to consider planting some herbs and wild flowers. These will always come in handy for ritual and magical use, as well as being beneficial to the local ecosystem.

Bathe in the Morning Dew

On Beltane morning, it is customary to pass your hands over the morning dew and rub it onto your face and body. This is believed to pass on the energies of love, fertility, friendship and springtime to you. You can also pass a knotted red cord through the dew, which can then be used for knot magic and other purposes in ritual. The morning dew is also believed to have regenerative powers, and the gift of youth. It also gives protection from troublesome imps.

Beltane Chants

Chanting is a lively way of getting into the Beltane spirit. Light a candle (or even better, make a bonfire) and try some of these chants. If you are musically minded why not try putting them to a drumbeat.

O do not tell the priests of our Art,
For they would call it sin;
But we will be in the woods all night,
A-conjuring summer in…
And we bring you news by word of mouth
For women, cattle and corn
Now is the sun come up from the South
With Oak, and Ash and Thorn!
'Puck of Pook's Hill', Rudyard Kipling (adapted)

Here we come a piping,
In Springtime and in May;
Green fruit aripening,
And Winter fled away.
The Queen she sits upon the strand,
Fair as lily, white as wand;
Seven billows on the sea,
Horses riding fast and free,

And bells beyond the sand.
'Traditional Beltane Song', author unknown

A Spell for Prosperity
From the Coven Book of Ways

This simple spell for prosperity is perfect for this time of year. A prosperity spell can be used for many different aspects within your life: a comfortable home, success in a new job, or good luck in general. Although prosperity spells can be used to help financially, one should be cautious about such spells. A greedy spell is likely to come with consequences, and asking for a large amount of money at one time could even cause money to come from somewhere you would rather it hadn't, such as a death in the family. If you do feel that a money spell is needed, it is best to ask for a reasonable amount that covers your requirements and nothing more. It would also be wise to read Chapter 14 of this book before attempting such types of magic.

Supplies:

Green Candle
Paper and Pen
Green Ribbon or String
Incense
Water
Salt

Calm your mind and feel at peace. Take three deep breaths; breath in peace, breathe out tension. First, light the green candle and focus on its energy. Then light the incense from the candle flame, and focus on the ability of fire to transform.

Now draw a picture to illustrate the outcome of your prosperity spell. For instance, if you would like success in your new career, draw a picture of you successfully carrying out your job role and receiving praise from your superiors. The picture does not need to be perfect – it can be as simple or elaborate as you wish, and your drawing skills are not important!

Now, place something of yourself on top of the picture to unite yourself with the wish. You could use a lock of your hair, a piece of your clothing, or simply blow on the paper if you have nothing else to use.

Now fold the paper up like a parcel enclosing the item inside and draw the symbol of Jupiter, the planet of fortune, onto the folded paper. Tie the parcel securely closed with the green ribbon.

Hold the parcel in your palms and focus on your aim. See yourself being successful, and see yourself prosper. Now keeping that image in mind, feel the power of your image flow down your arms, into your hands and into the parcel. Continue doing this until you feel that the parcel is fully empowered.

Pass the packet (carefully!) over the candle flame to empower, then through the incense smoke to purify. Then trickle three drops of water, then three pinches of salt, on the parcel to cleanse and manifest.

Now extinguish the candle and let the incense burn down. You should keep the parcel for three days, somewhere private to you but a place where you will see it regularly; a bedroom window is ideal. Each time you see it, focus on your aim and allow the power of the spell to grow.

After the three days is up, take the parcel and carefully light it.

Place it in a fire-proof container such as a small cauldron and allow it to completely burn into ash. As the spell burns, your wish will be sent to the astral plane where it will begin to manifest.

Once the ash is cool, turn it out onto fertile soil.

The Solar Year: The Sabbat of Litha

20th - 23rd June
Sun enters Cancer
Longest Day and Shortest Night
Doorway to the second half of the year

Midsummer
Summer Solstice
Festival of Summanus

The stang may be positioned in the south quarter of the circle and adorned with seasonal decorations.

The Litha Fires

Cloaked in darkness we wait, dressed in our finest robes, our fingers pressed to our drum skins in anticipation. Glowing embers in a dying fire the only source of light. Men and women with painted faces sway a solemn dance, awaiting the ascent from darkness into light.

A tiny slither of sunlight rises above the horizon and we begin to beat our drums purposefully, stirring the sun from its slumber, as we cheer on this most auspicious occasion. A chorus begins chanting songs of summer, exalting the Oak King as he reaches his height. All the while I continue to beat my drum, hitting harder and faster with every beat as the great disc of the sun rises steadily above the eastern skyline.

The masked dancers begin to dance fast and furiously, matching the frantic pace of the drummers, armed with great flaming torches; each symbolising the sun growing in its power - the great celebration of the Lord of Light, the benevolent and magnificent Oak King.

A young maiden pours mead from a large bull horn, preparing everyone for the toast once the sun has risen, as a Page takes around cakes and biscuits shaped like sun discs. We beat harder still as the sun furthers its climb above the horizon as we raise a large effigy; representative of the Oak King, crafted from the boughs of his sacred tree.

The Sun finally clears the skyline and we all cheer, our drum beats becoming erratic, matched by the masked dance and the chorus. All enjoying the rapture and ecstasy of this holiest of occasions. We all gaze up at the Oak King, as he towers above us in all his glory, clothed in lush green Oak leaves.

A Priest blows hard on a stout bulls horn, signalling everyone to attention: "Here ye, one and all, as the sacred day of Litha is upon us! The Oak King has reached the height of his power! Let us feast of his bounty, drink to his health and dance and be merry in his honour! Hail the Oak King!"

"Hail the Oak King!" The large crowd echoes in reply as music and dance fills the fields, joy and laughter filling every soul here present. I put down my drum and pick up my small drinking horn, toasting the Oak King. "And let us all thank the Great Goddess, who without which we would not be!" The Priest continues, holding high a drinking horn of his own. "Hail!" We echo his words once more as we take another swig of the sweet mead wine, thankful for what the Gods and the ancestors have given us, the bountiful harvest that is just around the corner, and the many hours of light and sunshine which we have been given.

"Now we must light the Litha fires!" The Priest utters, "For Litha is also a time of purification! Let disease and negativity perish

in the flames, and let us be purified in its presence."

With this we each light our torches and ignite the large belfire. It roars into life, a living symbol of the power of the radiant sun on this day. As the sun warms the earth, so do I feel the warmth of the flames clothing me. I gaze into the fire as if mesmerised, feeling strong and in my power as I listen to the merry sounds of pipers and harpists, summing up this most glorious day.

Twin horns sound out, signalling the start of the royal march, as the Oak King and Summer Queen begin to parade down an aisle formed between the crowds, throwing flower petals and luscious leaves out into the crowd, blessing us all with fertility. The crowd cheer loudly, enraptured by this great day and I again reach for my drum, drumming to sound of the pulsating sun.

Later the Holly King will emerge and challenge the Oak King for his right to rule our land. There will be a great battle and the Holly King will reclaim the throne. The days will grow darker and we will eventually mourn the loss of summer, as we are plunged into the cold and gloom of winter.

But that will come later, when evening is approaches. For the morning of the Solstice is about joy, fertility, life and love. Today is a celebration, not a time of mourning or loss. I smile to myself as I realise this and carry on as I began, beating at my drum with passion and joy; a perfect happiness filling me that only the height of summer can bring. This is Litha! And I feel truly alive!

'Litha' by Lugh Lamhfhada, from the Coven Book of Ways

Litha is one of the Minor Sabbats on the Wheel of the Year, and falls between June the 20th and June the 23rd. It marks the longest day and the shortest night, and is another of the Fire festivals.

Litha is analogous to that of the festival Yule, which is celebrated between the 20th and the 23rd of December. Both festivals are solstices and from the Saxon 'sol' meaning sun, and 'sistere,' meaning 'to stand'. The Winter Solstice, or Yule, represents the peak of the dark side of the year, but the Summer

Solstice, or Litha, represents the peak of the light. The word Litha comes from the Saxon word for the summer months of June and July, and so encompasses the nature of that part of the year.

As Litha marks the peak of the summer season, it also marks the start of the decline of the light. From this point forward, the days will begin to shorten and the nights will start to become longer, as the Wheel turns to the dark side of the year and we begin the journey towards winter.

Since the previous festival of Beltane we have enjoyed the growth of summer, the fertility of the land and the abundance of nature. The plants and trees are in full leaf, glossy and shining in the sun. The warm evenings have allowed bees and other insects to work for longer, and birds and animals are active late into the evenings. The forgiving climate of late spring and early summer gives their young a chance to grow and learn how to survive, before the year turns and the days become colder.

As the daylight hours have steadily grown longer towards the festival, it has given us the opportunity to do more outdoor activities in the warm evenings. For our ancestors, this would have allowed them more time to work in the fields, and more enjoyable social time once the work was done.

The Welsh call this sabbat 'Gathering Day,' as the festival also marks the first of the three harvests of the year – the collecting of young tender vegetables, peas and beans and early fruits. It is also the time to gather honey. The energy of plants harvested at the Midsummer was believed to be very potent, and so herbs for magical and medicinal use were often gathered at this time. Herbs such as mugwort and vervain were supposed to be particularly powerful, and to look at a Solstice bonfire through sprigs of Larkspur was said to keep the eyes healthy.

It is now at Litha that the sun is at its utmost power, and reigns over the land with strength and fortitude. It marks the peak of manifestation, expression and achievement and is a time of celebration. It was also celebrated as a time of fertility and sexual abundance – since the spring the Goddess has been gestating the child of promise, and her belly has begun to grow like the swelling corn.

At Litha, we also feel the return of the dark and we become prepared for the return of the passive principle of our lives. The dark will creep back over the land from this point on and the nights will begin to shorten. So this festival is of dual nature; the celebration and rejoice of the peak of summer, and also of the milestone which marks the journey toward winter.

The celebration of the Solstices was probably one of the most widespread of the festivals, with many traditions and customs being echoed throughout the world. The lighting of bonfires was often an important addition to the celebrations. Our early ancestors observed the weakening of the sun's power after the Summer Solstice and in response lit 'Sun Fires' in an attempt to supply the sun with 'fresh fire'. Sacred bonfires were also named by some as 'Need Fires' and 'Force Fires', both used for a similar purpose as the Sun Fires.

This custom continued on throughout the ages, with bonfires being lit to ward off evil spirits, to fumigate houses and to cleanse animals of disease. Aromatic herbs were scattered upon the fire to aid this cause. Often, the whole community was expected to contribute wood to the fire – to not do so would mean misfortune for that person during the coming winter. Torch processions would move through the village and around the crops to utilise the power of the sun at its strongest, before the dark side of the year returned. Often, nine different woods were used to kindle the fire, which had been taken from the previous years' Midsummer festivities. Once the fire was out, three pieces of remaining wood were chosen from the ashes to be 'planted' into the ground to ensure healthy crops.

Another popular custom was that of the Fire Wheel, which symbolised the solar wheel of the year and the power of the seasons. An eight-spoked cartwheel was wrapped tightly with straw, set alight and rolled down a hill as part of the Summer Solstice celebrations, a custom called 'tumbling the sun'.

The Sun Wheel has long been associated with the ancient Pagan Sun deities, with Gods depicted as travelling in flaming chariots and guiding the sun across the sky. The Pagan Spinning Sun Wheel also seems very similar to that of the firework the 'Catherine Wheel'. The firework was named after the legendary St Catherine, who was allegedly put to death upon an eight-spoked wheel by a Pagan Roman Emperor when she tried to convince him of the error of his ways. Although there is very little evidence that St Catherine actually existed, the use of the eight-spoked wheel as an instrument of torture during the Middle Ages was very real. But neither of these wheels were ever flaming, or spinning. It could be that the torture wheel named after St Catherine and the custom of the burning Sun Wheel became confused in folklore, resulting in the spinning flame firework.

The Golden Bough: Symbol of Life

They wing'd their flight aloft; then, stooping low,
Perch'd on the double tree that bears the golden bough.
Thro' the green leafs the glitt'ring shadows glow;
As on the sacred oak, the magic mistletoe.
Virgil, 'Sixth Book of the Aeneis: part 18'

The Golden Bough is a sacred branch of Mistletoe (or a combination of Oak and Mistletoe). It has been mentioned in various ancient texts and mythology as a powerful magical talisman and emanating supernatural glory; it was also considered as a symbol of prosperity, fertility and protection, and more importantly, the sun.

Midsummer Eve was a potent time to search for and to gather the Golden Bough, which would then be hung across the threshold in doorways to evoke its powers. But why Oak and Mistletoe? As we have previously discussed in this chapter, the Summer Solstice celebrations were of dual nature: to celebrate the height of the sun's power at its peak (and the peak of the Oak King's reign) and also to recognise the gradual shortening of the days as the year leans towards winter. The Oak King has been the reigning personification of the light side of the year since the Winter Solstice, when he fought his dark brother and regained control over the land. His power has continued to grow and the days have grown longer; the land has warmed and there is an abundance of food, fertility and prosperity. It is at the Summer Solstice, at the peak of the Oak King's reign, that his brother the Holly King will return to regain control and bring the dark half of the year to the land. The Oak tree was especially revered of all the woods in the forest during the Fire Festivals, and its close relationship with fire could have been for several reasons. Firstly, the Oak is the longest burning of all the woods, keeping a fire alight and for much longer than that of any other wood. Secondly, the Oak tree tends to be struck by lightening more than any other tree. Oak trees struck by lightening were immediately declared as especially sacred trees. Oak wood was also used more often than not to create aforementioned 'Force Fires' (in particular, fires created using the friction between two pieces of wood). The Oak was seen as a 'storehouse' for the sun's power and energy, and so to burn Oak wood at this time of year was to make the most of the power of the sun, and the Summer Solstice.

My growth is slow
Up and below
My roots shall hold fast
I shall last
I shall last
As long as the winds blow

They will fling my acorns low.
'The Old Oak Song', author unknown

But what of the mistletoe? Mistletoe is a parasitic plant that grows on deciduous trees. Although there are many forms of mistletoe, the rarer 'oak mistletoe' was the one revered by our ancestors. Although mistletoe is now more commonly associated with winter celebrations, our ancestors recognised its importance on both the Winter *and* the Summer Solstice. Looking at the Mistletoe by winter, we see that it remains green and bright, despite the lifeless appearance of its host the Oak tree – so then it symbolised the continuing 'life-force' and vitality/fertility of the tree through the winter. There it sits between heaven and earth out of harms way, hanging within the branches of the strongest tree of the forest. Our ancestors observed the oak withered and bare, and drew the conclusion that the spirits of the oak tree had withdrawn into the mistletoe for the winter.

So, if the oak was the 'storehouse' of fire and the sun, then the mistletoe was the 'seed of fire' which contained the power of the oak's solar energy within its berries and glossy leaves. After winter, the mistletoe would release the seed of the sun, and the oak would grow green once more. In this way, mistletoe gained its connection to fertility and so began the custom of kissing under the mistletoe.

So, looking at the comparative evidence given at the Winter Solstice, the mistletoe and oak gained an important connection to solar energy and the height of the sun's power. To gather the Golden Bough was to quite literally gather the emanation of the sun fire, which is why this custom was also performed at the Summer Solstice.

Another reason for gathering the Bough at the Summer Solstice was to symbolise the fall of the Oak King. When his brother returns to fight for the reign of the land the Oak King is slain, and so the dark side of the year returns. If the mistletoe was the seed of the oak's energy, it seemed logical that it should be collected to symbolise the cutting down of the Oak Kings power - as to slay the Oak King required the slaying of the mistletoe. After the mistletoe was collected, oak from the same tree was often used to build the perpetual Need Fire, Sun Fire or Force Fire.

Although the Holly and Oak King myth is relatively new (re-invented through the work of the anthropologist Sit James Frazer and the poet Robert Graves), it is based on very old folklore and mythology focusing on such dying and rising vegetation Gods as the Norse Baldr. Baldr was slain by a magical spear made from Mistletoe, the only thing on earth that had the power to harm. However, he was able to be reborn, completing his cycle as a dying-rising deity. James Frazer suggests the link between the Oak Spirit and the Norse God Baldr in *The Golden Bough,*

> *Grounds have been shown for believing that the King of the Wood personified the tree on which grew the Golden Bough. Hence if that tree was the oak, the King of the Wood must have been a personification of the oak-spirit. It is, therefore, easy to understand why, before he could be slain, it was necessary to break the Golden Bough. As an oak-spirit, his life or death was in the mistletoe on the oak, and so long as the mistletoe remained intact, he, like Balder, could not die. To slay, therefore, it was necessary to break the mistletoe, and probably, as in the case of Balder, to throw it at him. And to complete the parallel, it is only necessary to suppose that the King of the Wood was formerly burned, dead or alive, at the Midsummer fire festival which, as we have seen, was annually celebrated.*

Another dying-rising deity who was involved with the Golden Bough was the Greek Aeneas, son of Aphrodite. Aeneas used the Golden Bough – sacred to Persephone in this particular myth – to gain entrance to the Underworld, the realm of the dead. The bough represented the bearer's understanding of polarity, and that to enter the darkness was in fact to return to the light. Only by possessing such knowledge would Persephone embrace anyone trying to enter her realm. So in this way, the Golden Bough symbolises the entwined relationship of the dark and the light side of the year, and the power of duality.

TASK: Litha Activities
Try these Litha Activities to mark the Midsummer.

The Midsummer Seidh Fires
Our coven has a fire pit in our grove that we use for our Fire festivals. Using a fire pit is much safer than building a fire directly onto the ground, although for either practice the owner of the land should be consulted. Our fire pit was created very simply; by digging a circle of turf out of the ground, lining the bottom with gravel and then surrounding the pit with bricks. In this way the fire is contained and cannot spread onto the rest of the woodland floor.

It is also possible to use a cauldron set upon bricks to ensure that the fire is contained safely; a wonderful symbol of the creative aspect of the Goddess, and the fertile womb. In Norse Craft, the cauldron is called the 'seidh fire', meaning 'witch fire', or 'magic fire'.

These rites can be performed within the magic circle and directly after 'The Witch's Chant'. If possible, build your fire using some branches of oak. As the fire begins to grow, chant:

I build this fire
With flames so high
Protection of the Gods
Be upon these flames
I build this power

As I build the hearth.
Author unknown

If you have an open fireplace, this chant can also be used when building a log fire in the home. Other customs include jumping over the fire three times to bring prosperity and abundance, and passing ritual tools through the smoke to cleanse and empower them. Mugwort and vervain can be thrown upon the fire to aid purification, and juniper and sandalwood can be offered to the flames to aid fire and smoke divination. You can also perform this procession around the fire from our coven's Book of Ways, to carry out a self-purification:

> *Starting a good distance away from the fire; spiral your way gradually in to the center, repeating the chant until you reach the middle.*

> *Once you are at the middle, turn and spiral your way out again; taking either three or nine turns is traditional. Keep this going, a little faster each time, and visualise yourself becoming purified by the Midsummer fires.*
> *When the fire has burnt out and the pit is cool, choose three sticks from the ashes and drive them into the earth, scattering the remainder of the ashes upon the soil to promote health and prosperity.*

Children and pets should be kept well away from the fire. Extreme caution should be used with any sort of open fire and caution should be taken to keep the fire under control.

First Fruits
June is a great time for harvesting fruit, vegetables and herbs. Discover which fruit and vegetables are ready for harvesting right now. Why not find a 'Pick Your Own' farm near you, and go

and harvest your own fruit and vegetables? It's a great way to get in touch with the season, get out in the sunshine, and kids love it too.

The Litha Boughs

Litha marks the battle between the two great Kings of Holly and Oak. Go out into the countryside and cut a small bough of each tree. Once you have cut your boughs, take them home and cross the two branches. Using red or gold ribbon, tie the two boughs together in the middle to make an equal-armed cross. This creates the traditional equal-armed cross ritual garland. This can then be mounted on the stang or a pitchfork, or hung from a tree as an offering to the two Kings.

Solstice Fruit Fizz

Ingredients:

400g cherries
4 nectarines
250g strawberries
300ml lemonade
6 lemon balm leaves
A few cherries and strawberries, to serve
Ice cubes

Cut the nectarines and the cherries in half and remove the stones. Cut any leaves and stalks off of the strawberries, and wash all fruit thoroughly. Push the cherries, nectarines and strawberries through a juicer, then top up the juice with sparkling water or lemonade, and pour into a jug. Add a few ice cubes, the lemon balm leaves and extra fresh fruits. Pour into glasses to serve. This juice is also delicious served undiluted for a ritual libation.

The Solar Year: The Sabbat of Lughnasadh

31st July – 1st August
Sun mid Leo
Festival of Lugh, 'The Many Skilled'
First Harvest

Lughnasa
Old Irish
Lammas/Hlafmasse
Saxon meaning 'Festival of Bread'
Opiconsivia
Roman Harvest Festival of Ops

The stang may be positioned between the southern and the western quarters of the circle and adorned with seasonal decorations.

Lughnasadh is one of the Greater Sabbats on the Wheel of the Year, and falls between the 31st July and the 1st August.

Since the festival of Litha the days have remained warm and sunny; although we have aknowledged the returning dark at Litha, autumn has not yet become apparent. For us, the season running up to Lughnasadh (mid June – early August) has been a carefree and happy time. The sun is out, the land is warm, and we have made the best of the long, summery days.

However, for our ancestors this was a hungry month. Food stores were at their lowest as they awaited replenishment from the forthcoming harvest. The days were long and exhausting, and consisted of endless weeding in dry soil to ensure the best crop yield. The people longed for the festival of Lughnasadh, the Festival of Bread, when the first crops would be harvested with the sickle and the feasts could begin.

So it is at this point of Lughnasadh that these harvests began. The winter crops were harvested first - the wheat and rye, along with the first of the berry crops and followed by the spring crops of barley and oats.

> *I sleep in the kernel, and I laugh in the rain,*
> *I dance in the wind and through the waving grain.*
> *When you cut me down, I care nothing for pain;*
> *In the spring, I'll be the Lord of the Dance once again...*
> 'Lord of the Dance', author unknown

The holiness of the first harvest is firmly woven into the mythology and ritual celebrations of our ancestors, and much of the folklore and harvest celebrations are continue in many farming communities today.

There are several different Pagan myths that surround the festival of Lughnassadh. One of the most prominent is that of Lugh, the Harvest King, who lends his name to the festival. Lugh was worshiped in Britain, Ireland and other Celtic and Indo-European regions under the name of Lug, Lleu, and later, Lugh. He is also recorded in Gaul, Germany and Switzerland as Lugus.

The Irish Lugh was born of a union between his father, Cian of the Tuatha De Dann, and his mother, Ethniu of the Fomorians, and their marriage was a dynastic event between the two opposing peoples in an attempt to unite the two societies.

Before Lugh was born, a prophesy told his Balor, Lugh's grandfather and the evil King of the Fomorians, that he would be murdered by his grandson. So Balor locked his daughter Ethniu in a tower, to prevent her from meeting with Cian and becoming pregnant. However, Cian managed to gain entrance to the tower and Ethniu conceived triplets, one of whom was Lugh. When they were born, Balor discovered the babies and threw them into the sea. Two of the babies drowned, but Lugh was saved and was given to Mannanan Mac Lir, God of the sea and the Goddess Talitiu, who fostered Lugh as their own.

As a young man, Lugh travelled to Tara to train with the

Tuatha De Dann, and he soon became one of them, by demonstrating his many skills of craftsmanship, swordsmanship and magic. At the time, the Tuatha De Dann was oppressed by the Fomorians through slavery and high taxes. So Lugh decided to lead the Tuatha De Dann into battle to gain the people of the Tuatha De Dann freedom from oppression.

He lead a battle against the Fomorians using a collection of mystical weapons, such as a magical pigskin that healed all wounds, and a spear which if shed any blood no matter how little, would seal the fate of the victim and they would die.

Lugh faced Balor, his evil grandfather, who had a poisonous eye that would kill anyone it looked upon. But Lugh shot a stone into the evil eye with a slingshot and the eye was driven out of the back of Balor's head, turning it to look at the Fomorian army instead. And so the Tuatha De Dann were victorious.

After the battle, Lugh found Bres, a Fomorian and the former King of the Tuatha De Dann, alone and injured in the battlefield. Bres had been given the throne of the Tuatha De Dann several years before in a hope to reconcile relations between the two peoples, but instead he had enslaved the Tuatha De Dann to work for the Fomorians, and was exiled seven years later. So on finding Bres alone on the battlefield, Lugh prepared to slay him. But Bres begged for his life. He said that if Lugh spared him he would promise the Tuatha De Dann four harvests a year, and teach them when to sow and plough; a secret known only to the Fomorians at the time. Lugh said just one major harvest would be sufficient, and so the harvests of August began.

Lugh later instituted a festival to mark the August harvests, and also to mark the death of his foster mother Talitiu, who died as she worked hard clearing plains for ploughing. Lugh is said to have introduced the Lughnasadh games, part of the celebrations of the harvest, which are still an important part of the rites today.

Lugh is associated with the sun and considered as a sun deity – his name literally meaning 'shining light'. It is also interesting that the Old Irish word for Leprechaun is 'Lugh-Corpan', which means 'body of light'.

So, as the days become shorter and the wheat is cut down, Lugh may also be regarded as a God of Sacrifice and synonymous to another character of the season – John Barleycorn.

They ploughed, they sowed, they harrowed him in
throwed clods upon his head
and these three men made a solemn vow
John Barleycorn was dead.
Then they let him lie for a very long time
till the rain from heaven did fall
then little Sir John sprung up from his head
and soon amazed them all...
'John Barleycorn', author unknown

John Barleycorn is a folk name for the Corn God – the personification of the Corn itself. He is the maturing God who was born at Yule and courted the Goddess at Beltane, impregnating her with his successor (who is, ultimately, himself). The Goddess now changes to her dark aspect as the year turns toward winter, and she becomes the Death Wielder 'Old Mother Corn' who will sacrifice the Corn God to bring harvest to the land at 'the gathering', or, Harvest Whoam.

So, this is another story of death and resurrection, because along with the death of the Corn God comes nourishment for the people, and the gestating God within the Goddess' womb waits to be born again at Yule. For this reason, Lughnasadh was a time for both celebration and lament. The people would rejoice the coming of the first harvest, yet mourn over the cut corn and pray for its return.

In some customs it was believed that to cut the last sheaf of corn would endow the cutter with the temporary embodiment of the Corn Spirit. This person who represented the Corn Spirit was named Corn Man, Oat Man, or Wheat Man. Depending on which part of the county you were in this could be a good or a bad thing. Some customs would treat the worker like a king for the day; he would be decorated with corn, given a double serving at the dinner table and be waited on hand and foot for the evening, to thank the Corn Spirit for the harvest.

When corne is ripe, with tabor and pipe, their sickles they prepare; and wagers they lay how muche in a day they meane to cut down there.

And he that is quickest, and cutteth downe cleanest the corne, a garland trim they make for him, and bravely they bring him home.
From the 'Shirburn Ballads'

Most customs were harmless fun, such as wrapping the farmer up in the corn sheaves so completely he could hardly be seen except for the face, and then carrying him about the village to symbolise the harvest. However other customs would re-enact the sacrificial side of the festival, and in his book, *The Golden Bough*, Sir James Frazer reports of more ominous harvest customs such as men being seized, wrapped in sheaves and beheaded to symbolise the sacrifice of the Corn God. His blood or ashes would then be spilled upon the earth to represent the reseeding and success of the following years' crops. This holds some similarity to the Egyptian myths of the Harvest God Osiris, whose body parts were scattered about the land after his sacrifice.

However, symbolic sacrifice of the Corn God was also commonplace to represent the harvest, and these customs continue to be followed in folk tradition today. One such popular symbolic custom is that of the Corn Dolly, traditionally made with the last sheaf of corn. These are more commonly made in the image of the sacrificial Corn Mother, 'Callieach', although Neo-

Paganism also embraces the custom of making them in the masculine image of the Sacrificed Corn God. One such infamous Corn Doll is that of the Wicker Man, which, although today is more commonly employed during Beltane, must have originated from the sacrificial time of the harvest. The scarecrow is also said to hold its origin in the symbolic representation of the Corn Spirit, such 'Jack O' Lent' or the Slavic 'Kostroma,' a corn dolly that is dressed and then set alight.

The harvest is almost ready
The bread is almost done
The festival of gathering
Has only just begun
Corn Mother gives birth to the grain
Lugh shines down to bring them on
The corn heads begin to split
The harvest is almost done.
We renew our spirits
Regenerate our life
Harvest our good fortune
And banish troublesome strife.
South heats the seeds;
West waters them to swell;
North feeds the grain that lies beneath;
And east carries the grains' sweet smell.
'The Ytene Poem for Lughnasadh', from the Coven Book of Ways

The festival of Lughnasadh is the festival of harvest and sacrifice in order to bring nourishment and plenty, and effigies of the Corn God would also have been made in dough and eaten to represent the body of the Corn Spirit and the wealth of the first harvest. This is another custom that appears to run parallel with Christian practices, in this case Holy Communion, which has evolved from an earlier Pagan sacrament. The Aztecs also made images of their Gods in dough, particularly the God Huitzilopochtli, who represented the light side of the year that was fading along with the gathering of the harvest. The dough effigy was crowned and adorned, and there was a great deal of dancing and celebration, as well as lamentation and mourning for the sacrificed God, acknowledging both cycles of life and death.

TASK: Lughnassadh Activities
Try these Lughnassadh activities to mark this sacred day.

John Barleycorn/Lugh Doll

Supplies:

Dry straw (animal bedding is ideal)
String (natural, non-synthetic material)
Pen and paper
Cauldron (or other fire retardant container)
Ribbons and other decorations (optional)
Water to hand

Take a handful of straw, about 30cm x 15cm. Grasp the bundle in the middle, and then tie it tightly around the middle with some string. Now split the bottom half of the straw into two parts and tie string around the very top and the very bottom of the two bundles. This creates the legs of John Barleycorn. Now, leaving a space for the torso and arms, tie another knot further up the body to create the neck.

Now take a separate bundle of straw of a suitable size in relation to the rest of the body, lay it across the torso, and parcel tie it to the torso with more string. This creates the arms. Now trim the doll to make the shape neater. If you wish, you can decorate him with ribbons and other trimmings. When you are happy with the doll, place him inside the cauldron, somewhere outdoors where it is safe to have a fire (always have a bucket of water on hand just in case).

Think about what you wish to sacrifice at this time of year in order to reap the rewards of the things you have worked towards this year. You might decide to sacrifice a negative part of yourself that is holding you back, or ask for an old relationship to be put to rest so that it allows you to move on. Write the thing you have chosen to sacrifice on a piece of paper and meditate on its meaning to you. Now fold the piece of paper up and tuck it into the John Barleycorn. Now taking care; set the doll alight. The cauldron symbolises transformation and new beginnings, so as you watch your sacrifices burn know that you are removing past blockages and harvesting those things that you have worked towards.

Once the doll has burnt to ashes, you can scatter the soot upon your garden to encourage fertility and a good harvest for the following year.

Gaelic Lughnasadh Nut Bread

Ingredients:
12oz. malted brown flour
5oz. strong white flour
1 tsp. salt, sugar
1 tbsp. olive oil
1 tbsp. chopped nuts and sunflower seeds
1 pkt. yeast (7g)
300ml warm water
Sesame or poppy seeds
1 egg, 1/2-tsp. salt, 2oz milk and beaten together lightly and brushed on as below.

Before you start, bless the flour by holding your palms above it and drawing the pentagram of earth across it. Blessing flour, wheat and bread in this way is traditional at this time of year.

Mix all the ingredients together with 300ml of warm water (approx. 125ml boiling and 175ml cold) and turn out onto a clean kitchen work surface. Knead the dough for at least 10 minutes then form into the shape of a man, and brush on the egg and milk.

Remember to keep the shape simple and thinner than you want the finished bread to be, because it will grow in size whilst cooking! Now cover with cling film and allow it to rise in a warm, draft-free area; in an airing cupboard or on top of a radiator is ideal, until it doubles in size.

Prior to cooking, re-apply the egg and milk and sprinkle with the sesame seeds or poppy seeds. Cook at 230C (450F) in a preheated oven for approximately 30 minutes, or until golden brown.

O thou cereal deity, I worship thee. Thou hast grown well this year, and thy flavour will be sweet. Thou art good. The Goddess shall be glad, and I shall also rejoice greatly. O thou God, O thou divine cereal, do thou nourish the people. I now partake of thee, I worship thee and give thanks.

Traditional harvest blessing, author unknown

The Solar Year: The Sabbat of Hærfest

21st September
Sun enters Libra
Light and Dark in Equal Measure
Conclusion of the Harvest

Mabon
Alban Elfed meaning 'Light of Autumn'
Harvest Festival
Autumn Equinox

The stang may be positioned in the western quarter of the circle and adorned with seasonal decoration.

Hærfest, or 'Mabon', is one of the Lesser Sabbats of the Witches' Wheel of the Year and falls on the 21st September. The Autumn Equinox (Hærfest) is positioned directly opposite the Spring Equinox (Eostara) on the Witches' Wheel of the Year and marks the second time during the year when light and dark are in perfect balance. This time we see the sun waning, as this equinox marks the drawing in of the year.

During the previous festival of Lughnassadh we celebrated the beginning of the harvest and the bountiful grain. We gave thanks to the Corn King, who was sacrificed in order for the harvest to be plentiful. We recognised those sacrifices of our own that needed to be made in order for us to bring our projects to conclusion, and reaped the rewards.

Farewell O Sun, ever returning light. The hidden God, who ever yet remains. He departs to the land of youth, through the gates of death, to dwell enthroned, the judge of Gods and man. So dwelleth he within the sacred seed, the seed of new reaped grain, the seed of flesh, hidden in the earth, the marvellous seed of the stars.
'Gardnerian Book of Shadows, 1957'
Sourced from the works of Aidan A Kelley

It is now at Hærfest that we see the results of the harvest and the effect of the autumn upon the land. The trees begin to drop their leaves and the latter parts of the harvest – tomatoes, cucumbers and parsnips – can be picked. September is also the perfect time to harvest grapes, and this month marks the beginning of the wine making season; in Greece, it marked the beginning of the preparation for the Festival of Dionysus, the God of Wine. It is also traditional at this time to start preserving fruits, storing the harvest for the winter and cooking with the fruits of the season.

In Celtic Tree Lore the festival of Hærfest lies in the month of ivy, a plant which links this phase of the year with change and transformation, and the Full Moon nearest to Hærfest is named the Harvest Moon. Whereas Lughnassadh marked the beginning of the harvest, Hærfest marks the completion.

We can also see the reflection of the season's change within mythology and within ourselves. It is now at Hærfest that the Sun God sacrifices the last of himself, and descends into the dark womb of the Earth Mother. In some systems it is believed that the Dark Lord (sometimes described as a brother of the Sun God, or named the Holly King, brother of the Oak King) took control of the land at the Summer Solstice, and now at Hærfest brings much-needed darkness and rest. However, some other systems explain the increasing darkness at this time as the *disappearance* of a sun deity, rather than the appearance of a Dark other, such as in the stories of the Greek Kore and the Celt Sun God Mabon (see below). But whatever system we choose to follow, it is now at Hærfest that we really begin to notice the effect of the Dark Lord's power, as the land becomes colder and we feel the beginnings of winter.

The more popular name for this festival, 'Mabon', was adopted in the 1970's by writer Aidan Kelly, in response to the lack of a more descriptive name for the sabbat which all of the other witches' festivals shared. However, the word 'Mabon' was certainly a most appropriate choice, being named after the Welsh Sun God Mabon ap Modron, who was stolen from his mother and taken to the Welsh Underworld, Annwn. He is also known as (probably older) Maponos meaning 'Divine Son'. With the absence of the Sun God Mabon, so the strength of the sun weakens and the land becomes cold and dead. This Celt story is also synonymous to the Greek story of Kore, who was also stolen from her mother at this time and taken to the Underworld. The myths of both Kore and her Celtic counterpart Mabon tell of the change in the season at the point of their transition to and during their time in the Underworld.

Another Celtic myth that reflects this sabbat is that of the Sun God Lugh in his guise of Lleu Llaw Gyffes. Although this tale is connected with the previous sabbat of Lughnassadh, it can also be seen as being linked to the festival of Hærfest. The tale tells of the lovers Blodeuwedd 'the flower lady', and Gronw (a Winter God) who planned to murder Blodeuwedd's husband, Lleu (Solar God) – but because of his divine birth he is protected by a series of magical conditions. One such condition was that in order to kill him he must be stood with one foot upon the back of a goat (physical earth) and one foot upon the edge of a cauldron (the symbol of the underworld) as the fatal blow is struck. This balance between the mortal world and the under-world can be seen as a parallel with the balance of day and night before the year tilts towards winter. Coincidentally, the sign of Libra begins at this time: another symbol of balance. When Gronw defeats Lleu by tricking him into standing in this vulnerable position, and takes his place as ruler of the land; and so winter begins.

Magic during this time includes rites of wisdom, healing, rest and rituals of balance, as well as any activities involved in harvesting and cooking with the fruits of the season.

TASK: Hærfest Activities
Try these Hærfest activities to mark this sacred day.

Rites of the Underworld
Whilst it is the sabbat of Samhaine that is most commonly associated with the underworld, Hærfest is also a time to pay

homage to our ancestors. It is taboo to walk past a grave without paying respect to the dead during Hærfest; it is also traditional at this time to place an apple upon the grave of your ancestors, or upon ancient places such as tumuli and burial mounds. The apple has long been associated with transformation and the underworld, and is said to have the magical powers of eternal life. The apple can be seen as the native alternative to the Greek pomegranate, which gave the wisdom of the Underworld and life after death in the Greek myths; in the same way, Paris hands Aphrodite an apple, (the 'Golden Apple of Discord') just before the abduction of Helen in the Greek 'Judgment of Paris'. Aphrodite is the Greek aspect for the Roman Goddess Venus, and when sliced into two pieces the five pointed pentagram can be seen at its centre; the same five pointed star is drawn in the sky by the movements of the planet Venus over a 40 year period.

We all know the tradition of apple bobbing at Halloween (Samhaine in October) but it is likely that it was also played during the earlier festivities of Hærfest, due to the association of the apple with the defeat of summer and immortality. Ancient Avalon (modern day Glastonbury) was also attributed with the powers of immortality and was called the 'Isle of Apples'. The word Avalon became the Celtic word for 'apple', corresponding to the word *ablach*, which was also woven into the name of the mythical otherworld island 'Emain Ablach'. From the Welsh tale, *The Wooing of Olwen:*

> *Upon the steed was a four cornered cloth of purple, and an Apple of Gold was at each corner. Precious gold was upon the stirrups and shoes, and the blade of grass bent not beneath them, so light was the courser's tread as he went towards the gate of King Arthur's palace.*

The Festivities of Mabon Ap Modron

It was traditional to assemble for Hærfest festivities in high places, such as hills, mounds and viewpoints. There are many high points still open to the public in the British Isles, such as Cley Hill near Salisbury and Old Winchester Hill near Petersfield, both of which have round barrows at the top of them associating them with ancestral energy. Glastonbury Tor is another well known pilgrimage, in the heart of the 'Isle of Apples'.

However, you don't have to travel to a well-known site in order to celebrate Hærfest in this way, as any high place near you will do. Also, any place with 'Saint Michael' in the name may be relevant to ancient Hærfest festivities; like many other Celtic deities, the God Mabon was assimilated into a Christian Saint when Christianity came to Britain, and Mabon ap Modron took a new name of Saint Michael, and the places of his worship came to be associated with the Saint.

If you can, take a trip to a mount near you. Take a picnic to celebrate the bounty of the late harvest, and take berries to leave at the site as an offering to Mabon ap Modron. Feel the turn of the Witches' Wheel as the year hangs in balance: a perfect equilibrium of day and night, dark and light. Feel the gentle sunlight and the chill of the wind as the winter begins to draw nearer. Enjoy the variations in the weather and the changing seasons, which are so unique to the British Isles.

Making Hærfest Pie

This apple and blackberry Hærfest pie is made with the traditional fruits of the season. Serve with cream.

Ingredients:

(Pie Filling)
225g wild blackberries (handpicked)
4 sliced apples (also handpicked if possible)
1/2 tsp. cinnamon
1/4 cup sugar

Handful of dry sultanas
(Pastry)
175g plain flour
40g butter
Pinch of salt
Milk

9 inch baking tin
Greaseproof cooking paper
Pre-heated oven at 220ºc

Mix the flour and salt together and then add the butter, gradually mixing by hand until crumbly. Add 2 tablespoons of water and mix well into a smooth dough. Roll out the dough to a size slightly larger than the tin (say 11 inches depending on the depth of your tin). Place the greaseproof cooking paper into the tin to cover the bottom and sides, and then line the tin with pastry.

Simmer the apples on the hob until they begin to soften, and then strain them thoroughly through a sieve to extract the water. Once cooled, combine the blackberries and sultanas with the apples and place inside the pie. Mix the sugar and cinnamon separately, stirring well, and then sprinkle over the contents of the pie.

Cut another piece of pastry to lay across the top of the pie and seal the edges together by moistening them with a little water. Cut two slits near the centre, and use any excess pastry to make some decorative Hærfest leaves. Place these on top of your pie, again sealing with a little water. Brush the pastry with milk and dust with a few pinches of sugar. Cook at 220ºc for 30 minutes, or until golden brown.

Fate Cards

It is now at Hærfest that the tides of change turn the wheel once more, and we look towards Autumn. At Litha we celebrated the Summer Solstice, when the Holly King took reign over the land,

and since then nature has started to change. The trees are changing colour; the days are getting shorter and the air is getting cooler. All about us is change, yet there is more to come. At this time it is vital that we keep to our commitments, and make a pledge to ourselves which we shall keep.

This working is ideal for a group of people, although it can be done by yourself. Depending on the number of people taking part, cut several pieces of blank card, roughly playing card size, and copy the following four card designs so that you end up with at least two or more of each card:

Mix the cards up face down, and then one by one each person chooses a card at random. The cards will mean something different to everyone; a woman who has recently fallen pregnant might pull the cycles card, a symbol of her change to motherhood; someone starting a new job might pull the journey card, a symbol of their new career prospects; and someone who has fallen upon knowledge in some area of their life might pull the key card, a symbol of their wisdom.

Each person should look deep into the symbol, allowing it to sink into their subconscious, and focus on what they see changing and transforming now and over the coming months. When they are ready, each person should affirm their commitment in which ever area of their lives was brought to their attention by the card they chose.

The card which is chosen is a symbol of the change that is to come; it should be kept upon the altar or in some other special place, either until the matter has been concluded or the person feels the tides have changed again and the symbol is no longer relevant.

The Solar Year: The Sabbat of Samhaine

Sun enters Scorpio
Nutcrack Night
Snap-Apple Night
Shadow Fest
Witches New Year

Saven/Samhuin - Gaelic
Calan Gaeaf - Welsh
Feile Na Marbh – Pronounced 'faylu-nu-morv' meaning 'feast of the dead'

The stang may be positioned between the western and northern quarters of the circle and adorned with seasonal decoration.

Dread Lord of the shadows, God of life and the giver of life. Yet is the knowledge of thee the knowledge of death. Open wide, I pray thee, thy gates through which all must pass. Let our dear ones who have gone before return this night to make merry with us. And when our time comes, as it must, O' thou comforter, the consoler, the giver of peace and rest, we will enter thy realms gladly and unafraid, for we know that when rested and refreshed among our dear ones, we shall be born again by thy grace and the grace of the Great Mother. Let it be in the same place, at the same time as our beloved ones, and may we meet and know, and love them again.
'Gardnerian Book of Shadows 1949'
Sourced from 'Eight Sabbats for Witches' by Janet and Stewart Farrar

Samhaine is one of the Greater Sabbats of the Witches' Wheel of the Year and falls between the 31st October and the beginning of November. In a symbolic reflection of what is happening in nature, the festival of Samhaine also marks the Pagan New Year.

Samhaine marks a complete end to the farming year. The trees have dropped their leaves, the wind has started to become icy and the days grow even shorter. Since the previous festival of Hærfest, the crops having been harvested, the preserves have been made and the food has been stored for winter. It is said that any crops which have not been harvested by the eve of Samhaine will be ruined by the faeries, who start by urinating on the black-berries! All has been made ready for the winter, and it is time for indoor activities, story telling, arts and crafts and merriment.

At the time of Samhaine we begin to turn within ourselves as winter approaches. The period between Samhaine and the approaching sabbat of Yule gives us the chance to think about the year that has passed; we remember the good times we have enjoyed and allow ourselves to accept the mistakes we have made. Samhaine is also a perfect time to work with our deep unconscious, meditation and trance, and gives us the oppor-tunity to sacrifice our outer lives for a while so that we can develop our inner selves. It is a time for pause and reflection, and for using the power of the darkness the surrounds us to nurture us and allow us to rest. Indeed, Samhaine is also known as the 'Sabbat of the West Wind'; the west being the place of rest and renewal. The seed of potential is incubated within ourselves ready to be born at Yule, along with the birth of the sun.

Samhaine is a festival that pays homage to the nurturing power of the darkness; the darkness that allows rest and recuper-ation during the winter months, just as death offers rest for those who need it before they are reborn. In turn, this festival pays respect to those who have passed on before us. It is a time for us to connect with our ancestors, and invite our loved ones who have died to be with us again on this night. It also allows us to embrace the concept of death, and consider our own mortality.

It is at Samhaine that we celebrate the Goddesses of death and the underworld such as the Greek Persephone, the Welsh Cerridwyn, Norse Skadi and the Celt Cailleach. The Dark Gods are also celebrated, such as the Greek Hades, the Egyptian Osiris, the European White Lord, the Aryan Samana and the Semitic Tammuz. All of these Gods and Goddesses have something in common; they represent death and the decent into the Underworld. However, they also symbolise the mysteries of transformation and rebirth; they are the dying and rising deities. As witches we must begin to accept our own mortality and embrace death as a part of life. The deities of the Underworld (and their myths) demonstrate the journey from womb to tomb, and tomb to womb: a cycle of birth, death and rebirth.

The focus on womb-tomb imagery of the ancients is reflected in the ancient long barrows and tumuli of the British countryside. At Samhaine the veil between our mundane world and the other-worlds is thin, and this makes it a great time to visit such places and honour our ancestors; it was at Samhaine that people would visit these graves and commune with their loved ones and relatives who had died. It is also said that the doorways of the Sidhe open at Samhaine, allowing souls to pass from one plain of existence to another; these doorways are found at places of ancestral power, and many can still be visited today, including the Sliabh na Cailleach or 'Hill of the Hag' and the Hill of Tara, both in Ireland. It is at places such as these that we can feel our ancestors most prominently within the land; part of the earth all around us.

Samhaine and Halloween

Nowadays, Samhaine has largely been replaced by the popular 'Halloween' on the 31st October. The word 'Halloween' comes from the Christian 'All Hallows,' the festival of Saints. In an attempt to quash the Pagan festival of Samhaine, the date of All Hallows was moved from the 13th May to the 31st October by the Pope in the 7th Century. However, Samhaine's association with the 'supernatural', 'witches' and 'magic' persevered – all things that were forbidden by the Church. So, now chiefly a Christian country, Britain began to associate the 31st October – or Hallow'een – as a time of evil.

Late October to early November has always been time of misrule and contrariness. Previously called Mischief night, it was a time when minor rules were put on hold and people could play pranks on one another; children would stay up late and silly games were played. The origins of this British custom most likely came from the belief that all natural laws were unstable during Samhaine.

Nigel Aldcroft Jackson writes 'the world of the dead is an inverted image of the world of the living', and in reflection of this, some witches choose to raise two circles side by side on Samhaine night, one for the living and one for the dead. The circle for the dead also represents the Underworld, and the use of two circles can be effective when bringing our world together with the world of the dead. In our coven, we like symbolise the transition between the two worlds by using one circle, as follows; the rite is begun with plenty of candlelight and ended with a spiral walk into the underworld, at which point all light, except that held by the Gatekeeper, are extinguished. In this way, we make the transition from the world of the living to the world of the dead within the one circle.

Samhaine earned its reputation as a 'topsy turvey night', a time between the worlds, when the dead were invited back to be with the living and normal petty laws, such as rules against begging, were put on hold, and such activities were called 'gooding', 'mumping' or, later, 'clementing' – lawful begging . This British custom was eventually absorbed by the American Hallow'een custom, 'trick or treating'. In a similar way to Yule (Christmas) Samhaine has been turned from something spiritual and meaningful into something commercial. The shops are full of plastic masks and cauldrons, and the price of sweets rocket sky high. Many people dread the coming of Halloween due to the trick or treating, vandalism and association with the

Christian devil that has now comes hand in hand with the custom. The meaning of this ancient sabbat must now be reclaimed, so that we may honour our ancestors once again.

A Samhaine Meditation

In this meditation you are going to meet the dark aspect of the Goddess, and come to understand that the dark is not something to be afraid of, but a necessary part of life.

Close your eyes and take a few deep breaths. Focus on your breathing – in, and out, in an out. With every breath in, feel yourself calm, and at peace. With every breath out, feel the tension of the day drain away. Your heartbeat becomes slower, your body becomes heavier. Breathe in peace, breathe out tension. All thoughts of the day and other distractions leave your mind as you become completely relaxed and focused. There is no rush. When you feel completely calm and relaxed, you can begin.

Imagine yourself looking out into a deep forest. It is dark; you can see the silhouetted shapes of the trees, you hear the ghostly hooting of an owl and the rustling of tiny forest creatures beneath the leaf litter. You feel the forest is inviting you, an ancient calling which comes from deep within. Slowly, you make your way into the trees to explore.

You follow animal tracks through the forest, brushing beneath low branches as the dew drips off the leaves onto the back of your neck. It is quiet, dark, organic. You breathe in the sweet smell of the soil and the rotting wood that lies on the floor beneath you.

Soon, you find yourself coming to a clearing, where you spot a great earthen mound. You recognise it as a round barrow: a burial place of our ancestors. Yet, this one is different. As you draw closer, you see that there in the centre of the barrow is a carved stone doorway. This entrance is ancient; a doorway to the otherworlds and access to the mysteries of life and death.

The door begins to open and you see the Crone Goddess, grey and shrivelled, dressed in tattered shrouds and standing in the dim doorway. She beckons you to pass through over the threshold; at first you are hesitant, but you realise that to fulfil your true potential you must face your fears of shadow. So you pass through the doorway, and you enter the otherworld, and the body of the Crone.

The darkness closes around you and you smell the scent of the dark, rich earth. You are tempted to close your eyes but you keep them open, as shadows brush past you and make you shiver, like the cold damp air of a deep cavern. As they pass, you feel their cobweb-like fingers, which touch your face and the back of your neck.

You are passing through the Crone; you feel a nauseous sensation of death, decay and change. Yet you continue on. You see your fears; you see the faces of those who have passed on to the otherworld and those who are waiting to be reborn. Like a mothers womb, this place holds the earth's children, contains them in its body as they wait for rebirth.

Now suddenly you realise you do not fear the Crone, as she is the Mother of all, and the bringer of life as well as death. Upon this realisation, your surroundings change. You suddenly burst out of the darkness into a bright, sunlit meadow, with lush, dew-covered grass beneath your feet. You turn to observe the Crone, who is transformed: now beautiful, graceful, loving and laughing. Only those who do not truly know the Crone fear her. You have learnt that the fearful face of the Crone is an essential part of beauty, balance, and life.

You now turn back to the meadow to observe your surroundings. You are in the otherworld. Spirits of all ages, and ageless, move about this bright place in the sunlight and the warmth. Spirits enter and spirits depart, leaving the shadow lands to be reborn.

And now it is time for you to leave too, reborn and refreshed. You feel the warmth of the earth surround you and you begin to sense the forest again, and feel the leaf litter beneath your feet.

Now fully back in the forest again, you see the dawn

approaching. As as you begin to return to normal awareness you are at peace, and hold the memory of the beautiful woman who laughed when you exposed her disguise. You know that life is eternal, and that there is no death, only passage.

'The Crone Meditation', from the Coven Book of Ways

The Furious Horde

Samhaine brings many other native tales and myths to life. One such tale is that of the Furious Horde, an army of the dead who ride through the land collecting souls, accompanied by the sound of hunting horns and the baying of fierce black hounds.

In Germanic versions of the myth, the Furious Horde is lead by Gods such as Woden or Witch Goddesses such as Frau Holda. In Britain the Horned God Herne is attributed to leading the Horde, his 'Wild Hunt'. It is possible that Herne is an aspect of the Germanic Woden. Either way, the story of Herne is certainly one to tell on a Samhaine eve.

There is an old tale goes that Herne the Hunter,
Sometime a keeper here in Windsor Forest,
Doth all the winter-time, at still midnight,
Walk round about an oak, with great ragg'd horns.
From 'The Merry Wives of Windsor', Shakespeare

The God Herne was once a mortal, a Game Keeper employed by King Richard II in Windsor Forest. He was a fantastic huntsman and an important member of the King's hunting party. His skills to locate the prey were second to none, and the hunt always returned with a handsome kill when Herne was with them.

However, whilst hunting in the Home Park one fateful day, the King's hunting party shot and injured a fully grown white stag. Injured and crazed, the stag turned on them and charged at the King's horse. The King would have surely been killed, but Herne lunged forward and took the blow of the stag's antlers in his side.

It looked bleak for Herne, who was quickly loosing blood and would not survive the trip back to the castle. But suddenly, out of nowhere an old man appeared through the trees who offered to help Herne. The others in hunting party recognised him as a local magician, and the King bid him to step forward and do what he could to save Herne's life.

The magic used by the magician involved tying the antlers of the stag upon Herne's head – a process that, some say, brought Herne back to life as an alternate manifestation of the Celtic Horned God, Cernunnos. When he was back to full health, the magician advised he could remove the headdress and return to work.

The King reimbursed Herne very generously for the loyalty that he had shown that day, with a wealth of gold and a silver hunting horn. However, this favouritism made the others in the King's hunting party very jealous and they began to design a plan to frame Herne, and make him lose the favour of the King. First, they planted three deer skins in Herne's hut, to make it appear that he had been poaching during the night. Next they visited the magician who had saved Herne, and told him of the riches Herne had been given for saving the King's life. Why had the magician been forgotten, and given nothing for saving Herne? Their clever lies made the magician so angry with Herne, that he cursed him.

Next day, whilst out on the usual hunt with the King, Herne failed to find any deer for the King's hunt. The next day, it happened again. Herne had lost his hunting skills. This happened again and again, until the King grew suspicious. Was Herne hunting illegally at night and too tired to hunt during the day? He ordered a search of Herne's house, only to find the three deer skins which had been planted there.

Herne was instantly dismissed from his position, and sent away from the town for poaching and treachery. Herne took a horse and galloped off into Windsor Forest, and was never seen alive again. It is not known what happened that night; whether Herne ended his own life, or if he was followed by those who had double crossed him and murdered. But the next morning Herne was found dead, hanging from an old oak tree in Home Park.

Some time later when the King was out riding alone in the forest, Herne's ghost appeared to him. He told the King the story; how he had been framed by the other huntsmen and cursed by the magician. The King immediately ordered the other huntsmen to be put to death, and they were hung on the same old oak where Herne had lost his life.

The tale goes that the Horned Herne and his two huntsmen lead a ghostly hunt through Windsor at night, searching for other souls to join the hunt, and the appearance of the Hunt is also supposed to be bad luck for the monarchy.

There have been many sightings of the Wild Hunt in Windsor, and also of his horned, ghostly form stood beneath the oak trees. Although the original oak tree is now gone, there has even been sightings of a ghost of the oak tree itself, where Herne's oak once stood.

Some say the Herne name could be a distortion of the Celtic God, Cernunnos, who was also patron of hunting and who was associated with deer and also with the oak tree. It is possible that Herne was simply a translation of the word Cerne, which means 'horn' in Latin.

I like to think that the story of Herne is real; the Royal family certainly believes it, and King George III feared the ghost of Herne so much that he ordered the oak tree be cut down – which may have been a mistake as he went blind, deaf and insane soon after. A replacement oak was planted after his death, although during Queen Victoria's rule she had it cut down and furniture made from it. However, she quickly replaced it with a new oak, when warned of the family curse.

TASK: Samhaine Activities

Try these Samhaine activities to mark this sacred day.

Create a Lantern for the Ancestors

Its punky night tonight,
Its punky night tonight
Give us a candle,
Give us a light
Its punky night tonight!
Traditional folk song, author unknown

We all know the tradition of carving a lantern out of a pumpkin for Halloween. But how is it associated with Samhaine? Although pumpkins can be grown in Britain today, they were originally an American import which arrived along with other American traditions such as trick or treating. However, before the pumpkin, lanterns were carved out of other varieties of vegetable such as mangold-wurzel, squash and gourd. There are many stories that try to explain the origins of carving lanterns out of vegetables. As Christian folklore would have it, the first lantern was a carved turnip, which the devil gave to a drunkard and trickster named Jack. Jack could not enter heaven or hell, so the devil gave him the carved lantern with a single light inside it so that Jack might see his way through the dark. However, older Pagan folklore says that the lantern's purpose is to be placed at the window during the Dumb Supper, (see below) in order to guide the ancestors home.

Carving a lantern

Carve a squash, mangold-wurzel, gourd or pumpkin. If you are using a squash or pumpkin, use the insides to create a warming soup for the Dumb Supper. Once fully carved, position a small candle inside and place the lantern on a window ledge facing out, or outside the front door. Be careful with the candle, as placing the 'lid' back on the lantern can burn it and cause a fire risk. You can then perform the Threshold Evocation.

The Threshold Evocation
From the Coven Book of Ways

The Threshold Evocation communicates to the ancestors that you are opening your home up to them for a short period of time. The Evocation should be performed after dark on Samhaine Eve, and all who will be attending the Dumb Supper should attend the Evocation.

Set the table ready for the Dumb Supper, remembering to set an additional space for the ancestors. Go to the front door and fully open it, placing a small candle at the threshold. Watch it as it flickers in the wind. Then the Threshold Evocation should be performed, in a drum-like chant.

Ancestors, we welcome you, those who have gone before
Ancestors of blood - Ancestors of Spirit - Ancestors of this place
All who come in love and trust are welcome at our table
Ancestors, we welcome you, those who have gone before
Step to our threshold; show your presence by this light
Join us for our Dumb Supper, on this, our Samhaine night.

Watch the candle flicker and continue to chant the verse. Think of the ancestors whom you wish to invite. You may have someone in mind that has passed away. If not, invite a spiritual ancestor who you wish to pay your respects to. The ancestor should now show themselves, normally by the spirit casting a shadow around the flame, the flame becoming still as the spirit blocks the wind, or by the spirit blowing out the candle altogether. Once you are happy that an ancestor is present, stop chanting and say:

Ancestors, we invite you into our home for this, our Dumb Supper. We honour you, your wisdom and your messages. Know that you are welcome here until the stroke of midnight, at which time you will leave and return to your realms in love and trust.

Gesture the spirit into the house, and through to the dining table.

Note: If you feel uncomfortable with the presence that you feel at the door and do not wish to invite it inside, place one palm up facing the door in a 'stop' gesture and draw the banishing pentagram of earth across the door with the other hand. Then kindly ask the spirit to leave your doorstep and find another suitable Dumb Supper, and close the door. Remember, just because the spirit is an ancestor it does not mean that it is automatically friendly. Do your best to invite positive spirits in, and assess the spirit before you allow it to enter. Do not think you are 'obliged' to let it in; it is your home and your domain. Once you have invited the spirit to the table, the Dumb Supper should begin.

Feile Na Marbh – Feast of the Dead/The Dumb Supper

The Dumb Supper or 'Red Meal' should be performed in silence. The beginning of the silence is normally indicated by the single ring of a bell, or the chime of two glasses being tapped together. The Dumb Supper allows us to both pay respect to the dead and gives us a chance to receive messages from them. It also allows us to contemplate on the meaning of the festival, and the time of year. However, the Dumb Supper is *not* supposed to be a sombre occasion. Do not confuse this feast with the dismal mood of a funeral wake! The Supper is a celebration of the ancestor's lives, the things that they achieved and their wisdom after death. It should be a joyful occasion, when we can be reunited for a short time with people we have missed, remember them and eat at the same table once again. *Don't forget to lay a place for the ancestors, and give an offering of each piece of the meal on their plate.*

Some traditional meal ideas for the Dumb Supper are homemade winter soups, such as pumpkin and butternut squash, pomegranate, apples and Barm Brack. Barm Brack cakes are traditionally set out for the ancestors at Samhaine with a glass of wine. Foods of autumn colour and autumn harvest are also suitable, such as fresh bread, berries, organic meat, plenty of root vegetables, preserves and nuts.

Nuts can also be cast upon a fire for divination (after the silence has ended). A single hazel nut can be thrown into the flames to divine whether a wish will come true. If it burns brightly, the outcome is hopeful. If it fizzles out quickly or does not burn at all, it is likely the wish will not come true. Two hazel nuts can be carefully placed together over a fire to divine the result of a relationship. If they burn together, the couple are strong; if they burst apart, the relationship will not last. And if you are lucky enough to have an open fire in your home, it is traditional at this time to let the hearth fire go out, and then relight it from the Samhaine candles for good luck.

Once you have finished the supper, ring the bell once again to signal an end to the silence. You may then take the ancestor's dish of food outside and offer it to the ground, along with other offerings such as cider, pomegranates, nuts and tobacco.

At midnight, sweep the hearth and the threshold with your besom and visualise the ancestors leaving your home. Ring the bell three times to clear the space, and the sabbat is ended.

Crunchy Barm Brack – Irish Soul Cakes

Soul! soul! For a soul cake
I pray good misses, a soul cake!
An apple or pear, a plum or a cherry
Any good thing to make us merry.
'Souling Song', author unknown

Ingredients:

¾ cup butter
¾ cup caster sugar
¾ cup sifted plain flour
3 egg yolks
2 teaspoons mixed spice
2 handfuls currants
A little milk

Cream the butter and the sugar together, and then beat in the egg yolks. Mix in the flour and the spices, and once it is thoroughly mixed add the currants. Add a small amount of milk to soften the dough, and then split the dough into 10/12 small balls. Bake on a well greased baking tray for approximately 20 minutes or until golden. Traditionally, the soul cakes were left out for the ancestors on Samhaine eve, together with a glass of wine and some tobacco, or given to the poor. You can eat them yourself – but be aware they are extremely crunchy, and they might not be suitable if you have sensitive teeth.

TASK: The Wheel of Correspondences

How do the sabbats relate to the seasons, the elements, and the lunar cycle? What familiarities can you find between the corre-spondences that you have studied so far throughout this book? Using the template below, start to put together your own Wheel of Correspondences relating to the sabbats.

You should include:

• Elemental colours
• Elemental symbols (we have done the triangles for you to complete)
• Months of the year in relation to the elements (recommend

you put these around the edge)

- The sabbats on the 8-spoked wheel of the year in relation to the elements, the months and other correspondences
- Moon phases (we have done the circles for you to complete)
- The astrological symbols as the planets move through the Wheel of the Year (recommend you put these around the edge)
- Any other correspondences you would like to include, such as the elementals (i.e. sylphs, salamanders) and magical tools.

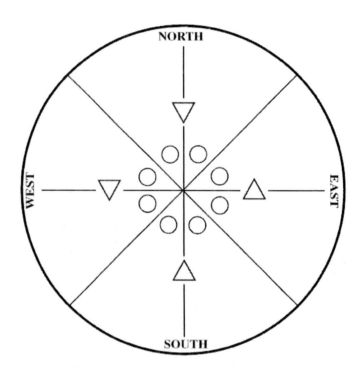

Chapter Eleven

Wortcunning: The Art of Herbs and Incenses

I know a bank whereon the wild thyme blows,
Where oxlips and the nodding violet grows,
Quite over-canopied with luscious woodbine,
With sweet musk-roses, and with eglantine.
From 'A Midsummer Nights Dream', Shakespeare

The art of wortcunning is a skill forgotten by most; however, this ancient craft is something that can be rediscovered. As Pagans, we believe in a close affinity between man and nature, and by reaffirming our connection to the earth and learning about the subtle energy of plants we can again begin to employ the art of wortcunning.

The Witches' Wheel of the Year is a parallel to that of the planting season. Together with an understanding of the solar year along and the effects of the movements of the moon, we can make the best of the omnipotent power of plants.

Herbs have been used for thousands of years as medicines, perfumes and dyes, preventative medicine and as treatment of all sorts of injuries and ailments. Our ancestors saw no separation between what we would describe as 'healing magic' and 'medicine', and they were often used hand in hand by the village wise woman or man to treat the sick. The wise woman, shaman or medicine man were usually skilled in the crafts of midwifery, counselling, and that of the art of herbs. Knowledge of herbal arts was usually passed on verbally from generation to generation: unwritten and received through the hereditary arts. Wood anemone could be used as a plaster for wounds, yarrow for preventing disease, knapweed for aches of the bones, feverfew to cure a common cold and groundsel for protection. All of the herbs that were used were common native species, most which are considered as common weeds to the modern gardener today.

It was not only the village folk who studied and use of herbs, however. Some great scholars throughout history made herbs the focus of their study, in the same way as doctors' work today. Medical texts written on papyri reveal that herbs were used medicinally in ancient Egypt, and Diascorides, a Greek doctor from the 1st Century, described over 500 plants and 1,000 medications in his works. Pliny, a Roman physician, also studied herbs and their medicinal uses. During the Dark Ages, herbalism was employed in monasteries where medical texts were produced and treatments practiced. One of the earliest recorded British herbalists was the monk Bald, who studied the use of magic and herbs, producing a compendium called the *Læceboc*. The book outlined a combination of herbal remedies and folklore. Doctor and Priest William Turner wrote *A New Herball* in 1551, and John Gerard's work, *The Herball*, was published in 1597. The apothecary John Parkinson wrote *Paradisus* in 1629, which later influenced the scholar Culpeper (1616-1664) who lead the way in bridging astrological botany with traditional medicinal uses, in his work, *The English Physician*, published in 1653. M. Grieves then wrote *A Modern Herbal*, which was published in 1931 following Culpeper's work.

Although some of the medieval accounts of herbal treatment have been discounted by modern science as being ineffective, the medicinal properties of plants have been extremely important to the development of modern medicines, which often contain plant extracts of one sort or another. Natural remedies can still be bought in chemists today as valid health aids in capsule, essence or tea form, such as valerian and chamomile for sleeplessness, and even prescribed synthetic medicines are usually based on older natural remedies.

So how do herbs work within magic? In the same way that we can connect with the Gods, we can also connect with the ever-present spirit of the plants and the trees. Once this connection has been made, we can then apply their power to our ritual and magic.

The energy that plants can offer is of immeasurable advantage to us, and our ancestors knew of their properties well. Mankind has learnt how to make the best of both the benign plants alongside their toxic and potentially lethal counterparts. The psychedelic properties of toxic plants, such as iboga and ayahuasca, have been used for thousands of years to induce vision and trance, allowing those who ingest them to visit super-natural realms and encounter their deceased ancestors. In this age of science we now know that it is the chemical properties of the psychoactive plants which cause these visions, however the question remains; does the plant cause us to 'hallucinate' and imagine false visions, or does it open our minds and allow us to reach the unreachable?

Ayahuasca and iboga, along with many other psychoactive plants of a toxic nature, are extremely dangerous to use. It remains a Class A illegal drug in Britain and the US. It must be remembered that the Shamans and medicine men who admin-ister the plant have a lifetime of experience with the plant, together with traditional antidotes and a keen eye which is able to match dosage to the individual. They also use the plant in countries where its consumption is protected under laws of religious freedom. The Egyptians also knew of the powers of plants to reach other states of consciousness, and often adminis-tered a hallucinogen composed of blue lily, opium and mandrake to aid their ritual and magic.

It would be foolish of us to experiment with these substances, just as it would be to try any other dangerous and illegal drug. However, many other herbs vibrate levels of energy and cause change within us, without causing us harm or breaking any laws. Just glancing through a herbal almanac we are spoilt for choice for common plants and herbs which display all sorts of different properties. Many aid us in trance and meditation, some banish spirits and others cleanse the soul. Some display miraculous healing properties, whilst others act as messengers to the Gods themselves.

When a herb is used within magic, it is usually described as a 'correspondence' to the aim of the spell. A system of correspondences is a set of similarities which different things share, and which reinforce and strengthen each others magical and ritual effects. Some things are directly connected whereas others are more distant, connected through a series of links of energy. Things which are more closely connected can be used as correspondences to one another as they effect each another on a metaphysical level whilst also symbolising the power of another thing within ritual or magic. The Heathen concept of the 'Web of Wyrd' can be used to explain this concept of the interconnectedness of all things, as can the 'Microcosm and Macrocosm' philosophy, and the Hermetic 'As Above So Below'.

Nowadays, it is all too easy for modern witches to go into the nearest herbal store or onto the internet to order the herb that they need. In some cases, this is the only way possible, as the herb we need is rare, difficult to harvest, or of foreign origin. However, our ancestors did not have this option. All of the herbs which they used, both magically and medicinally, were from the hedgerows, the treetops, fields and gardens. They were either harvested from the wild, or grown by hand. If they could not get hold of a particular herb, they knew which plant they could use instead.

An understanding of the plant itself is just as important to the witch as the end result, and a good witch should know how to grow the herbs that he or she uses and be able to recognise and harvest them from the wild. I always recommend that at least some of the herbs you use are home grown; many of them can even be kept in pots.

It is also important to know which herbs can harm, as well as which herbs can heal. Just because something is natural (and legal) does not mean that it is necessarily safe. Many common herbs can cause illness, or even death, if ingested. Be extremely careful even if you are handling them, and are in any way unsure.

Planting and Gathering

Planting

Many common herbs can easily be grown from seed without much trouble. Usually April is the best time to sow, but this can vary from herb to herb. Most seeds will be happy in fine, well-drained soil. Using special seed compost is recommended – all-purpose compost can be unsuitable for delicate seedlings; 'John Innes' is ideal.

Shallow seed trays are perfect for sewing your seeds, and since most seedlings need darkness to germinate, cover the seed tray with damp newspaper and lightly water daily. Once the first shoots emerge, remove the newspaper and place the seed tray in the window so that they can start to grow.

As soon as the seedlings have developed and a pair of leaves has fully sprouted, you can then prick them out and plant them into their own individual pots. It is best to handle the seedling by its leaves, rather than its roots or stem, as this can damage the plant.

Once your plants are big enough to be moved outdoors (and grown strong enough to withstand an attack from the slugs and the snails!), dig a larger hole than required for the root, place the plant in the hole and fill the space around the plant with a mixture of loose soil and compost. It is best to plant them out in warmer weather, but if you can't wait for that then you can harden off the young herbs; either cover them with a clear plastic bag over night, or keep them in pots for a while and bring them in to a warmer place (i.e. a shed) during the night, and plant them out after a few weeks.

Magically, when planting always think of the purpose of the seed, the place it will fill in your garden once grown, and the magical virtues it contains. And here's a tip – speaking to your plants really DOES help them grow! Why not design a chant to say over your herbs as you plant them and care for them. Generally, it is considered most auspicious to plant at either moonrise, or moonset.

Gathering

Traditionally, herbs gathered for ritual purposes are cut with the boline or bolline – the white handled knife. The boline blade can be either straight or sickle shaped, although you will probably find the sickle shaped version much easier for gathering herbs.

Folklore says that herbs should never be cut with blades of iron or steel, as this can discharge the plants' magical virtues. Contact with the floor or with the hands is also not recommended, so if you can cut the herbs directly into a basket or a paper bag this helps conserve their energy.

Drawing a circle in the soil around the herb with a wooden staff or wand and project your intention upon the herb itself, asking permission from the herb before cutting. Three circles should be drawn around the plant when harvesting mandrake.

Ensure that the wind is at your back as you harvest the herb. The wind should never be in your face when harvesting for magical purposes, and when cutting, you should never take more than you need. Always thank the plant for what it has given you. Some say that either spittle or blood should be left upon the cut branch as an offering to the plant.

The ideal time of day to begin your harvest is early morning just after the dew dries off the leaves, as herbs concentrate their essential oils in the night and release them when the sun warms the plant in the morning. If the herbs are going to be used fresh, you should collect them immediately before using them, as the longer they are cut the less potent they will be. If you are planning to dry them, you should lay them out to dry straight away after they have been cut, to avoid them withering before the drying process begins.

TASK: Methods of Wortcunning

Research the most auspicious time for planting and gathering herbs, according to the phases of the moon (Lunar Patterns) and the time of day (Solar Patterns). How does this correspond to our Witches' Wheel of the Year and sabbats and esbats, and how can we take advantage of the astrological phases when gathering herbs? If possible, I recommend reading *Gardening and Planting by the Moon* by Nick Kollerstrom, and *Herbs in Magic and Alchemy* by CL Zalewski. I would also recommend reading back over previous chapters in this book which outline the properties of the different phases of the moon.

Then choose a method, and then a recipe, from the following pages and harvest one or two of the ingredients, applying what you have researched regarding the time of day and the phase of the moon to how you choose to harvest. Carry out your chosen Wortcunning method and see how it turns out. Some are medicinal, others are magical; however, magical harvesting should be applied to either method in order to achieve the best from the herb. Some methods can prove more difficult than others, but with some practice all of these methods are achievable. As I have only provided an outline of each Wortcunning method, some additional research may be required.

Herbal Amulets

These are cloth bags filled with appropriate herbs and created with a magical aim in mind.

Taking a circular piece of fabric, approximately four inches across, lay it out flat and sew a circle of plain running stitches all around the edge. When you have finished, pull the thread through until the two ends are roughly the same length. Put the chosen herbs in the centre of the fabric then pull on both ends of the thread to draw the bag closed. Tie up into a knot. When you are sewing, always sew clockwise around the fabric and concentrate on the meaning of the amulet as you are making it. The bag can then be magically consecrated and empowered and placed somewhere that its energies will have a desired effect, such as upon the person, under a pillow, or in some other appropriate place.

Incenses

People have been burning incenses for thousands of years to scent the air, banish spirits, induce trance and reach a magical consciousness. There are several different forms of incenses which can be used including stick incense, loose incense, pebble incense and cone incense. Pebble incense and cone incense are usually made in the same way as stick incense, just shaped into a different form. It is possible to make your own cone, pebble and stick incense but requires some detailed instructions, which I will not cover here.

Loose incense is one of the easiest to make by hand at home, and is burnt on a charcoal disc. As long as the herbs and gums you use within the incense are safe and legal, there's really no rule as to what can and cannot be included within a loose incense. There are however a few key points to remember when making any loose incense:

- Choose an effective base gum or resin, such as Benzoin, Myrrh or Frankincense (this helps the incense burn for longer and binds the ingredients together)

- Make sure you don't crush the mixture too finely (else it smokes too much and burns too quickly)
- Devising your own recipes is a great way of developing new scents, but it is a process of trial and error; many herbs don't smell the same when they are burnt. Perhaps try some conventional recipes first, a few which can be found in this book and many more which can be found in good incense-making books such as *Oils, Incenses and Brews* by Scott Cunningham, before trying to invent your own.

By working with ingredients and listening to your intuition you can create some great incenses, by adjusting the proportions and testing each mix until you find the blend that works for you. Small amounts of essential oil can be added to the mixture; however, care should be taken as one or two drops too many can completely change the scent of the incense. Once finished, put the incense into an airtight jar and store it someplace where it will not be exposed to direct sunlight or extreme temperatures.

Baths, Washes, Soaps, Sprinklers

The method of baths, washes and soaps allows the person to clean with the essence and power of herbs, as a magical cleansing and preparation for the purpose of the ritual or spell which is to be performed directly after. We have used some simple ritual preparation salt baths previously in this book. Soaps are great fun to make; however, as with the incenses, these require detailed instructions that I will not cover here. Sprinklers are a preparation of rainwater and sea salt mixed with a herbal infusion, decoction or tincture, and used as a spray to cleanse wherever is sprayed. For easier sprinklers, oils can be used in place of herbal infusion, decoctions or tinctures.

Candles

We covered the basics of candle magic earlier in the book; however, candles can also be used as a vehicle for oils and other scented materials. The method of adding herbs and oils to candles in any way is sometimes termed as 'dressing' or 'loading' the candle.

Candles can be anointed with essential oils in order to combine the power of the oil with the power of the intent focussed upon the candle. In the same way, oil-anointed candles can be rolled in herbs to coat them with the herbs of our choice, or herbs can be carefully sprinkled into the flame during the spellwork. In this case, the more finely crushed the herb is, the more effective this method will be. Alternatively, coloured wax can be melted on the hob then herbs and essential oils added to the hot wax. A similar coloured candle is then tied to the handle of a long spoon or a knitting needle, and set across the open mouth of a large can. The special wax is then poured over the suspended candle, allowing it to dry slightly between coats. Continue pouring until you have achieved a good coating.

Infusions

These are made by pouring boiling water over fresh or dried herbs, and taken as a tea. Let the herb brew in the hot water for 10 minutes or so, stirring occasionally, then strain off the liquid. Leaves and flowers are most suitable for infusions. Infusions can be sipped hot or hold, but should always be freshly made.

Decoctions

A decoction is generally used to extract the properties of the tougher parts of plants, such as roots and seeds, which must be boiled or simmered to release their essence. Place the herb in a saucepan of shallow water and bring to the boil, then simmer for at least 10 minutes. Cool and then strain off the liquid, squeezing the herbs in order to extract all the juices. I sometimes find that placing the herbs in a smaller container and then within a pan of water means that you are able to bring the water to boil and heat the herbs without scalding them or bringing too much water into the equation. Decoctions can generally be kept longer than infusions (no more than 5 days), although adding an alcohol to the decoction can keep the decoction indefinitely.

Compresses

These are made by soaking a cloth in either a herbal infusion or decoction and applying it directly to the affected area. Both hot and cold compresses can be used, depending on the complaint being treated.

Liniment Rub

Make a liniment rub for tired and aching limbs by mixing one part herbal tincture with one part herb oil. Liniments are good for when an oil on its own would be too hot, i.e. in the treatment of arthritis. Rose and chamomile are soothing and relaxing, and thyme and rosemary infused with peppermint is good for aches and pains, especially after the flu.

Tinctures

Herbal tinctures are fairly concentrated extracts of herbs involving a mixture of water and alcohol, which is taken in small quantities, i.e. half a teaspoon three times a day. The chosen herb is chopped and powdered, then a solution of water/alcohol is poured over it (ratio water/alcohol depends on the herb). The jar is put in a dark place and left for two weeks and shaken every day. After this time, the herb is strained out and the liquid is transferred into a dark glass bottle, where it will keep indefinitely.

Ointments/Salves

A herbal infusion or decoction is prepared, sometimes with

essential oils added, and then stirred into to a mixture of slightly cooled melted beeswax with vegetable oil, petroleum jelly or lanolin, then mixed well and poured into glass jars. The ointment will gradually set and then can be applied to the body for either magical or medicinal purposes. 'Flying Ointment' or 'Unguenti Sabbati' was a common preparation used to anoint the handle of the broom, the wrists and the forehead before ritual. Nigel Pennick writes in his book, *Secrets of East Anglian Magic*,

> *In the trial of Lady Alice Kyteler in Ireland in 1224, a description was given of her 'pipe of ointment', wherewith she greased a staff, upon which she ambled and galloped through thick and thin'. This 'oyntment' was undoubtedly a psychedelic unguent prepared from the Nightshade plant which induced the 'flying trance'. The 17th century antiquarian Praetorius reported that witches are called 'grease birds', due to their use of such preparations.*

Gardner also gives a recipe for an ritual anointment in his *Book of Shadows*, as printed by Janet and Stewart Farrar in *The Witches Way*:

> *'Take some glazed pans filled half full with grease or olive oil. Put in one sweet mint, marjoram in another, ground thyme in the third, and if you may have it, Patchouli, dried leaves pounded. Place pans in hot water bath. Stir and cook for several hours, then pour into linen bags and squeeze grease through into pans again, and fill up with fresh leaves. After doing this several times, the grease will be highly perfumed. Then mix all together and store in a well corked jar.'*

Nigel Pennick also gives an old recipe for flying ointment – tansy, hellebore and wild ginger fried with butter and egg. Variations of Flying Ointment were also used by occultists and high magicians as a way to open astral doorways, using ingredients such as hashish, hemp flowers, poppy seeds, hellebore, cinquefoil and belladonna. Reginald Scot reports of water parsley, ginger, 'blood of a flitter mouse' (a bat) and tea vine.

Note – Herbs such as Hellebore and Belladonna are extremely poisonous! And bats are a protected species. Do not try to recreate these recipes yourself – instead try the safe and legal 'Visions ointment' or 'Sabbat oil' I have given on the next page.

Oils

Essential oils can be used within any herbal magical preparation as listed above, although care should be taken when using them in mixtures that will be applied onto the skin, as some oils can be irritants. Essential oils are also not suitable to be used neat upon the skin, and should not be taken internally. Oils are usually prepared using base oil, such as vegetable oil or almond oil, which can be bought in large bottles reasonably cheaply. Drops of essential oil are added to the base oil to create the required mixture, which can then be used for either magical or medicinal purposes. Other wet ingredients can also be added to oil recipes such as honey and wine.

Some Herbal Recipes

Fillet of a fenny snake, In the cauldron boil and bake; Eye of newt and toe of frog, Wool of bat and tongue of dog, Adder's fork and blind-worm's sting, Lizard's leg and owlet's wing, For a charm of powerful trouble, Like a hell-broth boil and bubble.
From 'Macbeth', Shakespeare

In the past, spells written by witches often contained items such as 'Bloody Fingers' (foxglove), 'Crow's Foot' (cranesbill), 'Snake Head' (balmony), 'Flesh and Blood' (tormentil) and 'Toe of Frog' (bulbous buttercup). In most cases these were simply common folk names given to herbs and plants (some say to keep the real ingredients secret), but it is easy to imagine how this lead to the misunderstanding that witches' potions included all sorts of ghoulish ingredients. Its not uncommon however for witches to incorporate more unconventional ingredients to spells, such as animal fur, snake skin, shedded cat claws and menstrual blood. For the purpose of this chapter I have outlined a few plant and resin recipes taken from my coven's *Book of Ways*. For measuring dry ingredients, I recommend using 1 level tablespoon as 1 part, to make a small, but adequate amount. *Make up as guidelines above.*

Antiseptic Oil

1 tablespoon honey
1 part powdered thyme
4 drops tea tree oil
2 drops myrrh oil

Sabbat Oil

Crush and steep in vegetable oil
1 part Wild Parsley Root
1 part Celery Root
1 part Cinquefoil
½ Saffron
3 drops Poplar oil

Egyptian Kyphi Incense

Easy Method

(Dry Ingredients)
3 parts Frankincense
2 part Benzoin
2 part Myrrh

1 part Juniper Berries
½ part Galangal
½ part Cinnamon
½ part Cardamom
½ part Cedar

(Wet Ingredients)
10 drops Lotus Oil
10 drops Red Wine
10 drops Honey
2 Raisins

Kyphi Directions:
Grind and mix the dry ingredients. Separately mix the wet ingredients. Pour both mixtures into separate airtight jars. Store both
separate containers in a dark place for two weeks. After two
weeks, take ten generous drops of the wet ingredients and add to
the dry, and mix well. Store for another two weeks, stirring daily.
After the two weeks decant into a glass jar and keep stored in a
dark place.

Cold Cure Tea Infusion
1 part Yarrow
1part Elderflower
½ part Peppermint
Pinch Cayenne Pepper
Tsp. Honey

Witches Ointment for extra power in ritual
Store in a pentagram marked jar
4 parts Vervain
1 part Carnation petals (ripped)
4 drops Frankincense oil
3 drops Myrrh oil

2 drops Sandalwood oil

3 drops Orange oil

Altar Incense

3 parts Frankincense

2 parts Myrrh

1 part Cinnamon

Sprinkler Recipe from Key of Solomon

Gather on the day and in the hour of Mercury at a Waxing Moon

1 part Fennel

1 part Lavender

1 part Sage

1 part Valerian

1 part Mint

1 part Basil

1 part Rosemary

1 Part Hyssop

Visions Ointment

Anoint to produce visions

1 part Star Anise

½ part Angelica

2 parts Kava-Kava

Exorcism Ointment

4 drops Frankincense oil

4 drops Peppermint oil

1 drop Clove oil

2 drops Pine oil

Condensing Method: Moon Incense/Sea Incense

To make on an esbat – from the Coven Book of Ways

The incense that results from this condensing method evokes the energy of both the moon and the sea, as well as producing a quality incense that takes its time to burn and doesn't create too much smoke. This incense can then be used in future esbat rituals.

Ingredients:

6 tsp ground Frankincense
Two ground Almonds
4 pinches of shredded Jasmine petals
1 shredded Lily flower
8 seeds crushed Lupin
8 seeds crushed Pumpkin
2 pinches Red Sandalwood
5 shredded Rose petals
3 crushed Star Anise
1 tbs Vervain
2 tbs Salt
¼ pint Warm Mineral Water
1 jam jar

In a mortar and pestle, crush the Frankincense resin into small chunks (no larger than 5mm pieces) but not to dust, as this causes the incense to become too smoky.

Add the other ingredients together and stir (always stir the incense clockwise). When mixing rather than crushing, it's best to use the other end of a spoon or a fork and not the pestle, so that you minimise the risk of crushing the incense any further.

Decant it all into a jam jar, and then pour the warm (not hot) mineral water in on top. Add just enough water so that the entire contents of the jar are just covered. Stir thoroughly, and then place on a window ledge; the jam jar should be exposed on the window ledge both day and night. Over a period of 2-3 weeks, depending on humidity, the water will begin to evaporate, and the mixture will condense. The seawater will also draw the energies from the ingredients, change the smell, and become empowered by the light of the moon.

It is vital that the incense is stirred at least once a day, to keep the mixture loose and moving. It is normal for the mixture to form crusts on the side of the jar; this is part of the process and when you stir it each day break these off the side with a butter knife and mix in with the rest of the mixture.

It will gradually dry out, and when you are sure that it is bone dry and moving loosely when stirred, you can transplant it out of the jam jar and into clean jars, ready for use.

This sort of method combines the ingredients to make low-smoke, high-energy incense that radiates the power of the moon and the power of the sea. Real seawater can be used for this recipe; however, as the salt content of real seawater is significantly lower the incense will not bind as well as it does with a higher content of salt. This method can also be used without the salt to create incense cones. In this instance, you crush the ingredients much, much smaller, and mould the incense into a shape before leaving it to dry.

Herbs for each day of the week:

Heliotrope: Sunday (Sunna's day)
Fern: Monday (Moon's day)
Vervain: Tuesday (Tiw's day)
Spurge: Wednesday (Woden's day)
House Leek: Thursday (Thor's day)
Maiden Hair: Friday (Frige's day)
Nightshade: Saturday (Saeter's day)

Chapter Twelve

Astrology

Astrology is the study of how the movements of the planets in the solar system relate to aspects of life on earth. It is a discipline which is thousands of years old, and holds its origins in the ancient Mesopotamian city of Babylon. Up until the 18th Century, astrology (the interpretation and divination of the stars) was studied alongside astronomy, which is accepted today as an academic science.

When people generally consider astrology, they often tend to think of the sun sign forecasts published in the popular press. This can give rise to all sorts of misconceptions; for example, that astrology is about dividing the six billion residents of the earth into twelve stereotypical sun signs; that the only thing you need to know to analyse a person is their birthday; or that your relationship with your partner is doomed to failure, just because they are an aries and you are a capricorn. This sort of belief gives the impression that astrology is very simple, crude and unchallenging, and it is perhaps fortunate that it only takes a little more digging to glimpse the true nature of this immensely complex subject. It would be remiss not to warn that its study is very challenging, but if you're prepared to work hard and persevere you will also find it proportionately delightful and rewarding.

In magic, each planet is considered in relation to the ruling zodiac sign. For instance any work performed during a Full or New Moon will be more successful if the magic is adjusted according to which zodiac sign the moon is in at the time. We can also choose a suitable day of the week in order to take advantage of a more helpful planet within the spell, and choose a time of day to suit our magic to ensure the most successful outcome.

We can also make the best of the positive attributes of that sign, no matter which sign it is, by adjusting our magic accordingly. So, if the ruling planet happens to be an obstructive influence for the magic – for instance, if you were doing a spell for love, and the period was ruled by Jupiter (not a particularly helpful planet for love) – then you might decide to do the spell on a Friday (ruled by Venus, for love) on the 11th hour after sunset (ruled by Mercury, for overcoming communication problems that may come with the period of Mars).

Tools of the Trade
Professional astrologers must be able to draw up and interpret a complete horoscope from knowing only the date, time and place of birth. As you might imagine, the whole process takes time, perseverance and effort, but it's a labour of love and there is an irresistible satisfaction in perusing the finished work. It may be useful to have the following items in your collection.

Ephemeris
A good ephemeris is essential because it tells you exactly where the planets are at a specified time each day. Try Raphael's Ephemeris, which is also very accurate and has an excellent reputation.

Books
Books are a very good thing for a beginner to have. *Parkers' Astrology* is a superb start, as it not only contains interpretive information, but a chart template, sidereal time tables and ascendant positions, along with a very easy guide on how to calculate the latter. There's also a basic ephemeris for when you're caught short.

Atlas
Because people rarely memorise the longitude and latitude of

their birthplace!

Calculator
Necessary for to-the-minute positions of the inner planets

Maths kit
Acquire compass and pencil, eraser, 360° protractor and a ruler

The Basic Building Blocks: Signs, Planets and Houses
This following portion of this chapter aims to give you a beginner's guide to the various components of the birth chart, or horoscope. The true horoscope, as opposed to your regular sun-sign prediction, is an astrological map of the solar system at the moment of an individual's birth.

The term 'zodiac' refers to the 'belt' on which the twelve star constellations, from aries to pisces, appear to sit, and which encircles the earth. These appear on the circular chart as twelve divisions, each containing 30°. Because our calculations assume the earth at the centre (*geocentric*), the sun and moon's apparent positions are included alongside those of the planets. The chart also includes the ascendant, which is the constellation on the eastern horizon at the time of birth. This measurement has at least equal importance to the sun sign, because it determines a further division of the chart into twelve houses. (Under the Equal House system, which we will use, these are also 30° each in size.) Therefore, each planet simultaneously occupies a sign and a house.

Planets, signs and houses all play different roles in bringing together the birth chart, and it is necessary for the astrologer to have some understanding of them all. A very brief explanation of each is given below; as you continue studying you will come to your own appreciation of their qualities through further reading and (more importantly) your interpretations of individual charts.

The Signs

These are the ones we all recognise. Many people will already know a little about the characteristics of their own sun sign, and possibly those of friends and relatives, too. In the horoscope, the sign occupied by any given planet determines the specific way in which that planet's energy will express itself. Each sign's basic characteristics are as follows:

Aries – the Ram

Ruler: Mars
Traditional Representation: Ram's Horns
Keywords: Self, expressiveness, activity, passion, confidence
Positive qualities: Enthusiasm, quickness, courage, energy, determination
Negative qualities: Selfishness, carelessness, impatience, anger, impulsiveness

Taurus – the Bull

Ruler: Venus
Traditional Representation: Bull's Head
Keywords: Steadiness, fixity, permanence, security, materialism
Positive qualities: Patience, endurance, reliability, warmth, carefulness
Negative qualities: Stubbornness, stolidity, possessiveness, slowness, over-indulgence

Gemini – the Twins

Ruler: Mercury
Traditional Representation: Two Children
Keywords: Communication, flexibility, intellect, logic, adaptation
Positive qualities: Cleverness, versatility, rationality, communicativeness, adaptability

Negative qualities: Inconsistency, superficiality, verbosity, deceitfulness, anxiety

Cancer – the Crab
Ruler: Moon
Traditional Representation: Breasts
Keywords: Family, sensitivity, emotions, protectiveness, intuition
Positive qualities: Affection, tenderness, generosity, humanity, caring
Negative qualities: Moodiness, reserve, resentfulness, over-sensitivity, clinginess

Leo – the Lion
Ruler: Sun
Traditional Representation: Lion's Tail
Keywords: Creativity, drama, leadership, expression, glory
Positive qualities: Assertiveness, creativity, expansiveness, decision, talent
Negative qualities: Attention-seeking, melodrama, aggression, pomposity, bossiness

Virgo – the Virgin
Ruler: Mercury
Traditional Representation: Female Genitalia
Keywords: Modesty, detail, perfectionism, analysis, practicality
Positive qualities: Accuracy, humility, thoroughness, diligence, intelligence
Negative qualities: Over-criticism, nagging, narrowness, nitpicking, carping

Libra – the Scales
Ruler: Venus

Traditional Representation: Pair of Scales
Keywords: Romanticism, peace, partnership, sociability, ease
Positive qualities: Friendliness, calmness, diplomacy, charm, sympathy
Negative qualities: Indecision, changeability, indulgence, petulance, gullibility

Scorpio – the Scorpion

Ruler: Mars/Pluto
Traditional Representation: Male Genitalia
Keywords: Intensity, energy, power, mood, complexity
Positive qualities: Passion, depth, strength, feeling, magnetism
Negative qualities: Jealousy, brooding, sulkiness, secrecy, obsessiveness

Sagittarius – the Archer

Ruler: Jupiter
Traditional Representation: Centaur's Arrow
Keywords: Humanity, spirituality, philosophy, optimism, quickness
Positive qualities: Charity, freedom, humour, honesty, cheerfulness
Negative qualities: Blindness, irresponsibility, tactlessness, restlessness, over-enthusiasm

Capricorn – the Sea-Goat

Ruler: Saturn
Traditional Representation: Goat's Head and Fish's Tail
Keywords: Conservatism, practicality, shrewdness, rules, tradition
Positive qualities: Discipline, wit, groundedness, caution, reliability
Negative qualities: Stagnation, gruffness, over-conventional, rigidity, pessimism

Aquarius – Water Carrier

Ruler: Saturn/Uranus

Traditional Representation: Bull's Head

Keywords: Independence, humanitarianism, originality, pioneering, idealism

Positive qualities: Free thought, compassion, self-reliance, intelligence, freshness

Negative qualities: Reserve, intractability, coolness, perverseness, lawlessness

Pisces – the Fish

Ruler: Jupiter/Neptune

Traditional Representation: Two Fishes

Keywords: Dreams, emotions, illusion, intuition, sensitivity

Positive qualities: Idealism, imagination, sympathy, kindness, intuition

Negative qualities: Delusion, escapism, passivity, wistfulness, weakness

The Planets

The planets themselves represent the various forces actually at work in a horoscope; the fundamental energies that exist within all of us and are manifested in different ways via the signs and houses.

The Sun

Keywords: Self-expression, life energy, conscious

Positive qualities: Creativity, self-reliance, health, generosity, affection, leadership

Negative qualities: Low self-esteem or overconfidence, selfishness, bad luck, authoritarianism, fear, weakness

Notes: Astrologers seem to disagree on whether the sun or Ascendant shows the conscious, open side of ourselves. Tradition has it that this role falls to the Ascendant, while the sun represents our hidden

qualities, but some say this has changed since sun sign personalities are now so widely known.

The Moon

> Keywords: Reaction, intuition, emotion, subconscious
>
> Positive qualities: Patience, sensitivity, caring, imagination, art, talents
>
> Negative qualities: Changeability, narrow-mindedness, over-sensitivity, confusion, fear, failure

Notes: The moon's circuit of the Zodiac takes slightly longer than a cycle from New Moon to New Moon – about 29.5 days. It represents the subconscious, the primal part of us. Together the sun, moon and Ascendant represent the essential integrated self.

Mercury

> Keywords: Mind, communication, movement
>
> Positive qualities: Intellect, perception, reason, versatility, communication, logic, humour, adaptability, craft
>
> Negative qualities: Learning difficulties, nerves, fickleness, lying, cunning, craftiness, speech problems

Notes: Astrologically Mercury is never more than 28° away from the sun, meaning it can only be in the same sign or a neighbouring one. It represents the rational, cognitive part of ourselves.

Venus

> Keywords: Harmony, love, beauty, refinement
>
> Positive qualities: Gentleness, friendliness, tact, beauty, artistic talent, affection, popularity, wealth
>
> Negative qualities: Laziness, infidelity, jealousy, selfishness, coldness, carelessness, indecision, over-dependence, need for luxury

Notes: Venus is always within 48° from the sun and so must occupy a position no more than two signs away. This also means that Mercury and Venus cannot be more than 76° apart.

Mars

Keywords: Physical force, Initiative, drive

Positive qualities: Courage, pride, strength, decisiveness, healthy sex life, fairness, energy

Negative qualities: Rashness, temper, aggression, violence, tyranny, ego, dishonesty, ruthlessness, rebellion

Notes: The placement of Mars often denotes where and how our greatest reserves of energy are likely to be spent.

Jupiter

Keywords: Expansion, popularity, success

Positive qualities: Optimism, loyalty, justice, generosity, happiness, wisdom, thoughtfulness, spirituality, honesty

Negative qualities: Recklessness, over-optimism, vanity, self-indulgence, extravagance, conceit

Notes: Whereas the position of Mars indicates the nature of physical energy in a horoscope, Jupiter brings enthusiasm and optimism to the relevant area of life. Its characteristics reflect its status as the biggest planet in the Solar System.

Saturn

Keywords: Stability, clarity, restriction

Positive qualities: Discipline, practicality, organisation, patience, success, reliability, honesty, frugality, humour

Negative qualities: Rigidity, narrowness, depression, fear, selfishness, cruelty, excessive limitations, stagnation

Notes: Until Uranus was discovered in 1781, Saturn was believed to be the outermost planet. Therefore it has come to represent boundaries and restrictions.

Uranus

Keywords: Change, disruption, shock

Positive qualities: Originality, versatility, independence, genius

Negative qualities: Delusions, perversions, rebellion, emotional outbursts, stubbornness

Notes: Because their orbits around the sun (and therefore their Zodiac circuits) take a long time to complete, Uranus, Neptune and Pluto are believed to have generational rather than personal influences through the signs, although their house position is still an individual matter. Uranus' effects concur well with the astronomical upheaval caused by its discovery.

Neptune

Keywords: Illusions, unreality, mist

Positive qualities: Arts, idealism, imagination, sensitivity

Negative qualities: Carelessness, indecision, deceit, delusions, drugs, 'victim' feelings

Notes: Neptune is the planet of illusions, its influence often lending confusion to a situation or decision. That it is now officially the outer planet in the Solar System may be suggestive!

Pluto-Charon

Keywords: Drastic changes, annihilation, explosion

Positive qualities: Overcoming difficulties, healing, regeneration, creativity

Negative qualities: Slyness, criticism, secrecy, cruelty, obsessive-compulsive disorders, extremism

Notes: Although Pluto has now been relegated to the status of 'dwarf planet', its astrological influences are still considered important in horoscope casting.

Chiron

Keywords: Wounded healer, Achilles' heel

Positive qualities: Inner power, bravery, daring, mirth

Negative qualities: Illness, weakness, psychological disorders, imbalance

Notes: The effects of Chiron, being relatively new to the astrological

family, are still being debated.

Planetary Days
Each experiment or magical operation should be performed under the planet, and usually in the hour, which refers to the same.

From The Key of Solomon

Monday	Ruled by the Moon
Tuesday	Ruled by Mars
Wednesday	Ruled by Mercury
Thursday	Ruled by Jupiter
Friday	Ruled by Venus
Saturday	Ruled by Saturn
Sunday	Ruled by the Sun

Planetary Hours
There are twelve planetary hours between sunrise and sunset, and the same between sunset and sunrise, which means the duration of each day and night 'hour' will change on a daily basis. Witches see the day as beginning at dawn and ending at dusk, and attribute the planet accordingly.

TABLE 12.1

Hrs from sunrise	Sunday	Monday	Tuesday	Wednesday	Thursday	Friday	Saturday
1st	Sun	Moon	Mars	Mercury	Jupiter	Venus	Saturn
2nd	Venus	Saturn	Sun	Moon	Mars	Mercury	Jupiter
3rd	Mercury	Jupiter	Venus	Saturn	Sun	Moon	Mars
4th	Moon	Mars	Mercury	Jupiter	Venus	Saturn	Sun
5th	Saturn	Sun	Moon	Mars	Mercury	Jupiter	Venus
6th	Jupiter	Venus	Saturn	Sun	Moon	Mars	Mercury
7th	Mars	Mercury	Jupiter	Venus	Saturn	Sun	Moon
8th	Sun	Moon	Mars	Mercury	Jupiter	Venus	Saturn
9th	Venus	Saturn	Sun	Moon	Mars	Mercury	Jupiter
10th	Mercury	Jupiter	Venus	Saturn	Sun	Moon	Mars
11th	Moon	Mars	Mercury	Jupiter	Venus	Saturn	Sun
12th	Saturn	Sun	Moon	Mars	Mercury	Jupiter	Venus

Hrs from sunset	Sunday	Monday	Tuesday	Wednesday	Thursday	Friday	Saturday
1st	Jupiter	Venus	Saturn	Sun	Moon	Mars	Mercury
2nd	Mars	Mercury	Jupiter	Venus	Saturn	Sun	Moon
3rd	Sun	Moon	Mars	Mercury	Jupiter	Venus	Saturn
4th	Venus	Saturn	Sun	Moon	Mars	Mercury	Jupiter
5th	Mercury	Jupiter	Venus	Saturn	Sun	Moon	Mars
6th	Moon	Mars	Mercury	Jupiter	Venus	Saturn	Sun
7th	Saturn	Sun	Moon	Mars	Mercury	Jupiter	Venus
8th	Jupiter	Venus	Saturn	Sun	Moon	Mars	Mercury
9th	Mars	Mercury	Jupiter	Venus	Saturn	Sun	Moon
10th	Sun	Moon	Mars	Mercury	Jupiter	Venus	Saturn
11th	Venus	Saturn	Sun	Moon	Mars	Mercury	Jupiter
12th	Mercury	Jupiter	Venus	Saturn	Sun	Moon	Mars

The Houses

While a planet's sign denotes the way in which it will operate, the house placing informs us of the sphere of life in which it will be most influential. In the chart, the house positions in the zodiac are determined by the Ascendant (and in some systems the *Midheaven*).

The first house

Corresponding sign: Aries

Natural ruler: Mars

Governs: Psychological motivation, self-expression

The second house
Corresponding sign: Taurus
Natural ruler: Venus
Governs: Security, finances, partners of all kinds

The third house
Corresponding sign: Gemini
Natural ruler: Mercury
Governs: Close relatives (but not parents), communication, travel, learning

The fourth house
Corresponding sign: Cancer
Natural ruler: Moon
Governs: Parents (possibly the mother in particular), family life, home

The fifth house
Corresponding sign: Leo
Natural ruler: Sun
Governs: Creativity, love, lovemaking, children

The sixth house
Corresponding sign: Virgo
Natural ruler: Mercury
Governs: Work, health, attitudes to people who work for us

The seventh house
Corresponding sign: Libra
Natural ruler: Venus
Governs: Romantic relationships, friendships

The eighth house
Corresponding sign: Scorpio

Natural ruler: Mars/Pluto
Governs: Deep psychology, sex, death, legacies

The ninth house
Corresponding sign: Sagittarius
Natural ruler: Jupiter
Governs: Spirituality, philosophy, learning, long term travel

The tenth house
Corresponding sign: Capricorn
Natural ruler: Saturn
Governs: Career, ambition, authority, parents (some say the father)

The eleventh house
Corresponding sign: Aquarius
Natural ruler: Saturn/Uranus
Governs: Charitable feelings, humanity, social circle, friends

The twelfth house
Corresponding sign: Pisces
Natural ruler: Jupiter/Neptune
Governs: Sacrifice, escapism, psychological issues

Divisions of the signs

A further way to understand the twelve zodiac signs is contained in their traditional divisions into categories of polarity (two groups), mode or triplicity (three groups) and element or quadruplicity (four groups).

Polarity is archetypal gender – positive/masculine and negative/feminine (note that *positive* and *negative* here do not mean the same as good or bad – in astrology all forces have the potential to be both). The word archetypal is used because the qualities of each are contained in both men and women; they are simply the divine principles of the masculine and feminine, equal in necessity and status. Modes, or qualities, are Cardinal, Fixed and Mutable. The Cardinal signs are indicators of leadership and authority; the Fixed signs of steadiness and stubbornness; the Mutable of adaptability and changeability. The elements are the well-known four elements of fire, earth, air and water, already covered earlier in this book. The element of each sign is linked to the polarity: earth and water signs are feminine or negative; fire and air signs are masculine or positive.

When these three divisions are applied to the signs, it will be observed that the combination is unique for each, as follows:

TABLE 12.2

Sign	Polarity	Quality	Element
Aries	Positive	Cardinal	Fire
Taurus	Negative	Fixed	Earth
Gemini	Positive	Mutable	Air
Cancer	Negative	Cardinal	Water
Leo	Positive	Fixed	Fire
Virgo	Negative	Mutable	Earth
Libra	Positive	Cardinal	Air
Scorpio	Negative	Fixed	Water
Sagittarius	Positive	Mutable	Fire
Capricorn	Negative	Cardinal	Earth
Aquarius	Positive	Fixed	Air
Pisces	Negative	Mutable	Water

Other features of the birth chart

Ascendant

The Ascendant is the degree of the zodiac on the horoscope that was rising at the time of birth, and is located on the left of the chart. It is the starting point of the birth chart, and determines the positions of the houses (sometimes accompanied by the Midheaven). Therefore, it is crucial to the horoscope. The Ascendant sign and the sun sign together give clues to the nature of the subject's outer expression and inner self. Traditionally, the latter has been the indicator of the hidden personality, but it has been argued that since people are generally aware of how the various sun signs are supposed to behave, this role has now shifted to the Ascendant. The opposite of the Ascendant is the Descendant, which is placed on the right hand side of the chart and is linked to the seventh house and its corresponding issues.

Midheaven

The Midheaven or Medium Coeli (MC) is the degree of the zodiac directly above the subject at the moment of birth, and will therefore be shown at or near the top of the chart. The characteristics of the MC are closely related to the tenth house, in that these are the qualities the subject tends most to respect, admire and wish to imitate. Career and ambition are associated with the MC as well.

The opposite of the MC is the Imum Coeli (IC), which is around the bottom of the chart and relates to family and roots, and other fourth house matters.

The North and South Node

The earth is tilted on its axis at roughly 23 degrees as it orbits the sun. The resulting changes in proximity to the sun between the North and South Hemisphere give us the seasons. However, what we see from earth is the sun appearing to move at an angle of 23 degrees relative to the Equator. The apparent path of the sun as it travels through the zodiac is known as the ecliptic.

The moon, meanwhile, orbits the earth at an angle that appears to differ from the ecliptic by 5 degrees. Consequently, the two paths cross at two points, known as the Lunar Nodes. Astrologically, the North Node is linked to Jupiter and represents our potential or ambitions, while the South Node is related to Saturn and restrictions or convention, or the status quo. The nature of the Nodes' influence is mostly based on their sign and house position.

Aspects

As if considering all of the above in interpreting a birth chart was not complicated enough, it is also necessary to examine how the planets, angles and nodes relate to one another using the aspects they form.

Where an aspect is present, it simply means that a significant angle has been formed between two bodies. The significance derives from being a notable fraction of the 360° total of the zodiac. The angle does not have to be exact; for each aspect there is an 'orb' of acceptable range either side of the optimal position. The most commonly used aspects are as follows:

Aspect	Quality	Angle	Orb
Conjunction	Neutral	0°	8°
Opposition	Negative	180°	8°
Trine	Positive	120°	8°
Square	Negative	90°	8°
Sextile	Positive	60°	6°
Quincunx	Weak negative	150°	2°
Sesquiquadrate	Weak negative	135°	2°
Semi-square	Weak negative	45°	2°
Semi-sextile	Weak negative	30°	2°

The interpretation of the aspects is assisted by using the quality given. Positive aspects suggest that the forces in question are working together harmoniously, giving the subject ease in that part of their life. Negative aspects set energies against one another, and therefore offer challenges. However, this is not considered to be a problem necessarily; there appears to be a consensus that such aspects bring grit and strength to the character. Most charts have a mixture of both types of aspect in them.

The conjunction is neither positive nor negative, but indicates that the forces involved are working on the same wavelength.

This can be either helpful or harmful in practice, rather like when two people live together: they can either tread on each other's toes or get along famously!

Aspect patterns

When examining the finished birth chart some patterns can appear, in which aspects effectively 'team up', offering yet more food for thought. Here are some to look out for:

Grand Trine – Three planets each making a trine aspect to the other, creating an equilateral triangle in the chart. A harmonious aspect but can make life too easy for the subject. Best when appearing alongside a T-square.

Grand Cross – Four planets forming a square on the chart, making squares and oppositions between them. This is quite rare and suggests the subject will face a major challenge. This could either be inspirational or harmful, depending on how the subject deals with the issue.

T-square – Two planets opposite one another with a third squaring them both. Looks like a right-angled triangle on the chart. This is a less heavy, and more common, version of the Grand Cross.

Stellium – A group of three or more planets in one sign (or less, usually one house), often involving multiple conjunctions, although this is not necessary. This gives an emphasis to the occupied sign or house. The more planets are involved, the stronger the emphasis will be.

Chapter co-written with Talenthia – Coven Maiden and Astrologer

TASK: Beginners Astrology

How would you interpret the following if you found them in a birth chart?

Jupiter in Sagittarius in the fifth house
Venus in Virgo in the seventh house
Mercury in Libra in the third house

Remember to consider the effects of aspects and rulerships. How might your interpretation change if the planet was well or poorly placed?

Chapter Thirteen

Manifesting Deity Within

The rivers I can make retire, into the fountains whence they flow, whereat the banks themselves admire, I make standing waters go. With charms I drive both sea and cloud, I make it calm and blow aloud The vipers' jaws, each rock and stone, with words and charms I avow. The force of the earth conjoined in one, I move and shake both woods and plain, I make the souls of men arise, whilst I pull the moon out of the skies.

'The Charge of Hecate', adapted from 'Metamorphoses' by Ovid

What do we mean when we say manifesting deity within? In previous chapters we discussed how deity is all omnipotent and transcending, yet has the ability to be in all things. In this way, deity is defined and given names and faces. Deity finds it's most recognisable face in the Gods and Goddesses, the archetypal spirits and energies which allow us to relate to deity directly.

Divinity is in everything: the rocks, the trees, the birds, the wind, the sea, and even within us. We don't need to be working witches to have deity within; each and every person on the planet is part of The All. No matter who we are we all display different characteristics and energies, all of which are part of divinity.

However, the difference between witches and the normal layperson is that as followers of the Craft, witches have the ability to tap into a particular energy of a deity that would normally be out of reach. For instance, somebody who is very timid by nature may decide to work with a God or Goddess of strength in order to deal with a particular situation in their lives. Someone who is finding it difficult to bond with their new baby may need to work with a God or Goddess of compassion and childbirth. By working with a particular deity and taking on their energy we are filled with that individual power; we can develop mentally, spiritually and physically. Different cultures call this practice of taking on a divine energy different names; as witches, we call it an Invocation, or an Evocation.

We have briefly touched upon Invocation and Evocation in previous chapters; however, this chapter is dedicated to these two magical arts and the differences between them. The words 'Invocation' and 'Evocation' mean two very different things, and are often confused by practitioners. I have given a detailed study of the two methods below.

- An **Evocation** describes the method of inviting a deity, spirit or other entity to join you either in or at the edge of the circle, to observe your ritual and offer their energies to help you perform it

- An **Invocation** describes the method of inviting a deity or spirit to enter your body. In this way, the Priest or Priestess becomes that spirit or deity itself, and speaks and acts for that which has been invoked.

Evocation

So what do we mean by Evocation? Let's first look at what it means to be evocative – to evoke.

One non-magical dictionary definition says to 'evoke' or to be 'evocative' is 'to bring a feeling vividly to mind' or 'to elicit or prompt a reaction, emotion, or memory.' So how does this understanding help us with our magical Evocations?

Think about things in your life which evoke certain memories, feelings and reactions. It could be the smell of the laundry that reminds you of your children, or those old photographs that always make you laugh. What about a certain place which always sends you down memory lane? A red wine that reminds you of your holiday in Italy? All of these things are very evocative, and, although they are not particularly magical, they are still sending you into a particular mind frame and consciousness.

So the method of Evocation is first based on our ability to enter a particular state of mind that allows us to access our higher consciousness, where we may then observe and interact with the energies that we have evoked. And this is the key to Evocation. It is not a matter of saying the words and waiting for something to turn up! When we are evoking a particular spirit or deity, we are conjuring their presence both physically AND mentally; that is, allowing our own minds to tap into a consciousness where we are able to see, feel and interact with the energies which we have evoked.

So the use of our senses – vision, touch, smell, sound and taste – can be very powerful triggers to help us get into a specific mind frame for Evocation. We have covered various correspondences for deities throughout this book; for example, associated colours and scents. On researching a particular spirit of deity, we may compile a list of correspondences associated with them. The use of these associations helps the Evocation on a magical level (by way of the 'collective unconscious') and also on a mental level (as our mind begins to create associations of its own). The power of our own minds in the practice of Evocation is just as important as the magical words or gestures that we may perform.

So then, a good knowledge of the spirit or deity that we are evoking is also of importance – the more we research, the more we can recognise and connect with the spirit. Researching their origins, mythology, family, correspondences, and their likes and dislikes is helpful. Try also to gain more than just a superficial understanding; what do their myths mean to you? How do you relate to that deity? How does the deity and their myths relate to the Wheel of the Year, and the cycles of life? Apply your knowledge, and use the correspondences to add to the experience of Evocation. Then, as you begin regularly working with a specific deity or spirit, your own mind begins to create associations, and Evocation will become easier.

Evoking Spirits and Evoking Deity: The Difference

The word Evocation has in recent years been more typically associated with the practices of High Magic. Very briefly, the art of High Magic focuses on the Evocation of spirits by way of complex rituals, employing ritual formulae from the Grimoires, such as the Lesser and the Greater Key of Solomon and the Goetia. High Magic focuses on the conjuration of spirits in order to direct them to do the bidding of the magician (and does not typically perform the Evocation of deity for the purpose of religious ritual). All sorts of spirits can be evoked through High Magic, both benign and malignant. The use of tools such as the Dark Mirror (similar to the witches scrying bowl or mirror) and the Triangle of Art are often used for the conjuration of spirits.

Although modern witchcraft does borrow some practices from High/Ceremonial Magic and visa versa, High Magic is not the same as practising Initiatory witchcraft or Wicca. Although it *is* considered a spiritual path, the practice of High Magic is typically not a religion. God Names are used: however, these are not usually seen as individual deities, more like Words of Power which evoke certain aspects of the One Power. Opinions vary.

Very simply, the differences between evoking deity and types of spirits are as follows:

- When we evoke a deity, we put our trust into that God or Goddess. They are a Higher Power. We ask them kindly to attend our rite and aid our workings. They have ultimate power, and we must treat them as what they are – Gods. Some old Grimoires include operations that appear to order the Gods around as if they were low spirits – this I do not agree with, and if you choose to follow such operations then good luck! When evoking a deity in our coven, we petition that God to attend our rite, and give offerings after the ritual to thank them for their presence.

- When we evoke other types of energy, for instance an elemental, a Daemon from the Goetia (not recommended!) or any other spirit, much more care must be taken. Spirits are not always benign and they are not easily controlled. As mentioned above, High Magicians usually conjure spirits within the Triangle of Art. Artificial spirits can also be created within the Triangle of Art, called Egregores, or Thought Forms. However – and this is an important point – the triangle is always placed OUTSIDE of the circle. This means that the magician is protected within the circle from the spirit he or she has evoked outside. This also partly explains why, when calling the quarters of the Compass, witches invite the elements and their associations (i.e. elementals etc) to the EDGE of the circle, and not within. This must to some extent impress the importance of a secure magical circle when performing any sort of Evocation of spirits. The banishing of any sort of spirit is VERY important.

For this chapter's task, we are only going to focus on the Evocation of deity – that of the Gods. The conjuration of other spirits is certainly an option open to you, but I will not cover it here. I would not recommend attempting the Evocation of any sort of entity without the help of an experienced High Priest, Priestess, or other experienced magical practitioner.

Operations of Evocation

When we begin an Evocation we combine our knowledge of the deity and its associations and then our own intent. We bring all of these practices together in order to empower our Evocation. So then, the operations for Evocation can be outlined as follows:

Scent: *Incenses, oils etc*

Sound: *The spoken word – Petition to the deity or Spirit, Vibration of God Names*

Taste: *Libation (blessed cakes and wine)*

Touch: *Tools, oils, robes etc*

Vision: *The circle, the magical tools, statues, talismans, etc*

Visualisation: *Quieting and centring the mind on the one focus*

The Mind: *The combination of these operations and reflection on their significance*

Trust: *Complete belief that the Evocation will work*

The element of TRUST is very important. We must know that our Evocation will work. Sometimes the spirit or deity will make themselves known to you, other times they will not. If you don't see something manifest, or you don't feel a distinct change in the energy of the circle, this does not mean that your Evocation has not worked!

It is also important to remember that Evocations of deity can occur at any point of a ritual when the God or Goddess is the focus of the proceedings. This could include *The Witch's Rune* (when the God names are chanted), or the reciting of the *Charge of the Goddess* or the *Charge of the God*. Evocation of deity does not necessarily only happen when we ask for it, and the God or the Goddess may well turn up when we are not expecting them.

Occasionally, we may even discover that the energy of the spirit or deity experienced first hand is completely different to what we expected from the results of our research. It is very important to remember that our own experience of a deity or spirit is just as valid as what is written in any book. What is in books (including this one) is only the opinion of one person and should be used as guidance only. Such knowledge should be approached with an open mind – you might experience things slightly differently, but that does not mean your experience was wrong. There is no 'right' or 'wrong' way to interpret the Gods.

TASK: Practising Evocation

I have listed below some Evocations from the coven's *Book of Ways* that you may employ in your rituals over the next month. As you gain experience of working with deities and Evocations, you will begin to find that you no longer need to use a pre-written Evocation. Most Initiatory Craft Priests and Priestesses find that as they work with the Gods they start to be able to receive inspiration on the spot, and most experienced covens do not work with scripts of any kind at all.

Remember to choose the deities who you feel comfortable with and you are drawn to. You may decide to write your own Evocations using these ones as a guide, or adapt one below to suit you and your chosen God and Goddess. An Evocation can be as long or as short as you like, and it can rhyme if you wish. You should try the same Evocation a few times, to monitor the difference, as you become more experienced at the practice. You should also practice evocations for both Gods and Goddesses; for simplicity I have outlined evocations for deities who work well together next to one another.

In our coven, we do not command the deities to leave the circle when the rite has ended; we allow them to make this choice, and simply thank them for their presence.

These Evocations should always be performed within a magic circle and with preparation as outlined previously in Chapter Eight.

Simple Method of Deity Evocation

Placing the palms on either side of the altar, close your eyes and still your mind. Employ one of the meditations beforehand if it helps. Listen to your breath, in, out, in, out.

Now open your eyes and look at your altar with fresh eyes. See the images that you have placed there; observe the colours of your chosen God or Goddess. Smell the sweet scent of the oils and incense you have selected. Use your entire sensory system to soak in the atmosphere that you have created, which is tailored to your chosen deity.

Now, closing your eyes for another moment, visualise that deity strongly. See them before you. Then recite your Evocation. Try a different one each Full Moon, and monitor how these Evocations went; what differences did you find between each of them? How did the energy differ, and how did each one make you feel?

A Generic Evocation to the Goddess

Gracious Goddess of the moon
Mistress of magic and rebirth
Lady of the harvest
And Mother of the earth
I invite you to join me in this, my rite.
I bid You, Hail and Welcome!

A Generic Evocation to the God

Shining God of the sun
Lord of warmth, keeper of the skies
You who are sacrificed
And then are born again
I invite you to join me in this, my rite.
I bid You, Hail and Welcome!
A European Evocation to the Goddess

Hail, Brigid
I call unto thee, Lady of golden hair
Bestow upon me the secrets
Of the sacred fires of creation
I invite you to join me in this, my rite.
I bid You, Hail and Welcome!

A European Evocation to the God

Hail, Cernunnos
I call unto thee, O Horned One
Lord of the wilds, come unto my side
So that I might know your nature.
I invite you to join me in this, my rite.
I bid You, Hail and Welcome!

An Egyptian Evocation to the Goddess

Great Goddess Isis
Lady of stars
Giver of life, beautiful in heaven
Rise in peace, rise in beauty
As I invite you to join me in this, my rite.
I bid You, Hail and Welcome!

An Egyptian Evocation to the God

Osiris, Beloved of Isis
Lord of resurrection, God of secrets
Darkness is banished
By the presence of your majesty
As I invite you to join me in this, my rite.
I bid You, Hail and Welcome!

Invocation

'Don't think of me. Never mind the human woman. Think of the Priestess in the mirror. All women are Isis, and Isis is all women. Watch the mirror...'
Dion Fortune, 'Moon Magic'

The word 'invoke' literally means 'voice inside', or 'to call inwardly'. An Invocation allows the Priest or Priestess witch to become one with the deity, speak their words and see through their eyes. Verbal prophesies are often given by the God or Goddess whilst they have the opportunity, as well as advice or messages to the other coveners.

For the benefit of the onlooker the invocation is said outloud, but for the purpose of the invocation itself it is just as effective if performed silently. The sound causes a reaction within the listener, whilst the inner meaning of the sound vibrates through the unconscious. To put more simply, it doesn't matter how loudly we call out; it is the intent that will reach the deity, not the volume.

It is important to remember that in order for Invocations to be performed the witch must be 100% confident in the circle that has been cast and the ritual that has been carried out beforehand. When we perform an invocation, we open up ourselves to allow the deity to reside within us. In the event of a circle not being properly made, we are leaving ourselves open to all sorts of other spirits to take up residence within our bodies.

Invocation was a common practice in Egyptian temples. David Rankine writes in his book, *Heka: Ancient Egyptian Magic and Ritual*,

Many of the spells and rituals (relied) *on the magician assimilating the deity into himself, effectively becoming the deity, and so gaining the powers associated with that deity. By becoming the deity a*

magician greatly increased his level of heka (magic) *ensuring the effectiveness of the magic he would perform.*

In a modern coven an invocation is usually undertaken by performing the five-fold kiss, adapted from the *Gardnerian Book of Shadows* and as published by Janet and Stewart Farrar in *The Witches Way*. In earlier records, Gardner refers to the Five Fold Kiss as the Five Fold Salute. The Priestess first prepares herself by connecting with the altar, then turns with her back to the altar and stands in the 'Osiris position' (arms crossed over the breast). The scourge and the wand are often used together at this point, to show command and magical power. The Priest then invokes the Goddess into the Priestess, by using the five-fold kiss. (The five-fold kiss is also used upon the Priest when invoking the God. In this case, the Priestess invokes the God into the Priest using a similar set of actions and words.)

The five-fold kiss symbolises of the adoration of eight points upon the body – the feet, the knees, the womb (or phallus), the breasts (or chest) and the lips – and creates a five-fold path across the body. The five fold kiss is immediately followed by an ad-lib call to the Goddess by the Priest, and then the standard invocation, all as follows.

The Five Fold Kiss & Invocation of the Goddess

The High Priestess takes up the wand and scourge and assumes the Osiris position. The High Priest, kneeling before her, performs the five fold kiss:-

Blessed be thy feet, that have brought thee in these ways.
Priest kisses her feet.
Blessed be the knees, that shall kneel at the sacred altars.
Priest kisses her knees.
Blessed be thy womb, without which we would not be.
Priest kisses her abdomen.

Blessed be thy breasts, formed in beauty.
Priestess raises her arms and Priest kisses her breasts.
And blessed be thy lips, that shall utter the sacred names.
Priest kisses her lips.

Priest steps back to adore the High Priestess and speaks the standard invocation:

I invoke thee, mighty Mother of of all life and fertility. By seed and root, by bud and stem, by leaf and flower and fruit, by life and love do I invoke thee, into this your High Priestess and servant.

The purpose of the five-fold kiss is an important one. Firstly, it opens up the Chakras of the body, to allow the Priest or Priestess to become a clearer channel. Secondly, it creates a connection between the Priest and Priestess who are working together. This partnership is of utmost importance to symbolise the love and the connection between the God and the Goddess. Thirdly, the five-fold kiss demonstrates the respect and the awe for the deity from the Priest and the onlookers.

The kiss is normally done directly upon the body, although some prefer not to make direct contact. This of course is a trust issue, and will rest upon whether you feel comfortable with the person performing the invocation. In any case, an invocation should only be performed when there is perfect trust between the two individuals involved.

Through the combination of actions and words by the Priest, the focus and chanting of the onlookers and the intent of the Priestess herself, the Goddess may then take residence within the Priestess for a period of time. The Priestess' voice may change, her posture may alter and physical changes are often seen within the face. It's common for physical reactions to occur in the Priestess, such as tremors and rocking.

Many hours of training is required to achieve an effective

invocation; just saying the words and performing the actions is not enough. For this reason, it is rare to witness a full invocation at an open ritual, as it is normally carried out in secret with inner members of the coven or those who have already received their First Degree.

Janet Farrar and Gavin Bone wrote that when we perform an invocation our mind enters 'Delta', the same state our brains are in when we are asleep and dreaming. It is also when we are in deep sleep that we exhibit REM, or rapid eye movement. These states of being, together with REM, are both reactions that occur when a deity descends into a human body. It's also common for the Priestess to have no recollection of what transpired during the invocation – another similarity with the state of Delta.

At this point in the ritual the Goddess then leads the proceedings through the Priestess and may direct intuitively lead workings, give prophecies, or energise the group. Messages can be given and stories told by the Goddess, which is sometimes called 'automatic speaking' or 'utterances', the Priestess herself acting as a conductor, or a channel, for the deity. Sometimes the messages are short and simple, and other times they can be long and complex. Sometimes they can take the form of words and other times the form of actions. Each experience is different. Energy can also be passed through to other members of the coven at this point. The Priestess can do this by simply touching the palms of another's hands and then crossing their palms across their heart, or another method where the Priestess touches the third eye (forehead) of another.

Invocation was also very common in the rites of the Egyptians; the Osiris and Isis poses used within modern invocation were used for the same purposes in ancient Egyptian times. The 'Lustration Rite' of the Greeks was also a form of recognising Divinity within, anointing points upon the body to cleanse and empower the Priest or Priestess with Divine Spirit. Invocation is also carried out within the Vodouan tradition, as well as other

Shamanistic belief systems. Their spiritual deities, called the 'Loa,' are described as taking possession of the individual. Unlike the average invocation, the physical reaction of the Vodouan invocation is more excessive, with the person often experiencing lack of control over their body and erratic movement. Voodoo, however, is another belief system that is misunderstood by modern society, and although their methods are somewhat more direct than western methods of invocation, their purpose is normally the same – for the good of the community, usually for healing or protection purposes.

Invocation and its relationship with Evocation

We have now discussed Evocation and Invocation and the differences between the two techniques, but how are they alike, and what methods of Evocation can be called upon to make our Invocations more powerful?

Dictionary definitions of the word 'evoke' include, 'to arouse' or to 'call forth' (emotions, feelings, and responses) for instance to 'arouse pity'. The Oxford Dictionary lists the word 'evoke' as meaning to 'bring or recall to the conscious mind' or to 'obtain' (a response). So in the same way that watching a romantic film can make us feel affectionate and 'loved-up' so can the presence of a specific Goddess or God arouse emotions and reactions exclusive to that deity. We feel the characteristics of that deity rising up within ourselves; for instance we may feel more magically powerful whilst Cerridwyn is present, or more courageous when Lugh is present.

Evocations are very helpful in demonstrating the energy of the deity to us before we attempt to perform an Invocation, and so we are able to create a relationship with that deity before taking the next step of inviting them to be within us. It allows us to feel the presence of the God or Goddess but without the trance-like experience that accompanies an Invocation.

The Evocation is also simpler and safer for a beginner to

perform, as we are not opening ourselves up for another entity to control. This means that the chance of an unwholesome stray spirit taking up residence inside us (due to, for instance, a badly cast circle) is substantially reduced!

TASK: A Simple Method of Invocation

You should be familiar by now with the methods of Evocation, and I hope that you have been incorporating those methods into your rituals. The next step is to take the energy that you have evoked and bring it into yourself, with the Invocation.

You may have already felt the effects of the Evocations in your daily life; if you have evoked Athena, you may feel more empowered and confident. If you evoked Cerridwyn, you may have begun to feel more psychic and attuned with magic. If you evoked Aphrodite, you may have started to appreciate yourself a bit more, and take better care of yourself. These are all ways that the power of the Goddess or God who was evoked at the Evocation has already affected you. So, in order to invoke deity without performing the Full Invocation, one must only make the next step and open ourselves up to that energy.

So far, I have touched upon the importance of experience, trust and competence when performing an invocation. The Full Invocation – consisting of the five-fold kiss and the rite itself – is very powerful and should only be carried out by an experienced High Priest and High Priestess (or in the presence of them). The power of the rite itself opens up our bodies to the spirit world and can make us vulnerable, so if we are not properly prepared, or if the circle is not cast correctly, or if we do not trust the people we are working with, an Invocation can be dangerous.

However, a beginner need not be put off working with the Gods and performing Invocations. To this end, I have detailed the Minor Rite of Invocation which allows the solitary witch (or group of witches) to perform an effective Invocation without the potential risks involved in performing the full rite. This form of

Invocation also prepares us for the next stage, when we may join a coven or begin working with a magical partner and start practising Full Invocation.

In order to allow an Invocation to happen, we must first be able to accept that we are one with the Gods. By performing an Evocation, we are simply evoking the energy of that God or Goddess from the universe, and from within ourselves. In an Invocation, we must see that there is no separation between ourselves and that deity; we must accept ourselves as one body, and one mind. The God or Goddess is you; and *you are* the God or Goddess.

Once we accept that we are part of the Divine, we begin to understand that the Gods and Goddesses are all aspects of ourselves, just as much as we are part of them. We are part of the earth, the air, the fire and the water. We come from earth, and we return to earth. Each one of us is an expression of a single strand of the tapestry of life; there is no separation.

The Minor Rite of Invocation
From the Coven Book of Ways

For this exercise, choose a deity with whom you are already familiar, or one that you feel you have a connection with and will enjoy researching. As a rule, if you are female, you should choose a Goddess; if you are male, you should choose a God. Although Invocations of a deity of the opposite sex is possible, it is not easy; it can be confusing for the psyche and is not recommended for the beginner. If you feel you would like to work more with a deity of the opposite sex, try to stick with Evocation for now.

Once you have chosen the deity, you will need to research the God or Goddess as much as possible. Try to discover more about them than is commonly known; don't just research what is easily available in mythology books, but really try to find the origins of the deity. Where do they come from? Where were they most commonly worshiped? What are their favourite colours and foods? Does the deity come from an older equivalent, or 'root' deity? Start to collect items, fabrics, images and food that relates to the Goddess or God. Depending on the deity you have chosen, you may be lucky enough to find a statue. If not, find something that represents them to you. Most importantly, don't spend too much – it's the thought that counts, not the price. Stick to charity shops, boot sales and the free supplies that nature offers; the Gods see no value in money.

When you have gathered the items together, build a small altar to that deity. If you already have a larger altar, you may decide to place the deity altar in the centre of your main altar – it can be as easy as a small box turned upside down and covered with fabric. Then decorate the mini altar to reflect the deity, their mythology and their energy.

An Invocation should always be performed within a magic circle and with preparation as outlined in Chapter Eight.

Once your circle is cast in the normal way, place your palms on either side of the altar; close your eyes and still your mind. Employ one of the meditations before hand, if it helps. Listen to your breath, in, out. In, out. Now employ the chakra cleansing that we covered in Chapter Seven. This will prepare your body as a clear channel, releasing any negative energy or blockages and keeping your intent pure.

Now open your eyes and look at your altar. See the images that you have placed there, observe the colours of your chosen God or Goddess. Smell the sweet scent of the oils and incense you have selected. Use your entire sensory system to soak into the atmosphere that you have created, which is tailored to your chosen deity. Now closing your eyes for another moment and visualise that deity strongly. See them before you.

When you feel the energy is at its strongest, turn your back to the altar, draw your hands out to the side, and visualise the energy of the God or Goddess filling your body. It is said that the deity steps into you from the altar. Feel the power of the deity within; you are one. See as the deity sees, feel the changes in yourself. You may have a vision, feel you wish to say something, or have an epiphany.

The deity may leave by him or herself, but if it doesn't and you have come to a point that you would like the deity to leave, intently visualise the energy stepping back out of you into the altar. If you feel residual energy left that you are not comfortable carrying, shake all your limbs out and dismiss the energy from you.

Turn back to the altar and thank the deity for filling you with their power and insight. Make sure you partake of libation to ground yourself fully. Leave an offering to the deity upon the altar, and cast it to the ground outside when you have finished the rest of the ritual.

Close the circle as normal. Try to take note of how the energy of that deity is affecting you on a day to day basis. Continue to commune with that deity; leave offerings, perform daily devotions and surround yourself in his or her correspondences. Eat appropriate food; wear appropriate colours. Keep a note of your experiences, both of the invocation itself and the positive affects in your day to day life afterwards.

Chapter Fourteen

Psychic Defence

What we call evil is simply ignorance bumping its head in the dark.
H Ford

What is Psychic Attack?

'Psychic Attack' is a term used to describe any sort of metaphysical assault toward another person or a coven. It can be intentional (i.e. through negative spellwork) or unintentional (i.e. the person does not realise that they are causing harm). The latter can occur when the strength of a person's dislike or negative thoughts are enough to cause change on the astral plane and affect somebody, without the attacker being aware of what they are doing.

A psychic attack can be initiated and received by both magical and non-magical folk alike. As witches, we may be able to more effectively deal with an attack, putting us at an advantage over the non-magical. However, it is also a sad fact that becoming more involved with other witches in the community can lead to it becoming more likely that you are intentionally attacked by others who are jealous, angry or vengeful. It is particularly sad when attacks bridge traditions in Paganism, and I have seen more than one dispute between Pagans who have offended one another because of their differing beliefs.

What is Psychic Defence?

Psychic defence can work in two ways. The first is *Preventative* – that is we protect ourselves routinely to avoid the risk of attack. This can include basic psychic protection such as cleansing and safeguarding our personal energy space on a day to day basis.

This sort of defence can protect us from the low risk negative energy that all of us are exposed to daily (such road rage, the office bully, the occasional troublesome spirit, etc!) and can also be used within the circle when we practice certain routine self-defence practices. After all, casting the circle is in itself a form of psychic protection.

In some ways the art of preventative psychic defence can go toward protecting us physically, too. Our spiritual state is often reflected in our outward appearance, and witches find that they are less likely to become victims of mugging or rape because their strong psychic defences are reflecting outwardly and giving them a more confident and strong appearance. However, I would recommend (especially to women) that you learn a martial art or some other physical self-defence to couple with your psychic practices.

The second form of defence is *Curative*. Sometimes, however much preventative work we do, an attack can get through our defences if we feel particularly weak (through illness, stress, etc) or if the strength of the attack is very strong. In this case we may then take action, and on identifying a psychic attack we employ methods to repel, reflect or dissolve the attack.

This form of defence is also used when protecting another person. It is often the case that if someone has got to the point of being badly, psychically attacked, he or she will need others to step in and help as they have gone past the point of being able to solve the situation by themselves.

Signs and Types of Attack

Psychic attack can manifest itself in several different forms. Sometimes we may just feel that everything has been going wrong – that we have had particularly bad luck in a short period of time. Other times it may be felt within the circle (particularly if the circle we have created has not been strong enough to act as an effective barrier for negative energy). We may feel uncomfortable in the circle, or things may constantly go wrong for us whilst we perform the ritual. We may feel the presence of energies and spirits whom we did not invite, or whom we do not feel happy entertaining.

In other situations, we might feel an attack through general psychic disturbance, such as becoming aware of the presence of 'ghosts' and 'spirits' (which can often simply be the manifestation of a thought, or of concentrated energy).

Another form of psychic attack is described as that of the 'Psychic Vampire': a magical or non-magical person who drains you of energy in one way or another. In some ways this is one of the worst sorts of psychic attack as it can create a permanent state of attack in which the attacker is 'feeding' off of the victim's energy and vitality. Again, this sort of attack can happen intentionally or unintentionally.

Sometimes an attack may come via our dreams, as we sleep. Several years ago we dealt with a psychic attack directed towards someone in our coven. The member of our coven was having repeated nightmares and waking dreams. This member of the coven had been practising psychic defence, and although she was a beginner, she had in some ways managed to create a boundary between the attacking energy and herself. It became apparent through more investigation that a particular individual was extremely jealous and vengeful toward our coven member and had, without knowing it, been sending harmful thoughts toward her. The attacker was very mixed up and confused, and much of the content of the dreams reflected the person and the situation. On identifying the root of the cause, the coven were able to work in a way that released the coven member from the attack, and also went some way to helping the attacker to sort out some of their own issues.

One last point is this. Just because you are having a bad day, it doesn't mean you are being psychically attacked! Look at the evidence objectively to see if it really points to an attack.

Although we train rigorously in defence, an intentional attack is quite rare.

Why and When is Curative Defence Used?

He who does not punish evil, commands it to be done.
Leonardo da Vinci

When working with curative defence, it is important that the ethics of the situation are examined thoroughly. First; why has this attack been initiated? Have we done something to the person that explains the attack? The answer to this may be no – people do not always need a reason to dislike us, and if they do have a reason it may well be unfair and unjust. However, if the answer is yes, then maybe the attack is our own 'just desserts'? In this case, we should think carefully before returning the energy which, after all, we earned for ourselves.

Secondly; do we think the person is aware that they are attacking us? If the answer is yes, then we may confidently return or reflect the energy back on them. However, if the person is unaware that they are attacking us (i.e. the person dislikes you for some reason, but would never wish to cause you harm) or they are a confused person who cannot help their actions (i.e. children, the elderly and those with learning disabilities) then we must re-evaluate the situation. We should then decide on the best action to take – this might be to send healing energy to the person to help them, rather than return negative energy to them – which, after all, they never meant to send.

In situations such as these, we need to look subjectively at the situation. Sometimes when we are being personally attacked it is very easy to get wrapped up in the emotions of the attack, and become angry. Sometimes it takes another person to step into the situation, to suggest another angle in which the situation could be dealt with. Other times, an advanced witch who is suffering a psychic attack may have attained the ability to be able to act with 'compassionate detachment' – that is to look at the situation from the outside, and deal with it as a third person.

In this way, we take any emotion out of the situation and can focus on the facts only. Often when employing this method a witch may completely change the way they deal with the attack, and the result is much better for everyone involved.

Another thing to consider is that of the Law of Return. Many cultures suggest that what is sent out by a person will be returned to the sender, in the right way and in the right measure. Buddhism calls this the 'Law of Karma'. Sometimes it may be decided that the best thing to do is, in fact, nothing at all. There is a fine line between what our coven considers as requiring spellwork and what we leave for karma and the Law of Return to sort out. We consider that to reflect energy back on a malicious attacker is a positive way of actively protecting yourself or the victim and then, in the long run, when you're out of immediate 'danger', let karma run its course. For more on ethics in spellwork, see Chapter 16.

I have listed below some common forms of both preventative and curative defence. In addition to these ritual forms of defence, other aids can also be used in conjunction, such as planting holly in the garden and hanging whitethorn boughs in the roof-space. Blackthorn is also a powerful plant of protection, and it's wood is used to make the Blasting Rod - a tool for use in hexing or turning back the energy of those who have harmed you.

Preventative Defence

Preventative defence describes any sort of activity carried out regularly to protect ourselves from possible attack, offering protection both from negative energy picked up from day to day interaction with other people, to more malignant occurrences, such as a psychic/magical attack from another practitioner or spirit entity. Some forms include:

- Setting boundaries

  As human beings, we naturally create bonds with other people; most of the time these bonds are positive and connect us with our friends, our family and our loved ones. Sometimes, however, we need to be able to set boundaries between our own emotions and the emotions of other people.

  For instance, we may be helping somebody with a problem in their life, giving advice, or working magic for them. No matter how close we are to that individual, we need to be able to step away from the situation. If we don't do this we may be dragged down too, and if that happens we are of no help to anybody. This is even more important when dealing with psychic connections built through performing magic for that person, or practising healing where we connect with a sick person for a period of time during the healing.

  Setting boundaries also applies when protecting ourselves from attack on a day to day basis. Creating a protected space around us can protect our emotions from everyday attack from strangers and familiar people alike, as well as 'Psychic Vampirism'.

- Working with energy and meditations

  It is possible to manipulate the energy around us in order to employ preventative psychic protection. By changing our aura, we can camouflage ourselves and even make ourselves 'invisible' to others. Energy meditations are a good way to practice manipulating energy, and can help us to become quicker at reaching a state of protection when it is needed. Working with protective energy can also be a good insurance against more direct and damaging psychic attacks, sent both from other practitioners and spirit entities.

- Protection whilst doing ritual, spellwork and healing

There are several rituals and ritual components specifically designed to protect the witch whilst he or she works on a magical level. The circle casting in itself is a form of protection, designed to create a safe and secure space that both contains the energy within the circle and blocks anything negative outside from entering. All magical ritual should ideally be performed within a sacred space, and spellwork and raising energy should always be performed within a magic circle.

When performing a magical operation, there are also certain fail-safes that we can use in order to assure that the spell does not 'turn sour' or come back on us; see later in this chapter for more details. All parts of your ritual should be undertaken with a strong intent and conviction, in order to make sure that it has been done properly. If in doubt, repeat that part of the ritual. There is no harm in doing something twice, just to make sure.

The Charm of Fire, Iron, Water and Salt
From the Coven Book of Ways, original author unknown

Three materials which are well known for their protective qualities are fire, iron and salt. The fourth element used in this spell is water, which protects by purification. This charm may well have originated from the blacksmith's trade, a livelihood associated with Wayland Smith, the Germanic God of Smithcraft.

Caution should be taken when working with this spell, as it involves heating metal. Using a pair of wooden tongs, pass an iron nail through a candle flame. Hold it within the flame for long enough that the metal begins to heat up; just a minute or so will do.

When you have reached the desired temperature, immediately plunge the nail into the cold water, a technique that blacksmiths call 'quenching'. Straight afterwards, dip the nail into a bowl of salt, and then lay it on a heatproof surface to cool for at least 20 minutes before you touch it with your bare hands.

When the nail has completely cooled, place it inside a red pouch or bottle and sprinkle a little more salt on the top. The bag or bottle should then be sealed, and placed in the home for protection. Placing it over the door is effective, but putting it under a floorboard or in the cavity of the wall is even better.

Curative Defence

Sometimes, no matter how much preventative defence we have done, we can still be victim to an attack. This can occur because we have let our barriers down due to having a bad day, or we are feeling unwell, or sad. In the case of being psychically attacked, we should first consider the ethical implications of anything we decide to do (as already discussed above). If we do then decide to retaliate against the attack there are various methods available, which include:

Direct Forms of Defence (methods specifically designed for use in curative defence)

I use the term 'direct forms of defence' to describe any ritual or ritual component which is specifically designed to either reflect or neutralize the energy of a psychic attack, such as the Lesser Banishing Ritual of the Pentagram. Although the LBRP can be used as preventative defence (cleansing and clearing a space entirely of any sort of negative energy) it is most often used in response to a negative presence being detected, or an attack being initiated.

Direct curative defence also includes reflective spellwork

(ritual designed to reflect the negative energy back upon its source). This form involves the use of mirrors, words of power, manipulation of energy, postures and visualisation. Other rituals place the victim within the centre of the circle whilst the rest of the coven remove the psychic 'cords' that connect the victim with their attacker. Psychic cords establish an ongoing psychic relationship of exchange of energy between two people, and this 'umbilical cord' can transfer both positive and negative energy. It is important to learn how to remove cords, which is then usually followed by healing work to heal both attacker and victim.

An old favourite for warding off negativity is 'The Curse' which, contrary to its name, is normally used as a method of protection rather than cursing. The practice is of Egyptian and Romany origin, and consists of raising the index finger and pointing purposefully towards the direction of the danger to ward it off.

Talismans/Amulets

Talismans and amulets can be used in many ways, and psychic defence is just one of them. The simplest and most popular methods are to either carry an amulet upon the person or place a talisman somewhere within the home. Placing the symbol across the threshold (i.e. above the front door or under the doormat) is a good way of keeping negative energy from entering the house, and putting a bowl of fresh water with a sea sponge inside in the corner of the room will absorb any negative energy which is already there. Talismans are also very effective when used in spells. More can be found on Amulets and Talismans in Chapter 16.

The Lepidotes Tooth

The Lepidotes Tooth is an amulet carried to evoke protection. The fossilised tooth of the Lepidotes fish was found on the seashores by our forefathers and was believed to be the legendary 'Toadstone', a magical gem which could be plucked from the forehead of a toad and worn for protection and power. This is just one of the customs which was followed by the 'Toadsmen', practitioners of traditional British witchcraft, and later continued in the practices of the 'Horseman's Word' secret society from the 18th century.

Nowadays, a Toadstone amulet is often set into jewellery and worn for protection against both physical and spiritual ills. I have a Toadstone necklace which was made for me, and I can vouch for its effectiveness.

Poppets/Bottle Spells/Binding Spells

All of these methods have one thing in common; they all use an image of the attacker within the spell. A Poppet is a small doll made to represent the attacker. It can be as crude or as detailed as you like; the most important thing is that the doll, in some way, represents that person to you. Usually, something from the person, such as hair, or a photo, is woven into the Poppet. 'Life' is then symbolically breathed into the Poppet and the doll is then used within a ritual either to bind, reflect, or communicate with the person to end the attack (see Chapter Five for more information on Poppets). Bottle spells can also be used within 'binding' spells in a similar way, containing the attacker or the negative energy within the bottle (See Chapter 16 for more information on Bottle Spells).

TASK: Using Preventative Defence

Begin to practice a form of preventative defence on a daily basis. Your practice need not take long, nor do you need to set up a sacred space. In fact, the point of preventative defence is, to some extent, to define a sacred space around you at all times which protects you from day to day attack. Notice as you practice over the next few weeks, how people act differently towards you. Are you feeling safer, and more confident? Monitor the changes.

Creating Boundaries

In protective situations one may wish to cast a circle mentally, often without giving any sign that one is doing so. This is not difficult with practice; as with the physically enacted rite, it is powerfully concentrated imagination and willpower (which enables you to cast the circle). Janet and Stewart Farrar, 'The Witches Way'

Casting a mental circle involves 'a rapid 'zipping up' of a sphere of blue light', (J&S Farrar): a sphere similar to that which is cast when we create a circle physically. With the practice of meditation and working with energy as suggested in this book, we become able to get into a trance-ritual state almost immediately: a state in which we can then cast a protective space around us and make a boundary between ourselves and the attacker. This sort of method is good in situations where we find ourselves caught out and suddenly at risk, whether that be from the negative energy of a passing stranger to someone directly trying to cause us harm.

The difference between this circle and the standard circle is that this one is flexible, and will move with you as you go about your daily business. This circle also need not be closed after you have finished with it; it will dissipate within 24 hours or so. If you do wish to shut the circle down, simply visualise the energy of the circle running down into the ground whilst you remain protected, energised and refreshed.

Breathe deeply, and begin to imagine the power of the earth drawing up from beneath you, and the power of the universe drawing down above you from the skies. Both of these energies mingle and centre within you at your solar plexus.

Now visualise this energy instantly surrounding you in a sphere of blue light, totally enclosing you in its protective energy. Outside energy will bounce off the circle. You can go about your daily business with the protection of this circle about you.

The aura can also be manipulated in order to create boundaries. No matter how patient and considerate we are, there are always negative people around us and sometimes we wish to keep them at a distance.

When faced with these people, my working partner Lugh will turn his aura grey, so that he becomes 'invisible' to the person. If I find myself troubled by a particularly disagreeable person, I will cover my aura with metal spikes, like a flail. It doesn't do the person any harm, but it does make them take a wide berth and pass me by!

Removing Cords: Group Method
From the Coven Book of Ways

This is a method for removing the psychic cords that can occur between people; this practice is where the saying 'cutting all ties' comes from.

Removing cords may be required if an unhealthy cord has formed (i.e. psychic vampirism). It can also be used to help someone get over an old relationship, or break ties with an unsavoury acquaintance. Within a coven, it is often used when a coven member leaves the group. Belonging to a coven creates strong bonds between the members, and no matter how amicable everyone was when the person left, it is best for everyone to cut the person's cords from the group mind.

The important thing to remember with this method is that it well and truly 'cuts all ties' with that person – that is, it is not to be used if you have any intention of being close to that person again, as bonds will be very difficult to re-form.

- Take a length of white cotton and a white candle. Light the white candle and place it in the centre of your designated sacred space, or upon the altar.
- If you are working on your own, fold the length of cotton in half, so you create a loop. If there are two of you, take one end of the cotton each and hold it taut.
- Concentrate on the centre of the cotton. Visualise the person you wish to cut ties with, see their face, smell their scent, think of memories you have of them.
- The cotton represents the psychic cord between yourself and the other person. If there are more than two or you, each person holds their end of the cotton with one hand, and in turn with the other hand takes a pair of scissors and cut the cotton confidently. If there are just the two of you, one person cuts the centre of the thread.
- As you cut, say '*I cut all ties with* [name]. *We are separate people, and we walk separate paths. For the good of all, I cut these ties. So mote it be.*' Each person repeats these words as the cords are cut.
- Once you have cut the thread, see the image of the person vanishing, until it is gone.
- The candle is then extinguished, and the thread destroyed in the cauldron.

Ritual of the Rose Cross
From the Hermetic Order of the Golden Dawn, original author unknown

This is a ritual of protection. It will also bring peace when distracted. For this rite, the 'Rose Cross' can be drawn as a simple, equal armed cross.

- Light a sandalwood incense stick in the centre of the room
- Move to the south-east and draw the Rose Cross

- Move to the south-west and draw the Rose Cross
- Move to the north-west and draw the Rose Cross
- Move to the north-east and draw the Rose Cross
- Return to the south-east and visualise the cross there, pointing the stick of incense to its centre
- Hold the incense stick high above you and walk diagonally across the centre of the circle from the south-east towards the north-west, at the centre of the circle drawing the Rose Cross above your head
- Continue to the north-west, visualising the cross you drew there and pointing the incense stick at its centre
- Holding the stick downwards this time, walk back to the south-east, now drawing the cross below you at the centre of the circle
- Continue to the south-east, visualising the cross you drew there and pointing at its centre
- Move to the south-west, visualising the cross you drew there and pointing at its centre
- Move diagonally to the north-east, visualising the cross you drew above you in the centre and pointing the incense stick at its centre
- Continue to the north-east, visualising the cross you drew there and pointing at its centre
- Move diagonally back to the south-west, this time visualising the cross you drew beneath you in the centre, and pointing the incense stick at its centre
- Continue to the south-west, visualising the cross you drew there and pointing at its centre
- Move to the north-west, visualising the cross you drew there and pointing at its centre
- Move to the north-east, visualising the cross you drew there and pointing at its centre
- Complete by moving back to the south-east, visualising the cross you drew there and pointing at its centre

- Move to the centre of the circle, face east and visualise the six crosses about you
- Then, stay in the centre, hold your arms out to the sides
- Then raise both arms up into a 'v' shape, with head thrown back
- Then cross the arms onto the breast and bow the head
- Slowly raise the arms, and when they are fully extended bring them back crossed upon the breast, saying *'the light of the cross'*
- Visualise the white light streaming down into the body, saying *'let the light descend'*. Keep up this visualisation for at least 2 to 3 minutes

Mirror Reflection Procedure

A mirror can be used in conjunction with any of the curative methods of self defence. Simply hold up a small hand-held mirror toward the direction that the danger is apprehended. Visualise any residual negative energy being channelled into the centre of the mirror, then being reflected back towards the sender. The mirror can then be left in a window facing outwards, to protect against the possibility of the negative energy returning. This method can also be used on its own, as a quick fix method.

Lesser Banishing Ritual of the Pentagram (adapted)

From the Hermetic Order of the Golden Dawn, and originated from the Key of Solomon, original author unknown

The Lesser Banishing Ritual of the Pentagram is a high magic ritual method that was developed to clear out negative energy all together, and reinforce a sacred space. It is a very powerful ritual and the complete version of the ritual can be a very exhausting, yet empowering, experience. It is best performed by an advanced and magically adept Priest or Priestess, and is not recommended for the beginner.

However, I have detailed the following simpler, adapted

version for you to use which is both safe and effective for the beginner. It is best not to perform the LBRP (this simplified version or the full version) too often; it should be retained for times when it is *really* needed in order to ensure the maximum effect when it is performed.

You do not cast a circle in order to perform the LBRP. If performing a cleansing of the whole house, I like to turn all the lights off and perform the LBRP in one room, usually upstairs, using a single candle for light. Then once completed we go deosil (clockwise) around the house gradually working our way downstairs, switching lights back on and scattering herbs and salt to mark that the cleansing is complete, and light is returned to the house.

Part One

- Holding your athame, stand with your back straight in the centre of your sacred space and facing east.
- Rest your awareness in the centre of your head and breathe deeply.
- Now visualise a shining ball of energy spinning above your head.
- With a deep breath, raise your athame straight up toward the light and charge the blade with this powerful force.
- Now bring the athame down and touch your forehead gently with the flat of the blade, visualising a shining light beginning to radiate there.
- Now direct the athame straight down so that it is pointing towards the ground, visualising a shining light beginning to radiate there.
- Now touch your right shoulder with the flat of the blade, visualising a shining light beginning to radiate there.
- Now touch your left shoulder with the flat of the blade, visualising a shining light beginning to radiate there.

- Clasp your hands across the breast, visualising a shining light radiating there and all around you. Concentrate on all of the points of the cross about your body glowing, spinning, energising and protecting you.

Part Two

- Turning to the east, make the pentagram of east
- Turning to the South, make the pentagram of South
- Turning to the West, make the pentagram of West
- Turning to the North, make the pentagram of North

Part Three

- Extending the arms in the form of a cross say:
- "Before me Raphael" *(Ra-Fay-EL)*
- "Behind me Gabriel" *(Gahb-Ray-EL)*
- "On my right hand Michael" *(Mee-chai-EL)*
- "On my left hand Uriel" *(Ohr-ree-EL)*
- "For about me flames the Pentagram"
- "And above me shines the six-rayed Star."*(visualise the hexagram)*
- Repeat Part One to finish.

An Exorcism by Salt, Water and Incense

Supplies:

Salt
Water
Loose Incense
Finely crushed dried bay leaves
Charcoal Blocks
Normal ritual tools

This ritual, which is adapted from the coven copy of the *Liber Umbrarum*, can be performed anywhere – indoors or outdoors, and inside or outside of the magical circle, depending on where you are exorcising, and for whom. If the exorcism starts in the circle but needs to be expanded out to cover the whole house or area, then a door should be cut within the circle at north-east before anyone leaves the circle. The doorway should be closed as you move about the house, and then reopened when you are ready to go back in to the circle. See *'a note on cutting doorways'* from Chapter Eight.

Cast some salt into some fresh water, visualising the water glowing with a purifying bright blue light. Hold your palms above the water and say:

Water and Earth, where you are cast
No curse nor adverse purpose shall last
Here my will, addressed to thee
As my mind wills; so mote it be.

Cast the loose incense and crushed bay leaves upon a glowing charcoal block, and visualise it glowing with the same powerful blue light. Hold your palms above the incense and say:

Creature of Fire and Air, this charge I lay
No phantom in thy presence will stay
Hear my will, addressed to thee
As my mind wills; so mote it be.

Moving about the house or the area to be covered deosil, sprinkle the salt water and censor the incense whilst chanting:

By water and fire I exorcise thee
Of adverse thought and enmity

Return to the place from whence thou came
Be pure of thought, and remain the same
Hear my will, addressed to thee
As my mind wills; so mote it be.

Chapter Fifteen

Planning, Practice and the Planes of Existence

Throughout the last fourteen chapters of this book you have learnt the origins of the Craft, the Gods and Goddesses whom we worship, our spiritual and magical methods, the aims and objectives of the witch, and the endless possibilities of Initiatory Craft practice. Although you have probably already begun to plan rites and celebrations on your own, I would now like you to design a complete Full Moon ritual using the skills and techniques you have learnt, this time, using the Astral Temple.

Plan the rite for the next Full Moon due by calendar month (unless it will pass within the next seven days, in which case work towards the next one, to allow yourself enough time). Then, on the night of the Full Moon, you can perform the ritual you have written.

Remember to utilise all of the applicable ritual methods I have shared with you, particularly the structure of the rite as outlined in Chapter Eight. You should add your own flair and creativity into the ritual and really make it your own, so feel free to add in your own ideas and workings.

Planning a Rite using the Astral Temple

How easy is it to plan a ritual? The simple answer is, not easy at all..! A ritual opens up limitless possibilities to its structure and content. How can we possibly decide what deities to choose, and which workings to perform? In this day and age, we live busy lives. It is all too easy to try to plan a ritual in a lunch break at work, or on the PC where you have access to the internet for quick reference. However, it is important to try and set time aside, to allow your own creativity to flow so that the rite comes from your heart. Setting time aside will also allow you to open yourself up psychically, enabling you to receive messages and guidance from the spirits and the Gods.

Some of the best rituals are designed by using altered states of consciousness, such as meditation, or trance induced by incense or candle scrying. Some of the most creative ideas for rites are often thought of whilst relaxing in the bath, or taking a walk in the country. One way, however, is to plan the ritual within your mind – within your own astral temple.

The astral temple is thought to be of Hermetic origin, although the use of permanent ritual spaces on the astral plane is common in most mystery traditions. It is a place beyond this world, on the astral plane and existing in accordance with your own belief.

The Planes of Existence

Although there are many planes of existence which are recognised by various different belief systems, there are five common planes which are recognised by most witches and occult practitioners. These are the Physical, Etheric, Astral, Mental and the Spiritual. Although they are identified as separate planes, they are in fact all interconnected and any change on one plane will lead to a change on the other. In effect, this coexistence of planes follows the laws of Web of Wyrd or Karma; in that each action has a reaction.

Like any spell, the first and most important part of bringing anything to manifestation is to project the intent onto the Astral Plane. In spellwork, we focus on the thing we desire and visualise having already achieved it; in doing so send that image to the Astral Plane where, with the will of the Gods, it will begin to manifest in the Physical.

The planes of existence also relate to our own levels of consciousness. When we meditate or perform ritual, we access a new level of consciousness; our minds move out of the physical world and enter a new plane of existence.

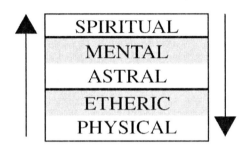

- The **Physical plane** is the lowest and the most material world of the five planes. It is the mundane world that we live in; the earth, the trees, the cities, our need to eat and drink, and even our mortality. As human beings, our bodies are tied to the physical; we are bound by the laws of gravity, our need for sustenance in order to survive, and our vulnerability to the elements and each other. Our souls, however, are not tied to this physical world, and can travel to other planes of existence. This plane of existence is called Assiah, the material world, and the place of physical existence.

- The **Astral Plane** is the world of endless possibilities; it is the place where all things develop and become manifest. It is the place of dreams and, in some beliefs, the place where the souls of the dead go to receive karma. It is the place where we send our hopes and our wishes so that they might become manifest. This is the place where magic is turned to form, and it is here in the Astral Plane where we create our Astral Temple. This plane of existence is called Yetzirah, the Astral World, the place of transformation.

- The **Spiritual Plane** is the highest and the most divine world of the five planes. It is the place of pure divine spirit; the place of the Gods and the place where we can communicate with deity. It corresponds to the tip of the Pyramid of Manifestation (see Chapter Six) together with our most spiritual self. This plane of existence is called Atziluth, the divine world, and the place of the Gods and the archetypes.

Once we have projected our will and designed the astral temple, it becomes a powerful place to design rituals, work magic and send our spellwork thereafter, and also acts as a gateway to other realms. northern European tradition speaks of nine worlds, which can be accessed through meditation, ritual and magic. These worlds are best approached through the Astral Plane, although at certain times of year such as Beltane and Samhaine they become accessible through the Physical.

TASK: A Meditation of the Astral Temple

Although there is a generic design for astral temples, you can adjust yours in the future to suit your own tastes. For instance, I have designed the temple outlined in this chapter to reflect its Hermetic origins and the temple is adorned with marble floors and silk wall hangings; however, the floors of your temple may be covered with leaves like to a forest floor, and the walls may be carved out of solid oak. You may also find that your temple trans- forms by itself, and each time you visit it something has changed. If a group designs an astral temple together, they can meet in the temple to perform workings on the astral plane, whilst their bodies stay home.

The following meditation allows you to build your own astral temple, a sanctuary that you can visit at any time to work magic, and where the impossible is possible.

For this mediation you need to find somewhere that you will not be disturbed. This could be a bedroom, a locked study, or maybe outdoors. Turn off the phone, and tell anyone who may interrupt you that you wish to be left alone for a while.

Read the text below several times so that you have a good idea of what will happen in the meditation. If possible, have someone read the meditation to you, or record it onto a tape and play it back to yourself. Listening to a meditation being read is by far the easiest way of following a guided meditation. When you have an image in your mind of the journey, you can begin. Don't worry if the meditation deviates from the original story; go with whatever happens in your mind, even if it is different to what you had expected.

If it is comfortable for you, sit cross-legged with your back straight; otherwise lie out flat. Close your eyes and take a few deep breaths. Focus on your breathing – in, and out, in and out. With every breath in, feel yourself calm, and at peace. With every breath out, feel the tension of the day drain away. Your heartbeat becomes slower, your body becomes heavier. Breathe in peace, breathe out tension. All thoughts of the day and other distractions leave your mind as you become completely relaxed and focused.

Feel the strength of the earth beneath you; the power of the rocks and the minerals which support all life. You can almost smell the earth, and feel it between your fingertips: soft and damp, like fresh black compost. Feel yourself grounded, solid and rooted like the mighty oak. Draw this energy up into your body, feel it follow the line of your spine as it refreshes and empowers you with emerald green energy.

Now focus your consciousness upon the sky above you; the purity of the air, the wisdom of the universe, the place of the Gods. Draw this golden energy down into your body. It passes through your crown chakra and fills your body with shining, divine light. It mingles with the green energy of the earth, making you feel pure, and complete. As Above, So Below.

As you breathe deeply, you start to feel yourself becoming lighter. You know that your body is only a material shell for your astral body, which constitutes your spirit and your soul.

Now, feel your astral body lift out of your physical body. You are not fearful, as this process feels peaceful and safe. Looking down upon your body now, you realise that you are still connected to your physical self by a silver, etheric thread – your connection to physical life. You know that at any time, you can return to your physical body as the etheric thread makes you inseparable.

Now feel yourself drift from this physical life and its limitations. Your aim is to travel to the other planes of existence, and other dimensions of our universe. Feel the breeze upon your face as you travel, knowing that you are passing through the very fabric of existence. You rise higher and higher, until the earth becomes a mere distant memory. You feel your mind open, your psychic awareness tune to the heartbeat of the universe. Now you can see so clearly, as if for the first time, the many hidden layers of existence.

Ahead of you, deep within the vastness of space, you see a mist of stars; as you draw closer you begin to realise that within the mist lays a door. It is not a conventional door of wood, bolt and key; it is an etheric door, a symbol of transgression from this level of reality to another. You feel drawn to the misty door of stars; it pulls you nearer. You pass though the door, expecting to find yourself still in space and surrounded by stars, but instead you stand in a corridor, lit by tiny lights upon the black marble floor.

You smell the evocative scent of burning incenses, a mixture of frankincense, eyebright and eastern incenses. Enchanted, you follow the corridor of lights which lead out to a great hall. Standing in the centre of the hall you look about you. It is a perfect square, with a bright white circle painted on the floor. Each wall is decorated with long silk hangings, which shimmer in the candle light and appear lighter than air. The silk is red in the south, yellow in the east, blue in the west and green in the north. Above the hangings, in the coving where the walls meet the ceiling, you see the astrological symbols of the planets and the zodiac. On the ceiling you see the circular symbol of the Yin-Yang.

In the centre of the hall in line with the northern wall you see a hexagonal table. It is carved out of ancient yew; the grain of the wood looks inviting and you run your fingertips along the surface to feel the grooves. Upon the table's surface lay the tools of the Craft: athame, two candles, pentacle disc, wand, scourge, bell, incense, water and salt – and a single lit taper.

Picking up the single lit taper, you light the two candles and the hall fills with warm, peaceful light. You realise that you have found your astral temple: the place of meditation, contemplation and transformation. Anything is possible here, and anything we put our mind to in the astral temple can be manifested in our physical lives. Stay in your temple for as long as you wish.

When you are ready to leave, extinguish the two candles, leaving the taper lit for next time. Now turn and walk back to the corridor, follow the floor of lights until you reach the misty door of stars, pass through the door into outer space.

Now see the earth beneath you and begin in travel down. Follow your etheric connection back to your body and begin to feel the connection with your physical self once again. Feel yourself float back into your body now. As you become aware of yourself in this room wiggle your toes, tune into the sounds of life around you, and open your eyes.

'The Astral Temple meditation', from the Coven Book of Ways

Chapter Sixteen

Magic and Spellwork

We have practiced various types of magic throughout this book, but I have left this chapter until last and some might wonder why. To the newcomer, magic is often the most intriguing part of the Craft and it is not unusual for them to want to skip ahead to try magic straight away. However, without preparation and knowledge, a spell is rarely going to have a positive outcome – if it is to have any outcome at all. I hope that the preparation which has been given in this book has helped you make a positive connection with the universe and the subtle ways of the Craft, all of which are so very necessary for magic.

An artist must know the way that colours work together; he must have studied perspective, and must have an understanding of light and shadow before he can create a masterpiece. A chef must know the purpose of the ingredients and the length of cooking time before he can create the perfect dish – it is not just a matter of reading the instructions and carrying them out blindly. So too must we have a good understanding of the background of the Craft if we want our rituals to be as effective as possible and the belief behind our religion to be strong. Too many books on modern Wicca ignore the background and core understanding behind the Craft and skip right to the instructions on how to conjure spirits, or cast a love spell. Working magic in this way will be a) irresponsible and b) probably ineffective, as you do not have the personal power behind the magic to make it work. It must be understood that although magic *can* be done by the inexperienced and uninformed, it is not advisable as magic can be volatile; if used incorrectly it can hurt others or reflect back on the sender.

By this stage, you should also have a full understanding of the history of the Craft and its purposes, together with experience of certain methods such as raising energy and meditation, which will help you achieve much more when using magic. Instructions have also been given for psychic protection and magical ethics. With all this in mind, magic can be incorporated into both your ritual and your daily life.

There are many definitions of magic and many ways of practising it, but ultimately magic is any method used to cause change. It is the mastering of the mind and the use of meditation, energy, symbols and gestures, together with our own personal power and intent. Whether we choose to recite a set of ancient words or create a simple, on the spot, chant or mantra, the first and most important point of power is that of our own intention. As Alistair Crowley described it, magic is 'the science and art of causing change to occur in conformity to the will'. Incidentally, it was Alistair Crowley who first put forward the idea of an alternative spelling for magic – 'magick'. He added the 'k' to distinguish his form of ceremonial magick (Thelemic) from what he described as 'low magic', the folk magic and lore of the common people. The alternative spelling has stuck with many practitioners of the Craft ever since; however, I choose not to use it, because, although we do incorporate certain elements of Thelema, what we practice is not Thelemic.

Every part of a ritual is part of the magic itself, from the setting out of the temple, the sweeping of the circle, to the blessing and consecration of the elements and even the closing of the circle at the end. In the same way, simply taking a walk on the beach and drawing a circle around you in the sand is a magical operation of its own. Magic is a natural vibration: a force which flows between us and throughout the universe. It is not something which can be switched on and off; it is a part of our lives – a source of energy and power which is never at rest. It flows through everything and can be used in conjunction with our will.

Some people consider that magic comes directly from the Gods, whilst others see magic as coming from their surroundings and from within themselves. The eclectic witch like myself (with a pantheist view) may call on both sources interchangeably. In my tradition magic is part of life itself: the turn of the seasons, the breath within us, the movements of the planets, the motions of the Wyrd and the threads of Fate.

Microcosm, Macrocosm and the Wyrd

The theory of microcosm and macrocosm describes how the macrocosm (the universe as a whole) and the microcosm (the tiny parts that make up the universe) are connected. That is, one directly affects the other as each is subject to the same laws. A similar concept is the 'Butterfly Effect': a theory that hypothesises that one tiny action can cause a ripple effect in the fabric of the universe and cause a much larger event to occur.

As witches, we believe that this extends to magic. Any conscious, unconscious, physical, mental or astral change we make effects the bigger picture. We believe in an interconnection between all things, and that the correspondences we use in magic and ritual (such as the colours, symbols, oils and planets) reflect these underlying similarities. The universe is ultimately a template for magic: a macrocosm and microcosm, forever entwined in each other's fate. It is the threads of Fate which cause magical occurrences, which are woven into all things and make all things a part of magic; a power that the Egyptians called Heka.

The Celtic and northern Craft describe this fate as the Web of Wyrd as the network of energy that connects all things and weaves cause and effect throughout the world. The word 'Wyrd' means 'to become' or 'to turn' and explains how everything emits energy and is ultimately made of the same material; and therefore, nothing is in isolation. Celt and northern Craft also speak of the link between actions and consequence; the ideals of fate and the power from within. Suffolk witch Rhys Chisnall described Wyrd as 'the process of unfolding the present, influenced and determined by the events of the past'. He explains the movements of Wyrd as patterns of action and interaction, which can be changed and redirected as time passes but will always be influenced by what has gone before.

Magic as Part of Life

For the seasoned witch, the practice of magic is not something that is separated from everyday life. To many outsiders what witches do is 'supernatural', but for us it is simply life; there is no separation. The idea of magic as a 'supernatural power' is alien to the real witch, for everything we do is in harmony with nature and does not supersede it. In the same way, magic is comparable with science; it works in harmony with the laws of nature, and through the knowledge of the practitioner it can create fantastic results. For the witch, the Craft should not be an escape from normal life, but a complementary art.

Our everyday lives are moved by the energies of nature and the power of magic, which is available to all whom genuinely seek it out and recognise it within the simplest of things. Magic is life, and life is magic; and to practice it is not to *master* but to *understand* the natural energies which surround us all of the time. Your can use your knowledge of magic and energy, particularly raising and grounding, to both energise and diffuse situations. Simple magic can be directed through the palms, so subtle that others may be unaware that you are doing anything at all.

In any event of magic, either as part of an elaborate ritual or used on the spot within our daily lives, our minds must first be completely focused on our goal with no distractions or other priorities. Performing a spell when your 'heart is not in it' will more than likely fail.

In this part of the book, I have outlined some more simple yet effective forms of magic which can be incorporated both as workings in a more complex ritual or used throughout your daily life, as and when the need arises. I have also included some 'fail-safe' gestures and rules which should be included in your spellwork, to protect you and those around you from a spell 'going wrong'.

Preparation

When we carry out any form of ritual or spellwork, the level of preparation can be very influential on the outcome of our workings. For instance, a cleansing bath with sea salt before the ritual will help prepare the mind, body and spirit; the bath cleanses you on a physical level whilst also purifying the spirit. A good, long bath with a few essential oils is also the perfect way to calm the mind and allow it to enter the Alpha state: a slower brainwave frequency that stimulates intuition and the psychic senses. One witch friend of mine told me that she does all her meditation in the bath, because she finds it the best place in which to be able to switch off and focus!

Preparation of the space is also important; if working indoors, a quick dust and vacuum round will make all the difference to the energy of the room. If you work with a permanent altar, it should be cleaned and any remnants from the last ritual, such as scattered salt and herbs cleared away. Fresh supplies can then be set out.

The preparation of the altar itself is also very important. We discussed in Chapter Four how the layout and appearance of the altar can affect the sub-conscious mind, and the items we choose to have on the altar also allow us to tap into the power of corre-spondences. For instance, if we were performing a rite for prosperity we might choose to light a gold candle and place images of coins upon the altar. In doing so, we are not only aiding our own thought processes by way of archetypal imagery but we are also making a connection with the underlying Wyrd of the universe; surrounding ourselves with the associations of prosperity in order to draw it towards us.

The Sight

'The Sight' or 'Witch Sight' is a way of preparing the mind for ritual and magic by altering and enhancing the consciousness. It should be developed over several months before it is ready to be used within spellwork, but once practiced the method is very effective. Within our coven, the person who has perfected this art and uses it within the coven is named the 'Seer'.

The first stage of developing the Sight is by heightening the awareness of your surroundings through touch, smell, audio and vision. Take a few moments now and again during the day to truly experience your environment; are you hot or cold? Are you comfortable, or do you have any aches or pains? What smells are around you, what sounds can you hear, and what small details can you see? Our modern minds can become so cluttered with mundane thoughts that they block out many messages which our senses pick up; but with practice, you will find that you are able to employ your senses all at once, and truly experience 'being'. The method can be overwhelming at first as your body is not used to taking in such a sensory overload, but with practice the method will allow you to sense both spiritual and physical elements around you, and give you greater control over your magic. Herbs which help gain the Sight include Cinnamon, Sandalwood and Myrrh.

The second stage is to then allow your etheric 'astral' body to move independently of your physical. This is done by visual-izing your movements before your physical body carries them out. For instance, visualise your hand move to the corner of this page and turning it. Almost immediately, allow your physical hand to follow the path of your astral and carry the movement out. The more detail you can give to your astral movements the better; which fingers will touch the page first, where will your hand settle after the page has been turned? This part of the method allows your astral body to take more of a role in your ritual and magic, and involves your astral self in ritual where your physical body might otherwise take over. Remember, it is the astral body which performs the magic, your physical body is a tool only. You may find with practice that you can start carrying out many magical tasks using your etheric body only, and you have no need to involve the physical.

Belief, Purpose and Intent

Of all the possible variables in magic belief, purpose and intent are by far the most important. For instance, someone who turns up at an interview convinced that they are not going to get the job is very unlikely to be offered the position. In the same way, if we perform a ritual or working without belief in our own abilities, it is just as unlikely that our spell will succeed.

Your intent is also very important. A spell that is driven by strong desire is much more likely to succeed than a spell which is less important to us. A witch performing two spells at one time may soon become testament to this, as they discover that one spell was successful whilst the other, less important one, failed. To get around this issue, if there is an important spell (such as healing) it should be given your whole attention.

Part of belief is also learning to trust in what we have done, and patiently allowing the spell to proceed upon its course. Ideally, once a spell is completed it should be forgotten about. Attempts to 'reinforce' the spell by doing it again or lamenting about what you could have done better will not help. Liam Cyfrin writes in his article, *The Psychology of Spellcraft*,

> *It's important to feel confident enough of our spells to let them go once they've been cast. A seed won't thrive if it's dug up every few days to see if it's sprouting and a carrier pigeon won't get far if you tie a kite string to its leg so you can yank it back periodically to make sure it still has its message.*

So be patient, and allow the spell to work in its own good time. If the spell does not work (and this could be for many reasons such as ethics, intent or even fixed fate) then it is just not going to work, no matter how many times you repeat it. Your belief in the spell and the powers behind it must be sufficiently strong in order for the magic to work - but if it doesn't work out, it doesn't work out.

Whilst magic can help move things along in our lives by altering certain situations and creating new opportunities, it is not an excuse for laziness; the hard work done on the physical plane is just as important as the work we do on the astral. As above, so below; what we are doing with our spell work on the astral plane must be reflected by our attitudes and efforts on the physical. For instance, if you wish to sell your house, you will still need to clean, tidy and decorate it to make the property appealing to the buyer; performing magic to ask for a quick sale is not enough. The Gods do not like laziness and will not be inclined to help those who do not help themselves. In the same way, if you believe someone is being harmed or is in trouble this should be reported to the police; simply performing a spell to help them is not acceptable.

It is very important not to overlook the practical ways in which you can achieve your goals. Janet Farrar describes in her DVD, *Discovering Witchcraft*, how she trains her students about the challenge of magic. Janet asks the student to use the power of their mind to move a flower vase from point A to point B. She watches them concentrate until they give up, obviously disappointed with their inability to move inanimate objects by the power of their mind. It is only then that Janet explains magic does not have to be something impossible to achieve, and simply picks up the vase with both hands and moves it manually from point A to point B.

Energy, Affirmations and Words of Power

Words of power are often used in the Craft. A word or phrase of power is any word or combination of words which declares a particular intent and is used to cause a particular outcome. Examples of power words include intoned mantras, God and Goddess names, creative words, repetitive words (such as chants) or words which have been used by many people for a very long time. These words are often described as being part of the universal consciousness, or Akashic Records. But it is not just the psychological effect of these words that give them power; the vibration of the sound waves given off by the word or phase can also have an effect on Wyrd, which then causes change in a certain way.

Words of power are of particular importance when used as affirmations. Affirmations at the end of spell work and ritual act as both an assertion of our will and also act as a mark to confirm that the working is complete. In modern Wicca, the most popular affirmation is 'So Mote It Be'. 'Mote' is an early word for 'Must' or 'May' from the Old English Moste or Motan, and is a phrase borrowed from Freemasonry meaning 'So Must It Be', or 'So Be It.' Its origins in modern Craft can probably be attributed to Gardner's friendship with the Freemason John Ward, who influenced Gardner's work. The phrase was later featured in *The Witch's Rune*, which was written by Gerald Gardner with the help of Doreen Valiente. Whilst it is accepted that Gardner did indeed have some old but fragmented Cunning Craft rituals from his own teachers, he also openly admitted that he had built the tradition by using other influences such as Freemasonry, the works of Margaret Murray, the Rosicrucian Order, the Ordo Templi Orientis and the poetry of Doreen Valiente.

Robin Artisson, prolific author and Traditional Craft practitioner, suggests the affirmation 'my will and Your power binds it so' which affirms both the will of the practitioner together with the power of the Gods. In our coven, we use a combination of our order and our intent 'As My Mind Wills, So Mote It Be' or 'As I Do Will, So Be It Done'.

Ethics and Magic

Resentment is like taking poison and waiting for the other person to die.

Malachy McCourt

When working on a magical level we must understand the possibility that any change we attempt to make by way of the magical arts may be returned to us. In some Craft traditions, and particularly in Wicca, it is believed that you receive three times whatever you send out – the 'Threefold Law of Return'. The true origin of the Threefold Law of Return is sketchy, and something that only you can decide whether to follow. It probably originates from the mythology of the 'Three Fates' and the magical significance of the number three, as briefly discussed in previous chapters. However, it isn't a bad rule of thumb to keep in mind that whatever we send out we are going to get back, and quite possibly somewhat more generously than we offered it. Whether what you get back is positive or negative is then, ultimately up to you. Opinions often differ within the Pagan and occult community regarding the concept of 'fate' and the influence of 'cause and affect'. Some believe that our fates are fixed, and no matter what we do in our lives there is no escaping the preordained plan. However, others believe that fate is changeable, transmutable, and we are able to design our own future by way of our present actions. For those that believe in the latter, the idea behind the concept of cause and affect sits more comfortably – namely, that which we put into the universe (whether good or bad) we should expect back, in one form or another. In this way, we are able to create our own path, and we reap the consequences of our actions.

Different ideas about fate, destiny, and cause and affect come from all over the world and from different traditions, however one of the most well known concepts is from Buddhism, that of 'Karma'. The word karma comes from the Sanskrit word for 'action', so then directly meaning that one action earns another. Although this is a Buddhist concept, it describes our Coven opinion on the matter well and that of many other Pagans alike. Like many other eastern traditions incorporated into Neo-Paganism such as the chakras, meditation and the Aura, the concept of karma sits well in progressive Pagan practice. The Buddhist concept of karma is that every living being lives a life determined by the accumulation of effects from past causes they have made. This applies to past lifetimes as well as the present one. The Egyptians also believed in a law of return, and their society emphasised the importance of good behaviour on the earthly plane in order to ensure their transition into the next life. The Egyptian source of magic, called Maat, was also the Goddess of justice; like the webs of Fate, Maat gave magic and power to her Priests yet punished those who used their power for evil.

Do not what you desire; do what is necessary.
Robert Cochrane

If we choose to believe in the power of cause and affect, then that means we must take responsibility for our own actions – both magically and non-magically – within our day to day lives. However, if we believe that our fate is preordained and fixed, then the possibility exists that we might revoke any responsibility for our actions and, in this way, cause someone to be hurt along the way. This sort of belief therefore can be a danger.

I am often asked when I read the tarot what my beliefs are regarding destiny. Many people believe that what is written in the cards is set in stone and cannot be changed. But it is quite to the contrary. The tarot allows us to see our present destiny – that is, how things are likely to turn out if we carry along upon the path that we have already started to tread. I believe that everyone's fate is changeable, and nothing in 'fate' is fixed.

As witches, it is our responsibility to work for the community and help others. It still amazes me how so many modern witches and other denominations of Pagans alike are so uninterested when it comes down to using our so-called gifts for the good of our fellow man. If we as witches are to make a positive contribution to the world it is vital that the showmanship and egocentricity, which has run so many circles over the past few years, is done away with and replaced with true spiritual and cultural advancement. It is an honour to be able to work on the path of the Craft, but we must earn the right to do so. My teacher and Elder of the Craft Maureen Wheeler is well known for testifying,

'It's a privilege to run a circle, not a power game, and I have no time for anyone who says otherwise.'

When working with magic and ritual, we are already accepting we believe that we have the ability to change something by the power of our own mind and our own actions in balance with the Wyrd. Therefore, the concept of cause and affect is, in my opinion, very much a part of magic and occultism and comes hand in hand with our responsibilities as practitioners of the Craft.

Fail Safes in Spellwork and Ritual

As witches, it our responsibility to ensure that we do not cause accidental harm towards ourselves or anyone else through our ritual and therefore spells should be carried out with the specific intent in mind. As witchcraft has become more popular in recent years, people have tried to 'sanitise' the practice and many books on modern Wicca in particular have given the impression that spells are harmless. This could not be further from the truth; the spell is in the hands of the practitioner and I have seen some disastrous consequences from people not taking their practice seriously. That is the downside to the growing popularity of the Craft; that there are too many students and not enough properly trained teachers.

When we decide to do a spell, we must first think about HOW the spell will reach the end goal. For instance, consider that you have done a spell for prosperity, so that you can get out of debt. If we don't specify HOW that money is going to get to us, it is statistically more likely that someone in your family will die and leave you money than you buy a winning lottery ticket. Magic is like electricity; if you do not give electricity a specific way in which to travel it will fit the quickest route to ground itself, which usually ends up with someone being frazzled. Do not let your magic find the quickest route to achieving its aim; give it specifics and a safe way in which it can achieve the goal without hurting you or anybody else.

For instance, a healing spell should work like a prayer; you should design it to do a lot of good but never have the capacity to do harm. And a protection or binding spell should work by changing a situation, rather than being performed with malicious intent towards the person involved. However, it is possible, particularly when working towards goals which are emotionally motivated, to accidentally cause harm without meaning to. It is also possible to cause psychic disruption, often simply by opening a ritual circle incorrectly. In order to prevent these sorts of things from happening, there are certain fail-safes that we can employ in order to ensure the safety of others and ourselves when working magically.

The first is a good circle casting. A poorly cast circle opens up a world of 'negative possibilities'. If a circle is not cast properly, the energies which are invited and evoked can cause major short term and long term problems for those involved. Casting a good circle (as per directions in this book) also ensures that any work done within the circle is performed within a properly cleansed and consecrated space.

The second is the use of words and affirmations. Many modern witches like to include phrases such as 'for the good of all' after their spellwork, to ensure that the working will not harm anyone. Whilst some witches find this sort of affirmation an insult on their own ethical standards, it is in fact a fail-safe action which means that if the working would have inadvertently caused harm, then its energy would have automatically been dissolved by the very words of your own spell. Whilst we would all like to think that we have good ethical standards, when a personal situation arises it is harder to make a unprejudiced decision. Of course, if a witch actually *means* to inflict harm, then they are unlikely to conclude their spell with this affirmation! However, this should be a very rare occurrence; there are times when a coven may take action to bind an individual when there is nothing else that can be done, but this would be under exceptional circumstances, and all of the coven would be consulted as to whether they felt that the action was acceptable.

The third is a good circle closing. In the same way that a good circle casting is essential, so is its closing. If a circle is not properly closed, and the energy is not properly dismissed, residual energy can remain and this can cause all sorts of problems.

Timing is also important in spellwork, and waiting for fortuitous influences such as the correct planetary aspects and moon phases can make a big difference to the success of our magic. But life isn't always as considerate as that, and sometimes we need to do a working right away – for example, we may need to do a healing ritual in an emergency, or do a spell for a sudden and unexpected job interview. In this case, decide on the best hour of the day to work on, then check the astrological aspects for that day and work out how best to approach the ritual or spellwork with the present influences in mind.

Always avoid hours of the day that are void of course. Depending on the astrological influence, you can approach the spell differently to make the most of the astrological energy, so you are not working against it. A list of the astrological influences and methods of ritual that can be partnered with each one can be found earlier in the book.

Forms of Magic

There are many different types of magic, some of which we have already covered earlier in this book. In this part of the chapter I have given a few other types of powerful magic which you can use within your rituals. Please take care with your magic, and always consult the magical ethics before taking action. Remember to keep the Gods involved, and always work for the higher good.

Witches Bottles

Witches Bottles have been used to heal, curse, protect and contain for at least 500 years. The bottle usually consists of various items which correspond to the purpose of the spell, such as herbs, planetary symbols, poppets and types of metal. Once filled and told its purpose the bottle is then sealed and buried.

The technique works by containing and amplifying power within the bottle. For instance, if the spell is for protection, the bottle will radiate that power around the designated area or person, surrounding them with protective energy. If it is for binding or cursing, it psychologically encloses the victim within the bottle and begins to subject them to the curse. The latter is not recommended, except in very extreme circumstances and in cases such as these the ethics and motivation of the spell should be closely examined.

One of the most popular uses for Witches Bottles is threshold protection: to protect the home from criminals and evil spirits.

These bottles can be buried under the doorstep, under a floor-board or placed in a wall cavity where they should remain undisturbed. It is quite common for builders renovating old houses to find witch bottles built into walls and door frames. They have even been found built into fire hearths – probably because the chimney was seen as a vulnerable point where evil spirits could enter. On finding one of these old bottles, most people err on the side of caution and leave the bottle where it is, or build it back into the house elsewhere.

We may also design a bottle which is aimed at a specific person, for instance for healing, protection or binding. We do this by creating a psychic connection between the bottle and the chosen person, which is done by including a strand of hair, a fingernail clipping, a photograph or a poppet of the person in the bottle. Iron nails are also used as they represent life blood, although real blood can also be used. Then other contents are added to the bottle:

- Thorns from the blackthorn bush are good for both protection and binding, although the thorns should be taken from fallen or cut branches and not snapped off a living branch. Holly can also be used to both protect and curse, as can pins, broken glass and black pepper. Garlic is another powerful ingredient for protection, as is sage and bay leaf.

- Tangled wool or thread is very effective for protection, as it causes confusion to the attacker. An absorbent material such as sponge can also be used to attract negative energy and spare the victim. Pieces of iron can also be used for this purpose, particularly when psychic attack is suspected.

- Talismans, amulets and photographs can be put into bottles for any purpose, as can a handwritten note outlining the intention of the spell.

- Coins can be enclosed for prosperity, as can sheaths of corn and other harvest grains. If you are working for a new job, perhaps place a payslip in the bottle for the salary you wish to get.

- To restrict someone's negative words or actions, use an elastic band which ensures that any negativity they send out will immediately be directed back at them.

- To aid healing, use soothing herbs such as lavender. Depending on the illness, items can be included to help fight off the sickness, and pins and thorns can also be used. Remember; always ask permission from the sick person or their relative before carrying out any healing.

The bottle which you choose is not really important. I have seen Witches Bottles made from old jam jars right the way through to ornate antique vases! Where you plan to put the bottle does need to be considered though – if you are planning to bury it then you need to choose a tougher glass, as thinner material will soon crack under the weight of the soil.

Ideally, the bottle should be constructed within a magic circle. By doing so we ensure that we are in the right frame of mind and that we are protected. As you place each item into the bottle, you should say what the item is for and how it will work, for instance:

This thorn is protection, to watch over my door.
This thread is to confuse all who mean harm.
This salt is to neutralise malevolence and evil.
This photo is our family, remaining safe and warm.
This house is protected! so mote it be.
'The Bottle Spell for Protection', from the Coven Book of Ways

Once you have instructed the bottle to its purpose and what each item is for, the bottle should be corked (or lidded) and then sealed with wax. The colour of the wax should correspond to the purpose of your bottle (see Chapter Four for colour correspondences). The bottle is now ready to be buried, or placed into a wall cavity or floor space. When working on another person, the bottle should ideally be buried on their own property.

Cord magic

Although the origins of cord magic are sketchy, there are some very good reasons for using cords within our spellwork. Firstly, the cord is a link between the worlds. It symbolically represents the umbilical cord that connects a baby to its mother, echoing the mysteries of birth and initiation. Secondly, the cord acts as a meditative aid; the act of knotting, weaving and plaiting cords aids the focus the mind. Thirdly, the cord is reminiscent of the etheric connection between our physical body and our spiritual body, which is often seen as a silver or white shining cord, and the threads of Wyrd which are constantly being spun by the Three Fates. The coven copy of the *Liber Umbrarum* states that the Cord is the magical tool for the fifth element, Spirit.

Knotted Cord

The most popular form of cord magic is the Knotted Spell, in which the cord is knotted whilst a chant is repeated. The chant normally differs from coven to coven, but many are variations of Doreen Valiente's *Spell of the Cord*. However, other chants can be just as effective. This nine-knot spell is from my coven's *Book of Ways*:

> *I tie this cord both strong and true*
> *One, Two..*
> *Knots one to nine to see it through*
> *Three, Four ..*
> *And by my will this spell create*

Five, Six ..
I tie these knots to seal this fate
Seven, Eight ..
And by this knot the thing is mine - Nine!

Some covens indicate a specific pattern in which the knots should be tied along the cord. I do not believe this is necessary, as it is the intent which is most important – trying to remember which order the knots are supposed to be in is only going to distract you from the work that is in hand. Instead, as a rule of thumb, you should tie your cord as follows:

To bring something into your life, tie the first knot in the end furtherest away from you and work your way towards your body

To banish something from your life, tie the first knot in the end closest to you and work your way away from your body.

The cord can then be wound around your athame and put away until the aim of the spell has manifested. In their book, *Spells and How They Work*, Janet and Stewart Farrar recommend using the verse 'I wind, I bind, this spell be mine!'

The Measure and other cords of Initiation

Another popular use of the cord in modern Craft is 'The Measure': a length of cord which was equal to the height of the initiate. The cord was then used to measure the circumference of the head, chest and hip and tied off with a knot at each point. The result was a length of rope with three knots which represented the vital statistics and measurement of the witch. In many covens, the Measure is seen as the coven's connection to the witch – an umbilical cord between the witch and the initiate which is kept by the leader of the group and destroyed if the witch betrays the coven. In our group we give the trainee their Measure to take home and keep as a reminder of their promises made under initiation.

Cords are also used to bind the trainee during their initiation. Three red cords are used – one at nine foot and two at five foot – which bind the wrists, neck, hands, knees and feet. Again, the binding is symbolic, a sign of the trainees willingness to learn and their promises made to the Craft. The cord is never tight. When the cord is removed at the end of the ritual, it symbolises the trainee's freedom from their past and their rebirth as an initiated witch. Both Measures and initiation cords are sometimes woven into the witches robe cord, so that it may be worn during ritual.

The Witches Ladder

Contrary to popular opinion, the Witches Ladder is *not* the same as the Nine Knots cord. The Witches' Ladder is a rope made of three yarns which have been plaited together, and whilst the braid is made goose or chicken feathers are woven into the cord; as standard, a three foot Witches Ladder can hold up to 40 feathers. The Witches Ladder can be used for protection, cursing, and also for controlling the spirits of animals, in particular deer and other wild game.

There is no specific chant or spell that goes with making the ladder, other than reciting your intention over the rope as you braid. The ladder is then hung up if it is intended for protection, or left for the victim to find, if it is a curse. Again, the latter is not recommended and you should examine the ethics and your motivation before you take any such action! A Witches Ladder was found in a Somerset attic in the early 1900s, which is now on show at the Pitt Rivers Museum in Oxford.

Healing Cords

Cords can be particularly effective for healing. A cord should be chosen in a colour which is appropriate to the illness, and then knotted nine times; you may choose to use the Nine Knots spell for this process. The cord can then be worn upon the person to aid healing.

> *A loaf in my lap*
> *A penny in my purse*
> *You are ever the better*
> *And I am never the worse.*
> 'The Healing Song', author unknown

A traditional cure for a sprained ankle was to tie black thread nine times and then wear it around the injured ankle, until it was healed.

The Witches Wheel

You can couple *The Witch's Rune* chant with a type of cord magic called the Witches Wheel, from my coven's *Book of Ways*. The Witches Wheel is made up of two lengths of white cord which are tied in the middle with a third piece of cord to create an equal-armed cross when held out. Each end of the rope should be held by a coven member who should step back so that the rope goes taut. As the coven processes round the circle, an effort should be made to keep the wheel taut and the arms at equal distances from one another. This method is better performed outside where there is more space, or alternatively the coven should have practiced spinning with the wheel as otherwise a great tangle can occur! When performed with grace, this method evokes the power of the four seasons and the spinning wheel of Wyrd and fate.

Amulets and Talismans

Many people get confused about the difference between amulets
and talismans. An Amulet is an item which is either carried upon
the person or kept in a special place as a charm. They can come
in all shapes and sizes, from rabbit's feet to three leaf clovers and
even lucky socks! A childhood rhyme echoes the superstitions of
amulets:

See a pin and pick it up,
All the day you'll have good luck.
See a pin and let it lay,
Bad luck you'll have all the day.
Author unknown

You might recognise this rhyme; it was later changed and the
amulet became a penny, rather than a pin. Pins in magic are well
recorded, particularly used in conjunction with witches bottles
and candle spells.

Talismans, however, are a little more sophisticated. Borrowed
from high magic, talismans use magical correspondences such as
planetary associations, numerology and are usually made within
a magic circle. The main benefit of using a Talisman rather than
an Amulet is that the Talisman, imbued with correspondences
and associations, will recharge and potentially last longer than
the Amulet. It also calls upon the underlying powers of the
universe – the planets, numbers, colours and sigils – which
means that a Talisman can potentially, although not certainly, be
more powerful than an Amulet.

A Talisman can be created from any sort of flat material such as
wood, metal, leather or card. A circle of about 6cm in diameter
should be cut out of the material.

On one side of the Talisman, the intent of the spell should be written. This could be done by creating a Sigil (see Chapter Five). On the same side, you should define who the spell is for. What is their full name? Are they male or female? What star sign are they? What is their date of birth?

Now on the reverse of the Talisman, the symbols of corresponding forces should be drawn. You could use the symbol of an appropriate planet, an influential tattva, element and moonphase (all of which can be found throughout this book) or appropriate God and Goddess names or symbol.

Once you have finished drawing the talisman, you should place it upon the altar in front of an appropriately coloured candle. Lighting the candle, visualise the aim of the Talisman coming to pass as you focus on the candle flame and the talisman beneath it. Then wrap the finished talisman in black silk, rotate it nine times to empower it and then uncover again.

The Talisman is now ready to use. Depending upon its purpose, the Talisman can be folded and worn upon the person, mounted on the wall behind a door to protect a house, or even left upon the altar until the goal has been achieved. If and when the Talisman becomes obsolete, it should either be cast into running water or set alight, both methods will ground any residual energy which remains in the Talisman and render it harmless.

GLOSSARY

Active Force: The active principle in magic. Usually described as male.

Agnostic: Someone who does not know, or believes that it is impossible to know, whether God exists.

Alchemy: Philosophical and spiritual discipline combining chemistry and mysticism.

All Seeing Eye: The image of the eye of God within a triangle or pyramid, and used as a symbol within Freemasonry and Rosicrucian traditions as a symbol of protection.

Alpha State: An altered state of consciousness which is achieved by activities such as meditation, ritual, and relaxation.

Ancestor: The term used to describe ancient people, or people who have passed away, or the ancestral spirit of a place.

Anima: The female inner personality, as present in the male.

Anima Loci: The soul or spirit of a natural place.

Animism: The belief that soul or spirit resides in every object, living or inanimate.

Animus: The male inner personality, as present in the female.

Archetype: An archetype defines an example of a personality type, i.e. Mother figure, Father figure. Often used in the Craft to epitomize a God or Goddess, or a group of Gods or Goddesses, and their place within our own Psyche. The accepted model of a person or concept.

Astral Projection: The process of leaving the body for a period of time, called 'Lifting' in the Craft. The physical body remains in a meditative state, whilst the Astral body or 'Fetch' travels to other places.

Astrology: The study of the planets and the Zodiac for divination.

Athame: Black hilted double edged blade, used for magical use only.

Bolline/Boline: White handled knife used for carving candles and physically cutting other items which are to be used for ritual purposes.

Book of Ways: A witches journal, normally handwritten although can also be typed, which contains records of rituals and magic. Usually kept private, although sometimes shared with coven members and students of the Craft. Also known as the 'Book of Shadows', 'Grimoire', or 'Secret Granary'.

Cakes & Wine: See 'Libation'

Cauldron: Pot used to symbolise the womb of the Goddess and often used to hold water for scrying, or to contain sacred fire.

Censor : Dish for containing loose incense burnt on charcoal blocks. Blocks are lit and the sensor carried around the sacred space to distribute the smoke.

Chakra: Sanskrit word to describe the energy points found on the body. Called the 'Sacred Wells' by followers of European Craft.

Chalice: Cup used to symbolise the womb of the Goddess and also used to hold wine or another drink which is to be used for libation and offering.

Charge, The: Charge of the Goddess/Charge of the God – special poems read out to the God and Goddess during ritual.

Chi / Prana: Eastern concept of the vital energy of all things.

Circle: The term used to describe the sacred space created for ritual.

Collective Unconcious: A concept which postulates that there is a 'collective memory' of our species, a place that we can access for knowledge. This is the place of symbols and dreams.

Cords: Different colour cords are often used to symbolise an individuals Craft Degree. Cords are also used to perform all sorts of cord magic.

Coven: A group of witches who choose to work together. Usually a hierarchal group with a High Priest and Priestess at the head.

Covenstead: The indoor place the coven meets, often the High Priest or High Priestesses' home.

Craft: A term often used to describe the religion of Wicca, but also used to describe older magical paths, such as Traditional Craft.

Crone: A woman who is wise, particularly in the Craft who is usually (but not necessarily) an older woman. The final face of the Triple Goddess.

Dedication: A rite of passage undertaken by newcomers to the Craft to dedicate themselves to learning the ways of the Craft.

Degree : A rite of passage undertaken by most coven-based witches. There are 3 main stages of Degrees: First, Second and Third: each Degree lasts at least 1 year, and with each Degree comes new responsibilities and stages of learning for the witch.

Deity/Divine: A term used to describe Gods and Goddesses, or all omnipotent androgynous spirit.

Devil: A Christian invention, not worshipped or recognised within Paganism or the Craft.

Divination: The method of fortune-telling or receiving messages with the aid of tools, such as Tarot, Runes or Scrying.

Divine Marriage: See 'Great Rite'.

Ego & Shadow: Terms used by psychologist Carl Gustav Jung to describe the parts of the mind which control our decisions, both consciously and unconsciously. The ego makes its judgements from past experiences to fulfil our needs and desires, whilst protecting us from potential harm. Our ego also decides how we portray ourselves to the world, containing and protecting the real person within. However by trying to protect us the ego can stop us from developing, by creating disowned, despised and repressed traits. This part of us is described as the Shadow, a 'dark side' which can suddenly surface when provoked. It is possible to 'make friends' with the Shadow, by recognising it; just some of the work undertaken during the Second Degree.

Elder: The term used for a practitioner of the Craft respected for their maturity, responsibility and experience within the Craft. The Elder is also a sacred tree for witches.

Elements: The five building blocks of life: Earth, Air, Fire, Water and Spirit.

Elementals: Personifications of the Elements.

Energy: A broad term used to describe the creative force within ourselves and the universe.

Esbat: Witches meeting/ritual held at either a New or Full Moon.

Evocation: Describes the method of inviting a Deity, spirit or other entity to join you either in, or at the edge of, the circle to observe your ritual and offer their energies to help you perform it.

Exorcism / Exorcise: To rid an place or person of a malignant energy, feeling or spirit.

Eye of Horus (litany): A chant based upon Spell 137B from the Book of the Dead.

Fundamentalism: The belief that a particular religion or path is completely true, or that a particular belief system is the only one true way.

God: The word to describe a/the Male Divine force.

Goddess: The word to descrive a/the Female Divine force.

Great Rite: A sexual act between two consenting adults to symbolise the marriage of the God and the Goddess. Also known as Hieros gamos, Divine Marriage, or Sacred Marriage. When the Great Rite is not possible or not suitable for the occasion, the Symbolic Great Rite may be employed. The phrases, 'Great Rite', 'Divine Marriage' or 'Sacred Marriage', are also used to describe the relationship between the God and Goddess, and so does not necessarily mean a ritual act.

Grounding: The act of bringing the self back to normal consciousness after a ritual, magical working or meditation.

High Magic / Magick: A form of ceremonial magic.

High Priest/Priestess (craft): An individual who has reached Third Degree in the Craft Degree system and has trained for at least 3 years. Entitled to run their own coven.

Hieros gamos: See 'Great Rite'.

Inner Mysteries: Secrets kept by mystery traditions. Also used to describe the discovery of one's inner self.

Intention: Complete dedication, commitment and focus for a ritual or spell. Without intention, magic is almost impossible.

Initiatory Witchcraft: An eclectic system that to aims develop occult understanding, and aid personal development through the mysteries of the Craft.

Intuition: To use the intuition is to act by way of feeling, rather than logic or reasoning; to follow the heart, rather than the head; to go with what we feel is right, rather than what we are told to do. The best rituals and magic are lead by the intuition.

Invocation: Describes the method of inviting a Deity or spirit to enter your body. In this way, the Priest or Priestess becomes that Spirit itself, and speaks and acts for that which has been invoked.

Karma: Sanskrit word for 'action', meaning that one action will earn another.

Kundalini: Instinctive force symbolised by the snake, and believed to rest at the base of the spine. Related to sexuality and earth power.

Libation: Food or drink offered to the Spirits and the Gods/Goddesses. Also partaken by witches in circle, normally at the end of the rite. Usually consists of a single chalice of wine, and a dish of cakes with just enough for each person present.

Lifting: See 'Astral Travel'.

Lustration: A form of anointment used particularly in ancient Greece and Greek ritual.

Maiden, Mother, Crone: The three phases of the Goddess and the three phases of womanhood.

Matriarchal: A social system based on, and usually governed by, women. Women seen as superior to men, physically and spiritually.

Maypole: A tall pole with ribbons used for traditional Beltane and

May Day dances. Used to celebrate fertility and encourage prosperity for the summer.

Meditation: Any process of quietening the mind, to achieve peace and enlightenment. Many forms of meditation are available, some of which involve stillness of the body and others that involve movement, facilitating focus.

Megalith: A large stone, sometimes forming part of a group or circle of stones, and usually important for social or religious reasons. Also called 'God Stone'.

Metaphysics: A philosophy about the understanding of existence and knowledge.

Monotheism: The belief in a single, universal, all-encompassing Deity/God.

Need Fire: A fire or bonfire lit for a ritualistic or customary purpose.

Neo Paganism: An umbrella of eclectic belief systems which are based upon the practices of the ancient people and cultures of the past.

Nun: Chaos, primeval waters, and sometimes can literally mean 'nothing'.

Occult: An umbrella term used to describe all sorts of activities relating to magical powers, the supernatural and the metaphysical.

Old Ones: See 'Ancestor'.

Paganism: An umbrella of eclectic belief systems practiced by the ancient people and cultures of the past.

Page, Father, Sage: The three phases of the God and the three phases of manhood.

Pantheism: The belief that everything in the universe is divine, and that 'God' is in everything.

Passive Force: The passive principle in magic. Usually described as female.

Pathworking: Guided meditation.

Patriarchal: A social system based on, and usually governed by, men. Men seen as superior to women, both physically and spiritually.

Phallus / Phallic: A symbol, object or tool that suggests the shape of an erect penis.

Phantom: Within Craft, used to describe negative energy of any type.

Polytheism: Belief in, or worship of, multiple Gods or Divinities.

Primiordial: A term to describe something which existed at or since the beginning of the world or the universe.

Psyche: The mind, or the deepest thoughts, feelings or beliefs of a person.

Pyramid of Manifestation: The concept that the shape of the triangle, pyramid and consequentially the number three are poignant in the movements of the universe and the power behind magic.

Reincarnation: The belief that a dead person or animal's spirit returns to life in another body.

Ritual: A word to describe any ceremony.

Qabalah: See 'Kabbalah'.

Sabbat: Festivals which are celebrated during the Witches Year. Sabbats are focused on both seasons and solar astronomical activity.

Sacred Marriage: See 'Great Rite'.

Sacrifice: Any offering to the Gods.

Sage: A man who is wise, particularly in the Craft who is usually (but not necessarily) an older man. A phase of the manhood, and the older face of the God.

Scourge: The traditional name for a whip or flail, used by ancient cultures to represent power.

Scrying: The art of seeing messages and images in water, smoke, crystal balls, dark mirrors, cauldrons, candle flame, etc.

Shapeshifting: The art of physically and/or psychically transforming into an animal or other form.

So Mote It Be: Expression borrowed from Freemasonry meaning

'So Must It Be', or, 'So Be It.' Mote is an early word for 'Must', from the Old English Moste or Motan. Its origins in modern Craft can probably be attributed to Gardner's friendship with the Freemason John Ward, who influenced Gardner's work.

Temple: Any indoor space that has been specially prepared for the worship of the Gods.

The Gods: A term to describe the Gods and Goddesses, or all omnipotent androgynous Spirit

Third Eye: The mind's eye; psychic sight/Witch Sight

Three Times Pass: The method of sealing a circle by three turns around its circumference after the circle has been cast. The Three Times Pass can also be used to release the circle, after it is closed.

Triple Aspect: The term to describe the three phases of Deity; Maiden, Mother and Crone of the Goddess and Page, Father and Sage of the God. Also used to describe the three phases of the Moon – waxing, full and waning.

Tumulus/Tumuli: A burial mound created by our ancestors in the shape of the womb. It was believed that a person buried within Mother Earth's womb – the mound – would be born again in another life.

Underworld: A place that appears in myths from around the world and from all different cultures. The definition varies culture to culture, but in general it is a place where the dead go before they are reborn. It is also often a place of judgment. It is interwoven with the myths of the seasons, particularly that of the winter.

Visualisation: The ability to create images within the mind, manipulate them and journey through them. Visualisation is also an important part of magic, and the witch must visualise the outcome of a spell.

Wand: Witches tool associated with the phallus of the God. Has links to the Symbolic Great Rite

Wheel of the Year: A term to describe the eight sabbats celebrated during the calendar year. Symbolic of the constant turn and change of the seasons.

Wica/Wicca: Traces back to the Proto-Indo word 'weik', meaning 'to consecrate', and 'to practice religion and magic'.

Witch: See 'Wica/Wicca'.

Womb – Tomb: The term used to describe the concept that the tomb is also the womb; within death lays rebirth. Also see 'Tumulus/Tumuli'.

Working: The term used to describe any additional work done within the circle such as meditation, healing, spellwork, chanting or magic.

Wyrd: The word which pre-dates the modern word 'weird' and means the Spiritual All.

Wryd, Web: The concept that all things are connected and that all action has a reaction.

BIBLIOGRAPHY

Aldcroft Jackson, Nigel, 'Call of the Horned Piper', Capall-Bann

Almond & Seddon, 'The Book of Egyptian Ritual', Thorsons Books

Armstrong, Karen, 'A Short History of Myth', Canongate Books

Artisson, Robin, 'The Witching Way of the Hollow Hill', Lulu

Author unknown, 'The Greater Key of Solomon', various sources

Berlitz, Charles, 'Atlantis: Lost Continent Revealed' Macmillian Publications

Black, Jonathan, 'The Secret History of the World', Overlook Hardcover

Bourne, Louis, 'Conversations with a Witch', Robert Hale Books

Buckland, Raymond, 'Complete Book of Witchcraft', Llewellyn Publications

Cabot, Laurie, 'Power of the Witch', Michael Joseph Books

Capra, Fritjof, 'The Tao of Physics', Shambhala Publications

Chumbley, Andrew, 'Leaper Between', article

Chumbley, Andrew, 'Qutub: The Point', Xoanon Publishing Ltd

Cochrane & Jones, 'Roebuck in the Thicket', Capall Bann

Conway, David, 'Magic – An Occult Primer', Chaucer Press

Conway, DJ, 'Advanced Celtic Shamanism', The Crossing Press

Crowley, Vivianne, 'Wicca', Thorsons Books

Cunningham, Scott, 'Earth Power', Llewellyn Publications

Cunningham, Scott, 'Incense, Oils and Brews', Llewellyn Publications

Dames, Michael, 'The Avebury Cycle', Thames & Hudson

De Martino, Ernest, 'Magick Primitive & Modern', Tom Stacey Ltd

D'este & Rankine, 'Circle of Fire', Avalonia Books

D'Este & Rankine, 'The Isles of the Many Gods', Avalonia Books

Ellis, Normandi, 'Dreams of Isis', Quest Books

Farrar & Bone, 'Progressive Witchcraft', New Page Books

Farrar, J&S, 'A Witches Bible', Robert Hale Books

Farrar, J&S, 'Spells and How They Work', Robert Hale Books

Farrar, J&S, 'The Witches God', Robert Hale Books

Farrar, J&S, 'The Witches Goddess', Robert Hale Books

Flowers, Stephen, 'Hermetic Magick', Weiser Books

Frazer, Sir James, 'The Golden Bough', Wordsworth Reference

Freke & Gandy, 'The Jesus Mysteries', Element Books

Friedland & Hemsher, 'Basic Psychic Development', Weiser Books

Gardner, Gerald, 'Gardnerian Book of Shadows', Various sources

Gardner, Gerald, 'Ye Bok Ye Art Magical', various sources

Gimbutas, Marija, 'Language of the Goddess', Thames & Hudson

Gray, William, 'Magical Ritual Methods', Helios Books

Gray, William, 'Seasonal Occult Rituals', Thorsons Books

Hancock, Graham, 'Supernatural', Arrow Books

Hawkins, J, Elemental Series, Capall Bann Publishing

Hutton, Ronald, 'Stations of the Sun', Oxford Paperbacks

Hutton, Ronald, 'Triumph of the Moon', Oxford Paperbacks

Jones, Kathy, 'The Ancient British Goddess' Ariadne Publications

Kalweit, Holger, 'Shamans, Healers & Medicine Men', Shambhala
    Publications

Kelly, Aidan A, 'Crafting the Art of Magic', Llewellyn Publications

Kightly, Charles, 'The Customs & Traditions of Britain', Thames &
    Hudson

Kindred, Glennie, 'Sacred Celebrations', Gothic Image Books

King & Skinner, 'Techniques of High Magic', Sphere Books

Knight, Gareth, 'The Practice of Ritual Magic', The Aquarian Press,

Knight, Peter, 'Ancient Stones of Dorset', Power Publications

Kollerstrom, Nick, 'Gardening & Planting by the Moon', Quantum
    Books

Kondratiev, Alexei, 'Celtic Rituals', The Collins Press

Kraig, Donald, 'Modern Magick', Llewellyn Publications

Leek, Sybil, 'Diary of a Witch', Prentice-Hill

Lewin, Roger, 'Human Evolution', Blackwell Publishing

Magnus, Olaus, 'Description of the Northern Peoples', Hakluyt
    Society

Matthews, John, 'The Quest for the Green Man', Godsfield Press

McCrickard, Janet, *'Eclipse of the Sun'*, Gothic Image Books
Metraux, Alfred, *'Voodoo'*, Sphere Books
Moura, Ann, *'Green Witchcraft'*, Llewellyn Publications
O'Kelly, Claire, *'Concise Guide to Newgrange'*, Houston Printers Ltd
Ozaniec, Naomi, *'The Elements of Egyptian Wisdom'*, Element Books
Paraskos, Stass, *'Aphrodite: The Mythology of Cyprus'*, Interworld Publications
Parry, Bruce, *'Tribe'*, Penguin Books
Pennick, Nigel, *'Magical Alphabets'*, Weiser Books
Pennick, Nigel, *'Secrets of East Anglian Magic'*, Capall Bann Publishing
Pierrakos, Eva, *'The Pathwork of Self Transformation'*, Bantam Books
Porteous, *'The Forest in Folklore & Mythology'*, Dover Books
Ramacharaka, Yogi, *'Hatha Yoga'*, Grange Books
Regula, DeTraci, *'The Mysteries of Isis'*, Llewellyn Publications
Ryley Scott, George, *'Phallic Worship: A History'*, Torchstream Books
Rysdyk, *'Modern Shamanic Living'*, Weiser Books
Sinclair-Wood, Lynne, *'Creating Form from the Mist'*, Capall-Bann
Sjoo & Mar, *'The Great Cosmic Mother'*, Harper Collins
Slade, Paddy, *'Natural Magick – A Seasonal Guide'*, Hamlyn Books
Spare, AO, *'Book of Pleasure'*, IHO Books
Telesco, Patricia, *'Advanced Wicca'*, Citadel Press
Telesco, Patricia, *'Labyrinth Walking'*, Citadel Press
Trobe, Kala, *'Magic of Qabalah'*, Llewellyn Publications
Valiente, Doreen, *'An ABC of Witchcraft'*, Robert Hale Books
Valiente, Doreen, *'Natural Magic'*, Robert Hale Books
Valiente, Doreen, *'Rebirth of Witchcraft'*, Robert Hale Books
Valiente, Doreen, *'Witchcraft for Tomorrow'*, Robert Hale Books
Wallis Budge, EA, *'Egyptian Magick'*, Arkana Books
Worth, Valerie, *'Crones Book of Magical Words'*, Llewelyn Publications
Zalewski, CL, *'Herbs & Magick in Alchemy'*, Prism Press